DOLLS AND HOW TO MAKE THEM

By the same author

MODERN SOFT TOY MAKING
TOYING WITH TRIFLES
WHAT SHALL I DO WITH THIS?
WHAT SHALL I DO FROM SCANDINAVIA?
MAKING OLD TESTAMENT TOYS
MAKING NEW TESTAMENT TOYS
MAKING AND USING FINGER PUPPETS
TOYS FROM THE TALES OF BEATRIX POTTER

The Christmas Crib

DOLLS
AND HOW TO MAKE THEM

BY

MARGARET HUTCHINGS

MILLS & BOON, LONDON
THE CHARLES T. BRANFORD CO., U.S.A.

First published . . 1963
Second impression . . 1964
Third impression . . 1967
Fourth impression . . 1970
Fifth impression . . 1974
© Margaret Hutchings 1963

I.S.B.N. 0·263·69983·8 (UK)
8231·3022·3 (USA)

First published in Great Britain by Mills & Boon Ltd., 17–19 Foley Street, London W1A 1DR.
Published in USA by the Charles T. Branford Co., 28 Union Street, Newton Centre, Mass. 02159
Made and Printed in Great Britain by Butler & Tanner Ltd., Frome and London

ACKNOWLEDGEMENTS

The author acknowledges with grateful thanks the willing and generous help given to her by so many people. In particular :

By Mr. Leslie Daiken, the late Rev. Denis Daly, Mrs. Beatrice le Huray, Mr. E. Lambourne, Mrs. Phyllis Robinson, Mrs. Emily Skipsey, The Guernsey Federation of Women's Institutes and the Trustees of the British Museum for information contained in the anecdotes which appear throughout the book.

By Mrs. Peggy Shortley for her research into embroidery cottons.

By Deborah Futter for modelling so charmingly for plate 9.

And by Mr. Paul Gallico, for so readily allowing her to quote passages from his delightful story " The Enchanted Doll ".

*   *   *

Colour plates by Studio Swain, Glasgow.

Black and white plates by E. Nixon Payne, Chelmsford.

Line Drawings by the Author.

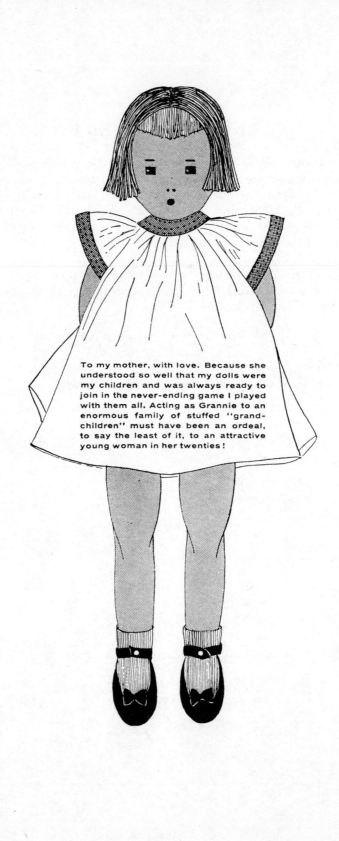

To my mother, with love. Because she understood so well that my dolls were my children and was always ready to join in the never-ending game I played with them all. Acting as Grannie to an enormous family of stuffed "grand-children" must have been an ordeal, to say the least of it, to an attractive young woman in her twenties!

CONTENTS

LIST OF PLATES

AUTHOR'S NOTE

SOMEONE ONCE SAID that every writer spends more than half his time reading, in order to write. I could not, by the wildest stretch of imagination, call myself a writer but rather a designer; however, I still find myself reading avidly everything I come across which is remotely connected with dolls and toys.

Thus it was that I recently found, among a collection of short stories, one of the most moving tales I have ever read. In it were contained exactly the feeling I have for those little creatures which as a doll maker I bring to life, feelings which I myself have never been able to put into words. I shall never cease to be amazed that they were written by a man; one who had never known the indescribable thrill of creating a doll, although the very fact that he wrote them proves that this "feeling" does get through to those who see and handle the results of our work.

"—No more than a foot long, she was as supple and alive to the touch as though there were flesh and bones beneath the clothes instead of rag stuffing.—Its creator had endowed it with incredibly lifelike features and lively grace, that gave one the impression of a living presence—was it possible for an emotion to have been sewn into the seams marking the contours of the tiny figure? I felt that if I did not put her down I should become moved by her in some unbearable fashion—for she was a creation that gave me the feeling that some part of a human soul had gone into the making of her." [1]

I am quite convinced that part of a human soul *does* go into the making of a doll. It is a task which can give utter satisfaction and absorption and is a relaxation second to none, during which one's dolls become one's children, with which one is almost as loth to part as one would be one's child! A hand-made doll, stitched with love, becomes a personality, and its individuality and character emerge in a way which can never happen in a mass-produced article. I hope *you* will experience this, as it is one of the aims of this book.

Modern Soft Toy Making was such a joy to prepare and I am indeed grateful for the wonderful reception it was and is being given by those of you who use it. Now you have asked for some dolls and, in so doing, have given me the delightful opportunity of writing a companion volume. Once again my family, friends and publishers have done all in their power to smooth the path for me, and I thank them all.

If those who make them, and those who play with them, experience even a fraction of the pleasure which I have done whilst designing the dolls—I shall indeed be happy.

M. H.

[1] "The Enchanted Doll". From *The Confessions of a Story Teller*, by Paul Gallico. Michael Joseph.

INTRODUCTION

No one seems certain why a doll is so called and many suggestions have been put forward. Some say that " doll " is a shortened form of " Dorothea " or " Dorothy ", and the *Oxford Dictionary of Christian Names* tells us that the use of the name as a description of a child's plaything was first recorded in 1700.

There are those who think that the word is a shortened form of " idol ". This sounds far-fetched, until one realizes how a little girl " idolizes " her dolls—then one wonders if there is, perhaps, some truth in the idea !

Up to about the 18th century, dolls were known more generally as " little ladies " or " babies ", which seems rather strange, as in those days most of them had adult features. They also wore grown-up clothes, but this is understandable when we remember that most *children* were then dressed in small replicas of their parents' garments—so were, in fact, " little ladies ".

The English " Puppet ", French " Poupée ", German " Puppe ", Dutch " Pop " and many more, all stem from the Latin " Pupa "—a girl, so it is easy to see why some forms of dolls are called puppets.

For those of us lucky enough to have children in our lives, it seems incredible that the doll as a child's plaything has not always existed. Yet historians tell us that the earliest dolls were funeral offerings, effigies, and symbols of departed spirits. Be that as it may—no one really *knows*, for we were not there to see ! The mothers among us find it hard to believe that every other mother, however primitive, has not at some time or other fashioned a miniature replica of the human form on which her child could lavish affection and care. Surely the little Roman rag doll (see plate 2) found in a child's grave and dating from A.D. 4, had been some little girl's constant companion during her lifetime !

It is interesting to notice that it is not so much children who insist that their dolls shall be perfect models and replicas of the fashion of their day, as the firms who make them and the parents who buy them. Children have vivid imaginations and love to use them, but mere " grown-ups " have an extraordinary way of presuming that only quite ordinary, natural imitations will please their offspring. Of course a little girl will enjoy receiving glamorous plastic brides and " teenage " dolls as presents, but in the long run and over the years, it is usually these beauties who fade and the tough, cuddly dolls, created at home, who survive as firm favourites.

More than half the pleasure of a hand-made doll is in the making, the whole family, even the children, taking a hand if they want to do so. In the past, dolls have been created from almost every imaginable material, birch bark, grass, clay, terra-cotta, bones, moss, wood, porcelain, tin, paper, wax, papier-mâché, leather, rag, cardboard, cones, seed-pods, breadcrumbs, gingerbread, ducks' bills and even withered fruit. The things which have stuffed them have been no less diverse—

sawdust, bran, cork, grass, straw, horsehair, wool, cotton batting, feathers, down and crumpled paper, all having had their day. For strength and real play value, only " down to earth ", modern materials have been used in the following chapters, but to the " unusual " list, corset laces and " Blakey's Segs " may be added as our contribution—for these form the basis of the " Doll's House Dolls " in Section XIII.

To prepare a book on doll making was a formidable task, inasmuch as there was so much material which could and should be included, but without the volume taking on encyclopaedic proportions, this was clearly impossible.

After much discussion and thought, the first choice was made by children, in the form of secret ballots as to which were their favourites, and the second by their mothers and grandmothers, godmothers and aunts, teachers and " big sisters ", who chose the dolls they would most enjoy making. A final sifting ensured that among the 80 designs contained within these covers, there was plenty of variety and that something had been included for everyone, whether at home, school or college, in hospital or convalescent home or if sewing in aid of good causes. It was also felt that no book on dolls would be complete without the figures for a Christmas Crib —yet these figures must be in a different category altogether from a doll designed to be played with on the nursery floor. As so many of the embroiderers and rug-makers of today are creating beautiful things for our churches and cathedrals, why not the doll makers ? So the Crib was included as a finale to the book, and here is your chance, doll makers ! It is hoped that Section XIV will be an exciting insight into the possibilities of wired figures, and the intention is that instructions for making many more dolls of this type shall be published later in a separate book of their own.

As a light-hearted " trimming ", short anecdotes of interest to doll makers have been added here and there, with the hope that you will enjoy to the full both aspects of the book—the stories behind the dolls *and* how to make them.

Section One

GENERAL INSTRUCTIONS

Before starting to make any of the dolls, spend an evening reading through Sections I and II, taking sufficient time to refer to all the diagrams mentioned. This will be a tremendous help in giving you a clear over-all picture of what the book contains and its methods. Then read right through the instructions given for the doll you have decided to make, being quite sure you understand each process before you start work.

PREPARING THE PATTERNS

ACTUAL SIZE PATTERNS for the dolls and their clothes will be found at the end of the book between pages 248 and 286, except for the shoes and hats, which are given separately between pages 43 and 61. In all cases make cardboard templates of the pieces of the pattern you are using, by tracing from the pages of the book and transferring the outline on to thin cardboard (such as a cereal box). Mark in all details such as the number of pieces required, letters, arrows and other directions, and cut out each piece carefully and accurately with small sharp scissors. Punch a hole in each template and thread them together in sets with a pipe cleaner. Keep tiny pieces like ears and eyes in an envelope for safety, punch a hole in the corner of this and thread it on to the pipe cleaner with the other pieces (fig. 1). Don't forget to mark each bundle clearly, e.g. "Felt Jester", or when you come to sort your patterns out on some future occasion you will waste a lot of time trying to find out which bundle is for which doll !

In the case of some of the larger pieces of clothing for the Crib figures, it has not been possible to show them full size. All these however are simple, straight shapes, and the measurements for cutting them are clearly shown by diagrams. The simplest way to cut out these garments is to first of all cut a piece of material the size of the basic outline shape ; e.g. for the King's Robe, fig. 89, cut a piece 13 in. wide and 22 in. long. Fold this in half widthwise, i.e. across top of sleeves and shoulders as shown by "FOLD" on diagram. Then measure 3 in. down from the fold and 3 in. inwards for the sleeve seam, mark this in pencil, then draw across to the lower hem to give the side seam. Fold the robe in half lengthwise before cutting along this line, so that both halves are exactly the same.

CHOOSING MATERIALS

Most materials are suitable for some part of doll making, but it is important to choose the right material for each type of doll, and in so doing the age of the future owner plays an important part.

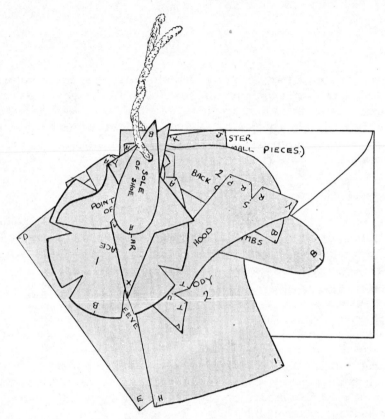

Fig. 1. *A set of cardboard pattern templates ready for use*

If using **second-hand** material, such as good pieces of worn clothes, make quite sure that they *are* good pieces or your work will be wasted, and the doll will not stand up to the wear and tear it is sure to receive. Hold second-hand material up to the light and mark any thin places with a pencilled circle, so that they may be discarded during the cutting out.

Many of the bodies are made of **cotton material.** Almost anything available may be used, as long as it is *strong*—calico, sateen and sheeting being particularly suitable.

When choosing **stockinette** for the dolls in Section VIII it is important to get just the right type. This material needs to be supple and " giving " and a good cotton stockinette, sold specially for doll making, may be bought from many handicraft shops (see page 28). It is sometimes 52 in. wide and sometimes 36 in., varying in colour from a very pale pink to a rather deep apricot—either is suitable for a doll's " skin ", and if making several dolls it is a good idea to make some in each colour (see the two colours in plate 11). Avoid a strong " rose " or " sugary " pink, this has a blue tinge and gives the doll an unnatural appearance; all pinks should be in the yellow range to look lifelike. When substituting material of your own for the stockinette used for the original models, remember that the body pattern for the dolls in Section VIII was specially designed for a very " elastic " material, so that although the pattern looks long and thin the finished doll is short and plump, for the material stretches sideways. If your material is too " solid ", your doll will look long, thin and emaciated ! This stockinette dyes well, so that you can make a brown piccaninny, and it is usually available in black, the same width and price as the pink.

Felt should be carefully chosen. The type needed for doll making is available from most large stores, drapers and handicraft shops. Avoid the thin, papery kind, which when held up to the light shows itself to be of poor quality, as this will split and tear. Avoid also the thick felt sold for slipper making; this is too solid and cannot be modelled. Felt is economical to buy, as it is available in small pieces in sizes from about 3 in. square upwards, or by the yard 36 in. and 72 in. wide.

Cotton prints and ginghams are the ideal material for simple dresses and knickers for little girl dolls, which will have much handling, as they remain fresh and crisp, wash beautifully, and are easy to sew.

Silks, satins, brocades and lamés are needed for glamorous robes of Kings and Queens—the more shiny and gaudy they are, the better they will look !

Fur fabric forms the basis of the babies' washable dolls. As well as being soft and cuddly, it has the advantage of standing up to repeated washing. It also cleans well with starch or a dog's dry shampoo powder. This material is usually 48 in. wide and there is a great variety of colours and " textures " available in wool, mohair or nylon. White was used for the original models of all the dolls in Section VI. Wool fabric is easier to work with than nylon, but collects the dirt during play more quickly. Which you use is really a matter of personal choice. If you cannot obtain what you want locally, an address is given on page 28 to help you. Sometimes good remnants can be picked up in sales or from market stalls. This is a very economical way to buy, and however soiled the pieces may be, they will come up beautifully clean if washed before the doll is cut out.

COLLECTING YOUR TOOLS (Fig. 2)

Scissors for doll making need, above all, to be sharp. Ordinary large dressmaker's scissors may, of course, be used for many of the clothes, where the pieces are fairly large, but for the smaller pieces, particularly the felt ones such as eyes, ears and lids, *very* small scissors are absolutely essential for accuracy.

Cutting nippers for cutting wire and pipe cleaners (scissors *can* be used for the latter but will be very quickly spoiled) are usually to be found in the family tool chest, as can a pair of **round** or **snipe nosed pliers**. These will be necessary for bending the wire into shape, when making the basic frames for the Crib figures. Make sure your pliers have small points or it is impossible to make small, neat bends in the wire.

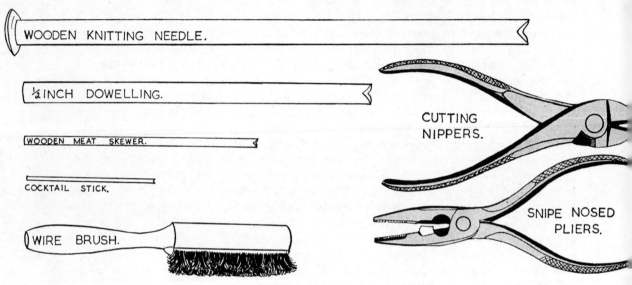

Fig. 2. *Stuffing sticks, wire brush and pliers*

A wire brush will give the fur fabric dolls an extra "finish", by bringing up all the pile flattened in the making. (A wire, suède shoe brush is ideal if kept specially for the purpose.)

Stuffing sticks are absolutely necessary to model and shape your dolls properly. If you try to push pieces of stuffing in with your fingers you will stretch the material, spoil the shape and in general find it an extraordinarily difficult process. Make a set of sticks, ranging in size from a large wooden knitting needle (for the dancing partners), ½ in. dowelling (for general use), wooden meat skewers and cocktail or orange sticks (Crib figures, etc.). Cut a V-shaped notch in the end of the sticks to help grip the stuffing, except for the very smallest—for these, file the ends blunt so that they will not pierce the material. For stuffing with sawdust, which needs to be rammed down very tightly, have a blunt-ended, very strong stick—this will push the fine "grains" more easily.

CUTTING OUT

Turnings have been allowed on all patterns, unless otherwise stated.
The easiest way to cut out most of the dolls is to place the cardboard templates on the material, draw round with a soft pencil (not a ball-point pen), and cut out on

the pencil line. Tailor's chalk may be used on dark material. There are, however, exceptions, when to facilitate the handling of slippery material or of tiny pieces, no turnings have been allowed—notably in the arms of the flat based dolls, page 256 and the bodies of the stockinette dolls, page 248. In both these cases the pattern should be drawn on to the material, then the machining done exactly on the pencil line—finally the shape is cut out about ¼ in. outside the machined edge (see fig. 43 A).

Remember when cutting out **stockinette** to have the stretch going *across* the doll, from side to side, so place the pattern on the material with the arrow on the pattern following the " grain " of the material.

Treat **fur fabric** in the same way, the arrows on the pattern pieces following the way the pile runs on the material (e.g. for the Baby Bunting, downwards on the body ; upwards on the ears). When cutting out this material work on the wrong side and cut only the backing, never the pile. To achieve this easily, use small, very sharp scissors and slide them along under the pile, taking short snips—not long, slashing strokes (fig. 3). The pile will be left to hang over the seams and cover them, whereas if it is cut off, the seams will have a raw, naked appearance. Remember, when cutting out pieces such as arms, to reverse one piece so as to make a pair—or you will have two right or two left arms !

When cutting pieces of **real fur** for hair, etc., work on the wrong side and use a razor blade, cutting only the skin backing.

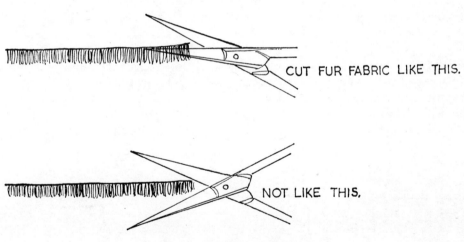

CUT FUR FABRIC LIKE THIS.

NOT LIKE THIS.

Fig. 3. *Cutting fur fabric*

STITCHING AND FINISHING

A great deal of the stitching in doll making can be done on the sewing machine —particularly the basic cotton or stockinette bodies. It is a good idea when stitching bodies and limbs to work round each piece twice for extra strength. When machining is mentioned in the text and for some reason you prefer to work by hand, substitute a small, strong **back stitch** (fig. 5 C).

When machining **stockinette** make sure you use a fine needle and a large stitch, so that the finished seam is " elastic ".

Felt is better stitched by hand, and whether working on the right or wrong side a small (*very* small !) neat stab stitch (fig. 4), using silk or Sylko which exactly matches the material, gives best results. Work as close to the edge as you possibly can, so that when stitched on the right side you have a tiny " ridge " seam, and when worked on the wrong side and turned, no stitches show when the seam is stretched, as they always do when oversewing is used. The hands and faces of the Crib figures demand *meticulous* stab stitching.

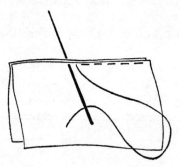

Fig. 4.   *Stab stitching felt*

Fur fabric needs careful pinning, tacking, then back stitching—all on the wrong side. Tacking for this type of material is done in the form of a large over-sewing stitch, which may be left in when the doll is stuffed and adds extra strength to the seams (fig. 5).

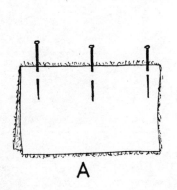 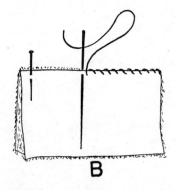 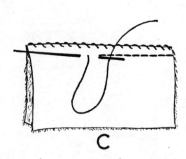

Fig. 5.   *Stitching fur fabric*
     A.   Pin
     B.   Tack by oversewing
     C.   Back stitch

For **closing openings** on felt or fur fabric, where these need to be invisible, use **ladder stitch** (fig. 6 A). This laces the two sides together firmly, turning in the raw edges at the same time. This stitch is also widely used throughout the book, for sewing one part of a doll to another ; e.g. head to body in Fat King Freddy, page 89. For this purpose one stitch is taken on the head, then one on the body and so on, the two parts being drawn neatly and invisibly together (fig. 6 B).

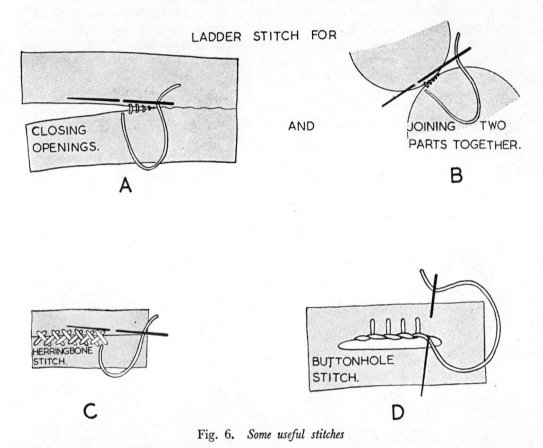

Fig. 6. *Some useful stitches*

When stuffing the fur fabric dolls, a piece of fine cotton or silk tacked round the opening will keep it from fraying. On completing these dolls, go over all the seams with the eye end of a large darning needle or the points of some small scissors, pulling out all the pile that has got caught in the stitching, before giving it a final brush.

Felt buttons, eyes, mouths, etc., are either stab stitched or hemmed in place— always neatly and as invisibly as possible, using a very fine needle. An 11 is ideal for the job, but if you cannot work with such a small size use the finest you can— nothing larger than a 9 can give good results for this job. You may find a small, curved, surgical needle a help in some of the more awkward places—these may be ordered from a chemist. However, these do take a little getting used to and all the originals were made with ordinary " betweens ".

For the dolls' clothes made of cottons and silks, use whatever stitching and seams you prefer. Quarter-inch turning has been allowed in all cases ; if you think you need more—allow it yourself. A narrow French seam is probably best.

Chamois leather may be stab stitched by hand or machined—as you prefer.

It is taken as a matter of course that all seams and other parts needing it will be pressed during making up, and the finished garments pressed carefully before putting on to dolls—just as you would if dressmaking for yourself.

When inserting **elastic** into such small circles as the legs of the clowns' tunics or the waists of the stockinette dolls' knickers, use a small gilt safety pin—a bodkin will simply not go " round ".

Sequins look attractive if sewn in place with a small bead in the centre. This hides the stitches (fig. 7 (2)), or they may be simply sewn on like a bead (fig. 7 (1)), using two or three stitches.

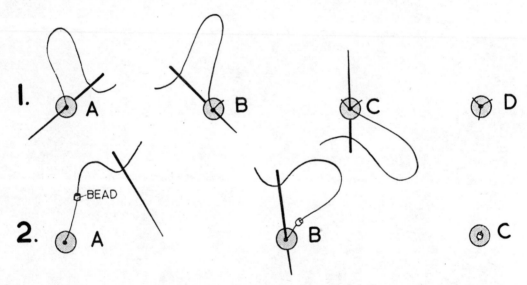

Fig. 7. *Two methods of sewing on sequins*

Pom-poms for the clowns may be made in two ways. Either gather up a circle of fur fabric and stuff it like a little ball (fig. 8 (1)) or make a small woollen ball by winding a length of wool round two cardboard circles, until the centre hole is filled up, cutting all round the edge and tying tightly at the centre (fig. 8 (2)). If you have an odd length of bobble fringe over from lamp-shade making, you will have several ready-made pom-poms.

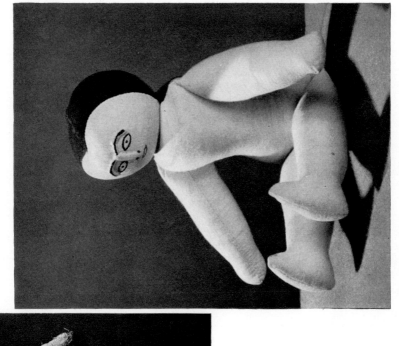

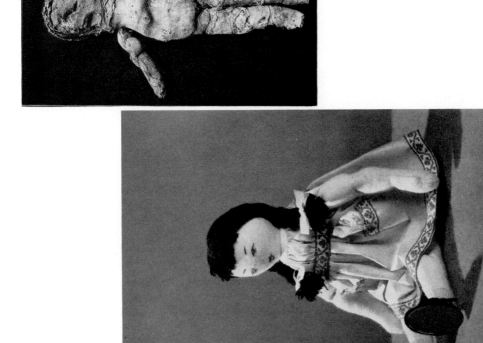

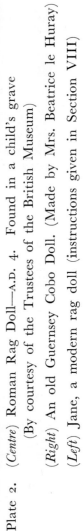

Plate 2. (*Centre*) Roman Rag Doll—A.D. 4. Found in a child's grave
(By courtesy of the Trustees of the British Museum)

(*Right*) An old Guernsey Cobo Doll. (Made by Mrs. Beatrice le Huray)

(*Left*) Jane, a modern rag doll (instructions given in Section VIII)

Plate 3. The Snowman and Eskimo Boy—both washable !

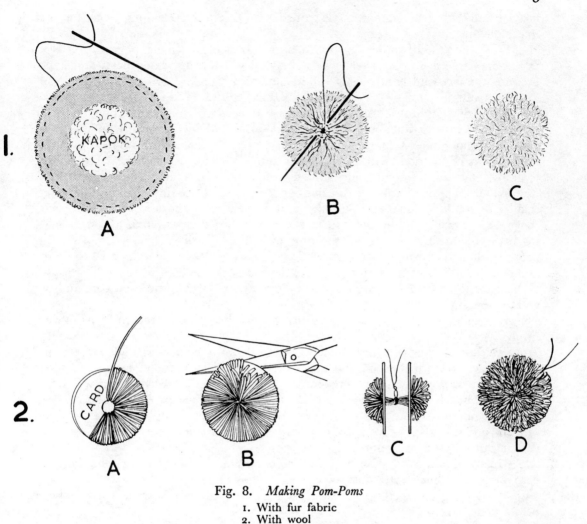

Fig. 8. *Making Pom-Poms*
1. With fur fabric
2. With wool

STUFFING

In general, dolls need to be light, and for most purposes good quality **kapok** is the best thing to use. It is not so expensive as it appears as it goes a long way. Most large stores and drapers stock it. A good substitute is **rayon strands** (see page 29). This is pleasant to use and less fluffy, so that it doesn't mess up yourself and the furniture in the same way as kapok does (until you have learned how to handle it !). It also has the advantage of being to a certain extent washable. But for all that, the preference for kapok still remains. Do not use cotton flock or any substitute you may be offered ; they sometimes appear cheaper but are in fact much heavier and "lumpy", so nothing is gained. Kapok is the *only* thing to use for such fine modelling as the Crib figures.

For a large doll, kapok can be expensive (Dancing Partners, page 179). *Wood wool*, obtainable from your greengrocer, may be put into the body parts and kapok used for the face and hands—this will also help to keep the doll lighter.

For washable dolls—(Section VI)—**foam rubber** is ideal. This is sold in furniture shops, multiple stores and drapers. It needs a little preparation. Discard any pieces with smooth, hard surfaces, and, using old scissors, chop up the pieces very much more finely than they were when you bought them. This is most essential, or the parts of the dolls with only a stockinette covering, such as the faces, will be "lumpy" instead of smooth and rounded (see page 23 for binding edges of openings).

Whatever type of stuffing you use, work slowly and carefully, using only a very small amount at a time and pushing it into place with the appropriate size stick (page 20). Start by filling the "furthest away" parts such as hands and feet, working inwards, turning the doll all the time to look at it from all angles, and shaping and modelling as much as you can, while you work. Washable dolls need to be soft and cuddly, so fill them sparingly—wired figures such as those in the Crib (Section XIV) need to be firm as a rock, so pack all you possibly can into each part and pay great attention to the shaping.

Throughout the text read "stuff firmly" for just that !—stuff these parts *really* firmly.

Sawdust stuffing is rather difficult to use. It must be packed and packed until not one more drop will go in, and then you must find room for more ! A teaspoon is a help in pouring it into the openings, and if you work over the tin in which you keep the dust, the surplus will fall back in the right place (see page 20 for stick). It is most important that you should obtain your sawdust—(almost any carpenter or timber yard will gladly give it to you)—several weeks before you need to use it, so that it can be well dried out (see page 135).

Bran makes a good substitute, and costs only a few pence per pound from the corn merchant, but it is "dusty" to use.

Avoid using chopped-up stockings or rags as a filling—the results can only be heavy and "unloving".

ENLARGING AND REDUCING PATTERNS (fig. 9)

It is possible that you will want to make some of the dolls larger or smaller than the size of the patterns given. To alter them is a very simple matter, and none of the elaborate charts and methods so often recommended are necessary.

Simply draw the pieces of the pattern to be altered on squared paper—for instance, ½ in. squares (fig. 9 A). Then draw the equivalent number of squares on a piece of paper, having each square larger or smaller as required, and copy the pattern pieces exactly on to it, making the curves identical with those of the original size pattern (fig. 9 B). Work carefully, checking constantly to make sure your lines are accurate, and the results will be perfect.

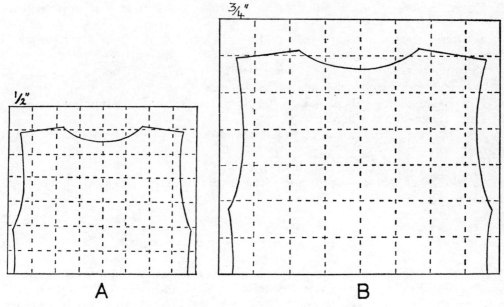

Fig. 9. *Enlarging and reducing patterns*

MAKING A " BIT BOX "

Every doll maker inevitably needs all sorts of bits and pieces from time to time, and it is a good idea to keep a box specially to hold them, so that you know just where to look when you want any odds and ends.

Things to collect:

Cuffs and any fine ribbing from old woollies and the tops of old white and bright coloured socks—for sock making.

Oddments of wool, Coton à Broder, Anchor Soft embroidery cotton, theatrical crêpe hair, fur and tow—for hair.

Good pieces of old towels or face flannels in yellow or brown—for hair for the ball toys.

Tops of nylon stockings and any good pieces of cotton stockinette from summer jumpers, etc., in pink, white or yellow—for bodies and/or faces of stockinette dolls.

Old pillow cases or similar—for binding wire frames of Crib figures.

Good pieces from worn kid, suède or chamois gloves—for shoe making.

Trouser buttons, *long* paper fasteners, coloured string and large beads—for the Jumping Jacks.

Ribbons and cords from Christmas and birthday cards—for hair ribbons and trimmings.

Beads, sequins and braids—for trimming.

Cereal boxes—for making templates of patterns; stiffening shoe soles, crowns, etc.

Sawdust—for stuffing hard dolls. (Immediately you get it, put it in a tin in the airing cupboard for several weeks, to thoroughly dry out.)

Tiny buttons and press studs—for fastening dresses and shoes.

Watch strap buckles—for fastening belts, satchels, etc.

Pipe cleaners—for stiffening fingers and using as " fur" trimming.

Lolly sticks—for the manger.

Ends of coloured nail varnish and paint, and corset and shoe laces—for the corset lace dolls.

Pill boxes—for hats and hat boxes.

All scraps of felt, however small—they will be useful for flowers and other trimmings.

SOME USEFUL ADDRESSES

As it is known that many people, especially those living in country areas, experience difficulty in obtaining materials locally, a list of addresses of firms which will accept postal orders is given below. They have been chosen from widely scattered parts of the country, and it should perhaps be stressed that these are not by any means the *only* firms which supply these goods.

Before sending an order it is of course advisable to write to a firm (enclosing an S.A.E. for a reply) to find out their stock situation, prices, postal rates and any other conditions they impose. Postal orders to The Needlewoman Shop, for instance, must be of at least £3 in value (at the time of writing, Spring 1974) and will normally take about 14 days to arrive.

FUR FABRIC: W. Shaw,
                     7 Cinder Hill,
                     Kirkburton,
                     Huddersfield, HD8 0UD,
                     Yorks.
                         and
                     Bristol Handicrafts.

STOCKINETTE: The Nottingham Handcraft Company,
                     Melton Road,
                     West Bridgford,
                     Nottingham, NG2 6HD.
                         and
                     The Needlewoman Shop.
                         and
                     Bristol Handicrafts.

FELTS: Nottingham Handcraft Co.
                                Bristol Handicrafts.
                                The Needlewoman Shop.
                                W. Shaw.

RAYON STRANDS: Bristol Handicrafts,
                                20 Park Row,
                                Bristol 1.

THEATRICAL CRÊPE HAIR:
                                Ellisdons Bros. Ltd.,
                                P.O. Box 52,
                                Kempston Road,
                                Dallas Road,
                                Bedford.

CLARK'S ANCHOR COTON À BRODER (the same shades and numbers as Clark's
    stranded cotton):
                                The Needlewoman Shop,
                                146–148 Regent Street,
                                London, W1R 6BA.

CLARK'S ANCHOR SOFT EMBROIDERY COTTON:
                                Messrs. Robert Sayle & Co.,
                                St. Andrew's Street,
                                Cambridge, CB2 3BL.
                                  and
                                The Needlewoman Shop.

DEWHURST'S SYLKO PERLÉ:
                                If you find difficulty in obtaining this, Anchor Pearl, stocked
                                by The Needlewoman Shop, is a satisfactory substitute.

*Did you know that if you go to the British Museum you can see a little
Roman Rag Doll about 4 in. long? (see plate 2). It is rather shabby
and made from a loose-weave, light brown material, not unlike our modern
scrim or hessian. It seems quite incredible, but this doll, found in a child's
grave, dates from A.D. 4 and was probably buried with the little girl to
keep her safe in her afterlife. It is a matter for speculation how many of
the dolls we make today will still be in existence 2,000 years hence!*

Section Two

NOTES ON VARIOUS PARTS OF A DOLL

MAKING THE HEADS

ACLOTH doll's head is usually thought of as a round or oval " knob "—and in most cases this is all that is needed. However, even a " knob " can be arrived at in several ways and a number of variations will be found as you work your way through the book.

Pom-Pom Heads

The flat based dolls' heads (Section IV) are made just like a " pom-pom " (fig. 8 (1))—a circle of material being gathered up and stuffed—the pulled-up gathers coming conveniently at the back, under the hair. This method is also used for the corset lace dolls.

Ball Heads

As their name implies, all the dolls in Section V have just a ball for a head, made by either the pentagon or orange peel method.

Oval-Shaped Stockinette Heads

Stockinette is such a pliable material that two ovals sewn together all the way round the outside edge, are all that are needed to make a head in this material (fig. 43). When stuffing, it is possible to push out the front to form a good " chin ", without having to make darts. All the dolls in Section VIII have heads made in this way.

Darted Heads

Cotton material or felt made up in the same way as stockinette would make a very flat head, as it has not sufficient " give " to be suitably moulded during stuffing. A series of darts all round the front of the head, and either a shaped back or more darts, give " breadth ". To understand this, look at the golliwog and felt doll patterns, pages 273 and 279, then at the pattern for the heads of the Crib figures, page 286 and at fig. 83 H, I and K.

Silhouette Heads

Sometimes, especially in a character with very accentuated features, a " silhouette " type of head is an advantage. This is specially so in the case of the Witch, fig. 64—but it has also been used for her other end—the Fairy Princess, to show that this method *can* produce a pretty face. Felt is used for these heads and very neat stitching is needed as a seam runs right down the centre of face.

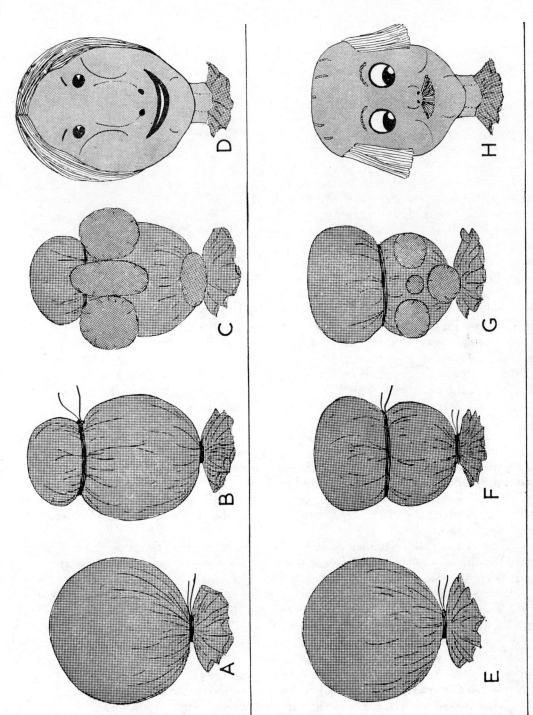

Fig. 10. *Padded heads*
1. Wobbly Winnie
2. An idea for a " little man "

Padded Heads (fig. 10)

For a comic figure, a head which is padded to incorporate nose, cheeks and chin is fun to make and can produce the most amusing, as well as pleasing results. This type of head is used for Wobbly Winnie (page 185), and illustrated by fig. 10 D.

A large double handful of kapok is moulded into a ball and tied up into a bundle, covered by a piece of muslin, curtain net or some similar fine material. Use strong thread for tying. The ball for Wobbly Winnie should be about the size of an average eating apple (fig. 10 A). Then tie a further thread several times round the head at a point near the top and pull tightly (fig. 10 B). This is where the eyes will come. (Note, they are caricaturized and come in an impossibly high position.) Now make two little balls of kapok, similar to fig. 10 A, and tie up in the same way, but have them very much smaller. Stitch in place for cheeks (fig. 10 C). Make a large oval " knob " for nose and a smaller one for chin and stitch in place (fig. 10 C). Finally cover the whole head with stockinette, following fig. 11, and stretching it *very* tightly over the face. Embroider the features.

All sorts of weird expressions can be achieved like this, merely by varying the position in which you tie the second string and the size and position of the small " knobs ". It warrants a lot of experimenting and will cause a great deal of fun.

Fig. 10 E, F, G, H show a funny little man—Wilfred perhaps—who would make an enchanting wobbly husband for Winnie. Although these heads are really more suitable for comic faces, experiment will show that they can be made into delightful baby and child heads with care. In this case, of course, much smaller " knobs " of kapok will be needed, and great care must be taken as to their position.

Moulded Heads

Many people become frightened when it comes to making the head of a doll and buy a mask—or even a whole head, thereby sinking their doll into the oblivion of a mass-produced article. What a pity !

Masks which are attractive are expensive to buy and add much to the cost of the doll. Those which are cheap, *look* cheap and give the doll a rather nasty " bazaar like " appearance.

None of the dolls in the pages which follow have moulded heads, because of the inevitable difficulty of individual people finding the right size mould to fit the body of the doll in question. However, you might like to experiment by yourself.

Select, first of all, a mould for the face. See that this is in proportion to the body of the doll you are making and that its characteristics are suitable. For instance, for a " little girl ", use a bought china or plastic doll, for an oriental face a carving on a piece of furniture, for an old man a toby jug. It is quite amazing, once you start to search, what a lot of household objects will be found suitable for this purpose. Having selected your mould make the face in this way :

1. Grease the mould very thoroughly—using a good face cream. See that every odd corner is well covered, so that the material will not stick.

2. Cut a piece of felt, a piece of muslin and a piece of paper (writing paper will do well) large enough to cover the mould completely.

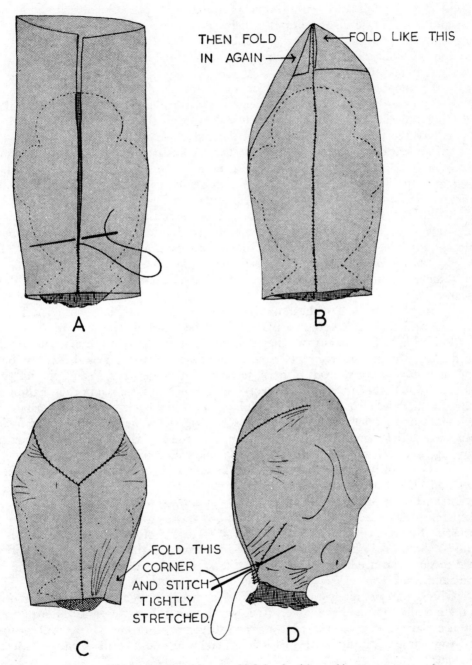

Fig. 11. *Covering a padded head with stockinette*

3. Soak the felt and muslin very thoroughly in paste. Polycell, home-made flour and water paste or any brand sold by a stationer are all quite suitable. Both pieces must be so saturated that it is possible to wring the paste out. (If the felt does not absorb it easily, soak this in water for two or three hours first, then wring it out. It will then take the paste well.)

4. Thoroughly paste the paper on both sides.

5. Squeeze the muslin gently to remove the surplus paste and place it so that it completely covers the mould, pushing it well into all the corners.

6. Lay the pasted paper on top of the muslin and repeat the process.

7. Squeeze the felt gently to remove the surplus paste and lay it on the mould, on top of the paper and muslin. Press carefully into position, making sure that it fits tightly against the mould. Using a match stick or knitting needle, go over the entire face pushing the material into the contours of the nose, eyes, mouth and wrinkles.

8. Put the covered mould away for two or three days in a warm place such as the airing cupboard and leave until completely dry and hard. You will then be able to pull it easily off the mould, which may be washed and put away. Trim the edges of the mask to make it a good shape (fig. 12 A).

(Stockinette may be substituted for felt, but has less " body ", so use a double thickness of paper in this case.)

To make the back of the head needs a certain amount of thought—the join between this part and the mask being so placed as to be covered by the hair.

Referring to fig. 12, cut two shapes as given (in fig. 12 C) from material to match the mask. The measurements of each straight side between Y and X must be the same as from the centre front of mask to base of neck between Y and X (fig. 12 B). Starting from Y at centre front and working on the wrong side, join each half of back of head to the mask from Y to X (fig. 12 D). Turn the backs away from face towards each other and ladder stitch centre back seam (fig. 12 E and F). You may find the chin needs adjustment—particularly if you have used a wide-faced mould such as a toby jug. A pair of tucks or darts usually takes care of this.

This type of head needs firm stuffing, especially in the protruding parts like the nose and cheeks, or dents will appear during play.

Features are added in the normal way—appliquéd in felt for comic faces, or embroidered—but usually painted for a little girl face—using the original mould as a pattern. Sometimes it is easier to add the features before sewing the back of the head to the mask, especially if stitching is involved, as the masks are stiff and it is hard to push the needle through, but the task is made easier if you can get to both front and back.

This is quite definitely a type of head which needs individual treatment, according to the moulds you have available. It is worth trying, however, and the experimenting necessary will give you pleasure and become absorbing. You will probably find you are making the heads first—then making up dolls to fit them, and after all, why not?

Oil paints, or any household type, are suitable for indicating the features.

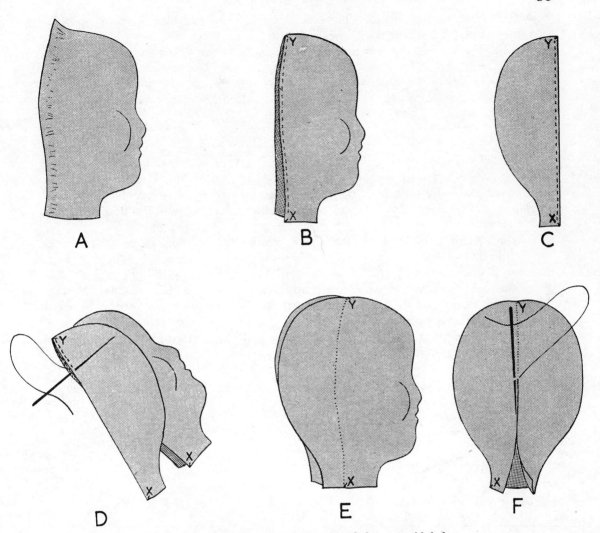

Fig. 12. *Making the back of the head for a moulded face*

ADDING THE FEATURES

Making the face of a doll seems to be the part which puts most people off attempting this very exciting branch of toy making. They buy a mask and are then surprised when their effort looks mass produced and just like the doll next door! No one can be honestly said to have made a doll unless they have created its face—the very part which gives it life and character—so do try, it really is not difficult.

Children for the most part are extremely easy to please, and ask only that their dolls shall have pleasant faces. They do not ask for all the detail that is so often put into a doll and which sometimes spoils the final effect.

Look, for instance, at some of the faces in cartoons appearing in newspapers and magazines and at the enchanting expressions of the " caricature boys and girls " who daily advertise the necessities of life on our television screens and take a cue from them—utter simplicity, just a few strokes and circles making a face brimful of character.

PLAIN EMBROIDERED FACES

Dolls' faces can be made in so many ways. Plain heads, simply embroidered, are perhaps the easiest for a beginner to start on, and the simple circles, squares and lines which make the stockinette dolls' faces (figs. 44 and 45) form a good beginning. A glance at the Eskimo Boy (fig. 36) will also show what a few well placed lines can do.

When making this type of face, if you are unsure of yourself, pencil the lines *very* lightly on to the doll first, then embroider over them, using *one strand of cotton only, at a time,* and working very neatly with a small, fine needle. Work lines in very small stem stitch and thick parts in very close satin stitch (fig. 13). The Ball Dolls in Section V are worked in exactly the same way, also the Flat Based Dolls (Section IV) and the Jumping Jacks (Section VII). Figs. 75, 76, 77 and 78 show how faces can be simplified even further, for the corset lace family do not even possess noses, and do not look amiss without them !

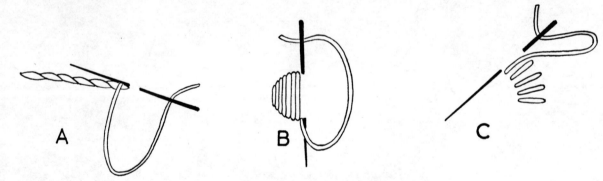

Fig. 13. *Stitches used for embroidering features*
A. Stem stitch for lines
B. Satin stitch for filling in
C. Straight stitch for lashes

Felt Appliqué

The Giant Clowns and Bertie Beacon (Section XII) have the addition of pieces of felt appliquéd in place. A tiny hemming stitch is best for this. Always stitch these pieces *all the way round*, never, as is so often done, with a stitch just here and there. In this way they become loose and eventually detached in play.

Gathered Noses

Noses for above dolls, and those in Section IX, are circles or ovals gathered up and stuffed to form little knobs. These are made just as for the pom-poms (fig. 8 (1)) but on a much smaller scale—then ladder stitched (fig. 6 B) to the face.

Modelling

Having made flat faces you may like to try a little modelling (although the simple ones are often more successful).

Baby Bunting and "Twinkle", the Star Fairy, have soft stockinette faces, on which the cheeks, nose and chin may be raised to give "shape". This should be done with a long fine needle, and silk or Sylko which exactly matches the colour of the face. A series of invisible stitches are taken from side to side of the nose and pulled tightly so that the material between the stitches is raised up (fig. 83 K, L, M). In most cases the outline to be followed when taking these stitches is shown by a broken line on the diagram concerned. These should not, however, be followed *too* rigidly, for according to the amount of stuffing in the head and just how you have shaped it, your doll may need different treatment. Cheeks are raised in the same way—but naturally you will work from top to bottom instead of sideways. Chins are raised like noses, but a little more material left between the stitches.

A Pouting Mouth adds charm to a baby face. Fig. 14 shows the method of making these. *A*, embroider a circle (for the dolls in this book ¼ in. diameter is a good size) using one strand of red cotton. *B, C, D, E,* and *F,* surround this circle with six stitches,

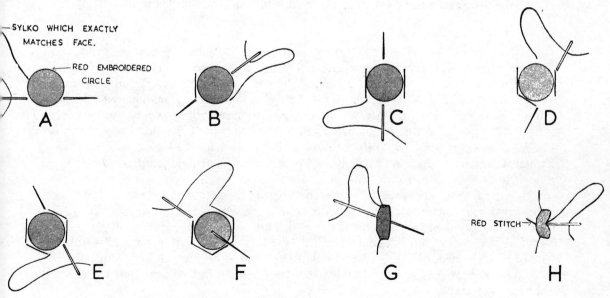

Fig. 14. *Making a "pouting" mouth on a stockinette face*

using Sylko which exactly matches the face, and pulling each one tightly to raise the circle, so that sideways it looks like *G*. Bring the needle out at centre of circle *F* and *G* and put it in again just a little way away from where you brought it out, pulling tightly to sink the mouth in the middle. Finally take a tiny red stitch each side of mouth *H*.

Sinking Eyes

When making realistic faces such as those for the Crib figures (Section XIV) and felt dolls (Section XI) the eyes need to be set back into the head to avoid a " pop-eyed " unnatural appearance. This is done by taking two straight stitches, reaching right through the head from the back to the front and back again, and pulling them very tightly to form eye sockets (see fig. 83 N). This will naturally make a " dimple " at the back of the head, which will be covered later when the hair is attached. The eyes are then either embroidered or cut from felt and sewn in place, and the lids sewn on last of all.

Sometimes the eyes may be sunk *after* attaching to the face, as in the case of the Golliwogs. In this case stitches are taken from the front to the back of the head, pulling tightly and working all round the outside edge of the eye.

Artificial Cheeks

Small felt patches hemmed to the face and raised by a little padding can often be used to give a doll a comic or naïve appearance. Fig. 58 shows that they do a lot to improve a Golliwog. In some cases they are helpful in giving a clown expression—but only, of course, if it has a felt face. The golliwog's lips are attached and padded in the same way, which gives them a full and rich appearance.

Using Paint

Care should be taken, when using paint, that the child is beyond the sucking stage ! Used with discretion, a little red water colour on the face of a stockinette or felt doll adds a lot of life and gaiety. The paint should be nothing more than red water and should be placed high up on the " cheek bones ", reaching well outwards, also a little on the chin. Always do this job in the daylight—or you may have a shock. Be prepared for the paint to sink in and lose itself the first time you apply it, for when you come back after the paint has dried, it will look much paler than when it was wet. But work slowly and give several coats, rather than overdoing it the first time—you can put more on, but can't take it off.

The painted faces of the dolls in Section IX are the greatest fun to do and they have the advantage that if not satisfied with your work, you can wipe the offending part off with a corner of rag, while it's still wet, and start again. Almost any odds and ends of household paint or enamel will do for this work. Just a word of warning—make sure the heads have been meticulously prepared and are stuffed with bone dry sawdust, so that they are hard as wood. If not, dents will appear and the painted surface will crack.

Needless to say, these dolls are not intended for the *very* young.

Beginning and Ending

The addition or modelling of features naturally messes up the back of the doll's head—one has to begin and end *somewhere*. All knots, odd stitches and dimples at the back caused by the tight stitches modelling the front, will eventually be covered by the hair, so they need not worry you as long as you bear this in mind and do not let them stray down the neck or round to the front.

Position of Features

In most cases one wants a little girl doll to look young. It is important therefore to keep the features very low down on the face, giving the doll a high forehead. A glance through the book at the various diagrams illustrating faces will show you that placed low they give a young face (fig. 44 (3)) and the higher they get, the older the appearance of the doll becomes (fig. 45 (4)).

Padded Faces such as that used for Wobbly Winnie, page 185, will be found under HEADS (padded heads page 32).

Making Masks at Home

Good imitations of bought masks may be made at home and instructions for making these appear under HEADS—(moulded heads page 32).

Finally, whatever type of face you choose to make, work slowly. First sketch the features on paper, even if you are copying exactly those given in one of the diagrams, as this will help you to grasp the general plan. Then, if you are a beginner, make up a rough head (without a doll) and experiment on this before working on the actual doll. If you are unaccustomed to needle modelling practise it carefully, for only in this way will you learn the pitfalls of pulling too tight or placing your stitches wrongly. Trial and error shows just what is needed for *your* doll—after all she is different from every other doll and needs individual treatment.

Above all, keep a sense of humour over the whole thing. Don't be put off by a few faces which don't please you. It is our mistakes that teach us far more than our successes, and *your* sense of humour will eventually come through on to the doll, so that you will be delighted with the result.

CHOOSING AND CREATING A HAIR STYLE

Everyone knows what a great deal of difference a pretty and, above all, a neat " hair do " makes to the appearance of any human being—the case is just the same in the doll world. A little time spent finding a colour and style to suit the doll you are making is immensely worth while.

Wool

Probably the greatest stand-by and in many cases the most successful material for dolls' hair is wool. This is easy to handle and stitch and fun to arrange. 2- or

3-ply knitting wool and small skeins of darning wool are all useful, and your " bit box " will probably contain odds and ends you will be glad to use up.   Figs. 44 and 45 show clearly six ideas for styles and how to arrive at them.   Instead of stitching the wool directly on to the head, it may, in some cases, first be machined to a piece of tissue paper (the machine stitching being the parting), then the paper torn away and the prepared wool back-stitched to the head, working on top of the machine stitching.   The length of the wool must be varied according to the style you are making, so that for the village gossips (fig. 20) and Wobbly Winnie (fig. 71) sufficient length must be allowed for the twists, buns and plaits.   Even if creating a short style it is always advisable to start with the wool much longer than is eventually needed, then trim it to the required shape.   Rug wool or " Double Quick Knit " is used for the Giant Clowns in Section XII.

Embroidery Cotton

There are many embroidery cottons which are useful for hair, probably the best being Coton à Broder, which has the great advantage of standing up to combing very well, so that the young owner can try out various styles for herself.

Anchor Soft is thicker, but a good texture for many dolls.

Dewhurst's Sylko Perlé, which comes in a 50-yard ball, works out cheaper than the above makes, but is perhaps not quite so effective.   (Addresses for obtaining these are given on page 29.)

Colour

The above cottons and, of course, wools are obtainable in a wide range of shades. Care should be taken in choosing a colour suitable for the complexion of the doll you are making.   Black, soft browns and gingery auburns look well (we see all too few auburn-haired dolls and they make a change—Judy, plate 11).   For fair-haired dolls avoid the bright, strong yellows and choose rather the soft honey tones.   Remember, lots of little girls have " mousy " hair and this colour looks natural and right on a doll.   Remember, also, that far more little girls have straight hair than curly ! Straight woolly or cotton hair makes a welcome change from some of the glamorous curly mops on commercially made dolls.

Bought Dolls' Hair

It is possible to buy dolls' hair in skeins or packets from many handicraft shops. Some is good, but some presents problems.   Make sure, if you do buy it, that the hair is not one mass of short ends which will pull out in play and become stuck all over the doll's clothes.   In most cases this hair is not nearly so successful as wool.

Crêpe Hair

Crêpe hair, sold in plaits by the inch, for theatrical purposes, is useful for some dolls.   It is definitely better than the hair sold specially for doll making.   When the string which binds the plait together is pulled, the hair unravels and the required length can be cut off and teased out. This is used for Joseph and the Old Shepherd in the Christmas Crib—it being very suitable for beards and hair on a doll which will not be brushed and combed. (Address on page 29.)

Fur and Fur Fabric

These two materials are useful for the sort of hair which stands up all over a doll's head—clowns (figs. 52 and 53) and golliwogs (fig. 58). If real fur is not available in large pieces it may be bought quite cheaply in narrow strips and, starting at the centre back of the head, sewn round and round in a spiral until the head is completely covered (see page 21 for cutting these materials).

You will probably think of many more things to turn into hair. Tow, for instance (from the plumber), is wonderful for an old man (fig. 95). Straw, raffia, string and even real hair can sometimes be utilized to advantage.

Be very careful not to have hair too thick or it will look ugly and plaits or " bunches " will be quite out of proportion to the size of the doll—on the other hand be sure to cover the head well so that no bald patches show through.

The material for the dress of a doll should always be chosen in conjunction with the hair-style. For instance, dolls with long, straight, dark hair do not look attractive in dresses with stripes running downwards—they look too tall and thin. In this case make the stripes run *round* the dress to give breadth to the doll, and reserve downward stripes for dolls with short, curly or " bunched " hair. It is by giving thought to these details that your dolls gain that little extra " something ".

When using hair ribbons, remember that nylon ties and stays put more easily than satin and is easier for small fingers to manage. Make sure that your ribbon is very narrow and therefore of the correct proportions for the doll. If you tie your bows in a " shoemaker's knot ", i.e. twisting the ribbon *twice* round the first loop before making the second loop, they will stay in place and not keep coming undone.

For tiny dolls like the doll's house family (Section XIII) old knitted jumpers or socks in appropriate colours are useful. Chop up the knitted material very finely with sharp scissors, so that it is a mass of tiny woollen curls. Cover the doll's head with glue, then press the curls in small handfuls to the head, until it is well covered. This is often a less " fiddly " way of making hair for such tiny dolls than the methods suggested in Section XIII, but it does not of course have the finish that the other styles do, and would not be suitable for a doll that was going to have a great deal of handling.

MAKING SHOES AND THE PATTERNS FOR THEM

Almost any solid material which does not fray may be used for doll's shoes. Scraps of felt, chamois leather, suède, Rexine, Vynide and kid were all used for the originals, and you can, of course, use whatever you have available. Old gloves are a wonderful source of supply.

The type of fastening used must depend on the age of the small owner. Little fingers can often cope more easily with press studs than buttons, and in this case, size ooo are ideal. Tiny buttons (or beads) and buttonholes may of course be used if you feel the child in question will be able to fasten and unfasten them. Button-holes should always be worked round for reinforcement or the slits will stretch and become useless—especially on a felt shoe. Lace-up shoes of such a small size are fiddly and not practical for tiny hands to tie up, so they are not included here.

The shoes in this section have all been designed to fit various dolls which appear in the book. They have been grouped together so that a " shoe shop " could easily be stocked, and to this end a box has also been included.

The sandals, welted ankle strap, dancing pumps, bar shoes, ankle straps, sandal shoes, moccasins, and bedroom slippers fit the stockinette dolls in Section VIII, and the box on page 51 will fit these shoes.

The casual shoes fit Meg in Section IX.

The four pairs of clowns' shoes fit any of the clowns in Section IX.

The mules, strip sandals, rustic sandals and oriental sandals fit the male figures in the Christmas Crib in Section XIV.

The Jester's shoes and Cowboy's boots fit the felt dolls in Section XI.

Preparation of Soles (fig. 15)

Cut two sole shapes in cardboard for each pair of shoes and two in the material to be used for soles, slightly *larger*. Run a gathering thread all round the edge of material and placing cardboard inside, pull up gathers tightly and work a few " criss-cross " stitches to hold the cardboard stiffening in place. Cut another pair of soles, slightly *smaller* than the pattern, from some material suitable for lining the shoe. Felt or even stiff paper will do. Stick this in place. (White lint makes an effective " fleecy " lining for bedroom slippers.) Make up each type of shoe as described under its own separate heading.

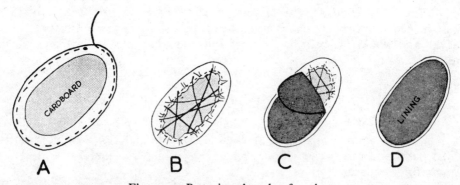

Fig. 15. *Preparing the sole of a shoe*

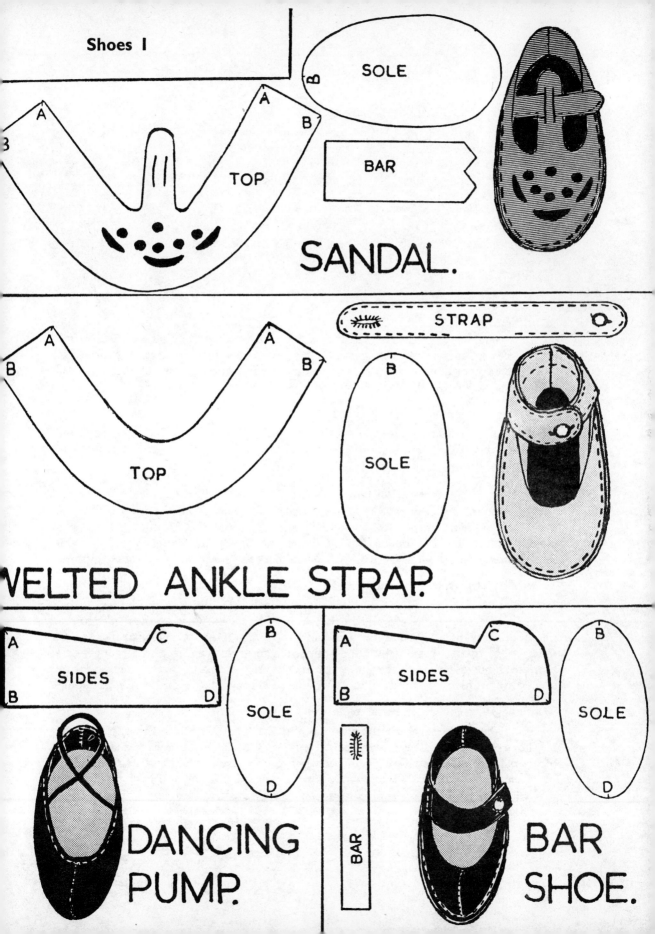

Shoes 1

SOLE

B

B
A

A
B

TOP

BAR

SANDAL.

A

A

B

B

TOP

STRAP

B

SOLE

VELTED ANKLE STRAP.

A   C

B   D

SIDES

B

SOLE

D

DANCING
PUMP.

A   C

B   D

SIDES

B

SOLE

D

BAR

BAR
SHOE.

Sandals (Diagram and pattern page 43)

Prepare soles (fig. 15). Join back seams A–B on wrong side of tops. Cut decorative holes and slots. Place tops on top of soles and stab stitch all round on right side to form a " welt ". Fold bars in half and stitch. Stitch bars to side of tops, thread through slots and sew on fastenings.

Welted Ankle Strap (Diagram and pattern page 43)

Prepare soles (fig. 15). Join back seams A–B on wrong side of tops. Cut two straps for each shoe. Stab stitch these together all round except for a small portion as shown on sketch. Slip centre back of shoes between these open portions and stab stitch in place. Stab stitch tops to soles on the right side. Attach fastenings.

Dancing Pump (Diagram and pattern page 43)

Prepare soles (fig. 15). Cut two sides for each shoe and stab stitch these together on the wrong side C–D. Turn in a tiny hem all round top edges and stab stitch. Stitch soles to sides on the *wrong* side. Ease sides over soles so that the pumps are the right side out and neatly turn in and ladder stitch the back seams B–A. Attach a short length of round, black elastic to cross over foot.

Bar Shoe (Diagram and pattern page 43)

Prepare soles (fig. 15). Cut two sides for each shoe and join these on the wrong side C–D and A–B. Stitch completed top to sole on the right side to form a welt. Attach bar to one side of shoe and fastening to the other.

Ankle Strap (Diagram and pattern page 45)

Prepare soles (fig. 15). Cut two sides for each shoe, remembering to slit along E–D–C to form the straps. On the wrong side join seams E–F. Stitch sides to soles on the wrong side. Ease sides up over soles so that the shoes are right way out. Neatly ladder stitch back seams B–A. Make fastenings and add " bow " trimming.

Sandal Shoe (Diagram and pattern page 45)

Prepare soles (fig. 15). Cut two sides for each shoe and join on the wrong side seams C–D. Stitch sides to soles on the wrong side. Ease sides up over soles so that the shoes are right way out and neatly join back seams B–A. Cut two straps for each shoe. Fold two of these in half and stab stitch together leaving a small loop at the top, the same width as the strap. Stitch these folded straps to front of shoes and the other two straps to the inner sides. Slot these through loops and make fastenings.

Moccasin (Diagram and pattern page 45)

Fold the two bases so that A meets B and C meets D. Stitch these small seams on the wrong side. These form the " heels ". On the right side gather up front of bases all round from E–F. Pull up tightly and fasten off. Stab stitch flaps in place on the right side. Oversew two pipe cleaners all round top edge for fur and, if liked, decorate front with one or two beads or a little embroidery.

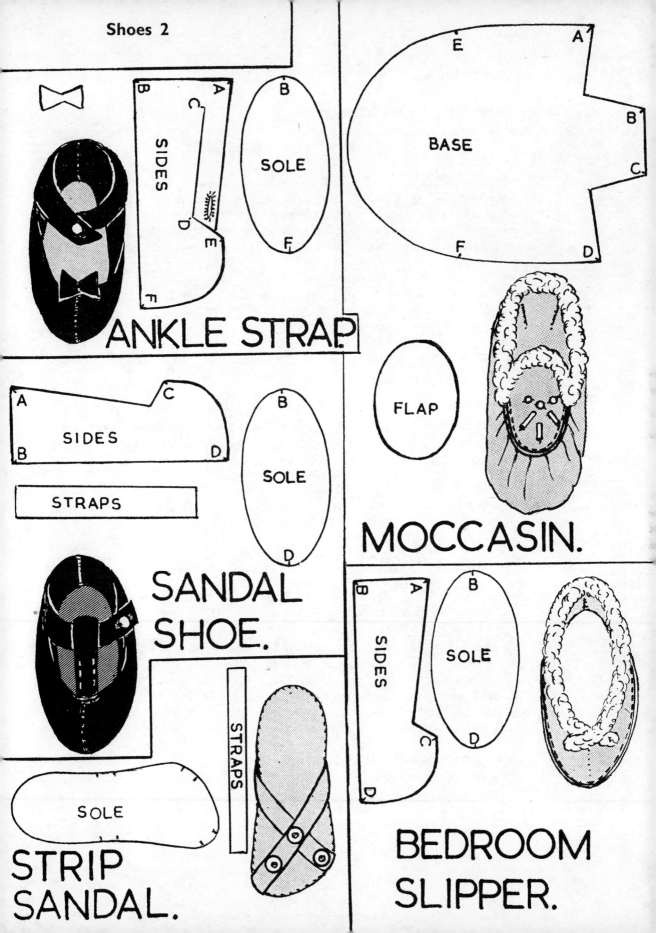

SIDES

B — A
C
SOLE
B
D
E
F
F

ANKLE STRAP.

E — A
BASE
B
C
F — D

A — C
SIDES
B — D
STRAPS
SOLE
B
D

FLAP

MOCCASIN.

SANDAL SHOE.

B — A
SIDES
SOLE
B
C
D — D

STRAPS
SOLE

STRIP SANDAL.

BEDROOM SLIPPER.

Bedroom Slipper (Diagram and pattern page 45)

Prepare soles (fig. 15). Make up slipper exactly as given for the bar shoe on page 44, but omit bar and oversew two pipe cleaners all round the top for fur.

Strip Sandal (Diagram and pattern page 45)

Prepare soles (fig. 15 A and B), but do not stick on the lining. Cut two straps for each shoe and stitch these to top of sole as shown on diagram, so that they cross at centre front. Add lining, oversewing in place instead of sticking, and decorate straps with beads and/or sequins.

Casual Shoe (Diagram and pattern page 47)

Make just as for bar shoe, but omit the bar and sew a small shanked pearl button on the front.

Clown's Shoe No. 1 (Diagram and pattern page 47)

These are large ungainly shoes with toes that turn in. Make as for bar shoe, but omit bar and turn a tiny hem all round top edge.

Clown's Shoe No. 2 (Diagram and pattern page 47)

A large, plain shoe which turns up slightly at the toe. Make as for bar shoe, but omit bar and add a large red " pom-pom " (see fig. 8). Turn in a tiny hem all round top edge.

Clown's Shoe No. 3 (Diagram and pattern page 48)

A large plain pump, turned up slightly at the toe. Make exactly as for dancing pump, but omit elastic and add a few sequins on front.

Clown's Shoe No. 4 (Diagram and pattern page 48)

A typical clown's "outsize" shoe. Make just as for bar shoe, but omit bar and turn in a tiny hem all round top edge.

Mule (Diagram and pattern page 48)

Prepare two *pairs* of soles (fig. 15 A and B). (No linings are needed for these shoes.) Cut two tops, one for each shoe, and turn back neatly where shown by broken lines along *long* sides ; press, but do not stitch. Stitch tops to one pair of soles, where shown by broken lines across short ends, tucking the " extra " pieces underneath. Now oversew the second pair of soles to the first, having the wrong sides together and the " extra " pieces on the tops between the two soles. Decorate with beads and/or sequins.

Rustic Sandal (Diagram and pattern page 49)

Cut one sole, one toe strap, two ankle straps and one sole lining for each sandal. Also one cardboard " stiffener " for each sole. Using a good glue or Copydex,

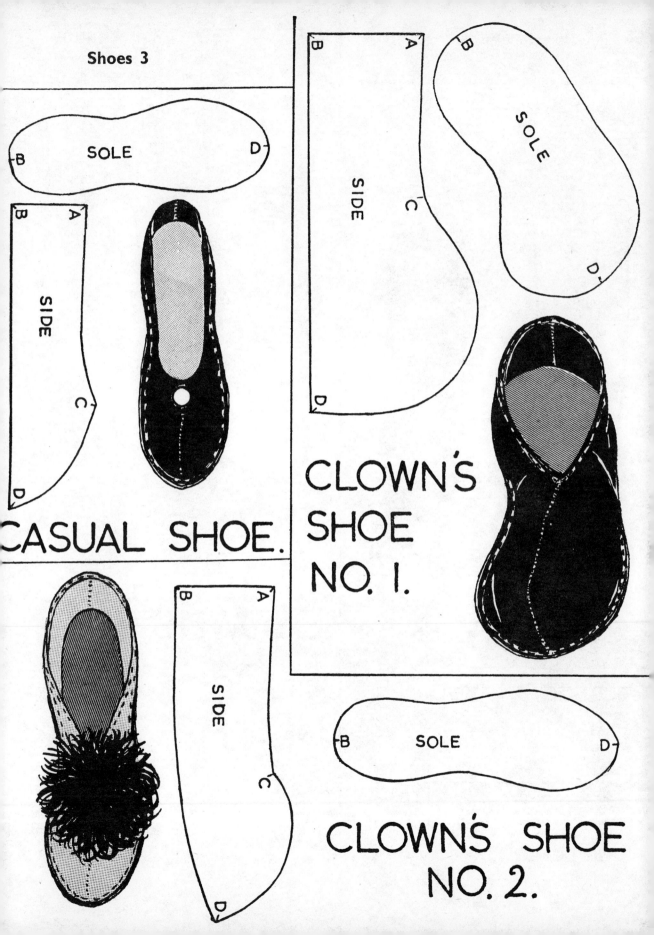

Shoes 3

SOLE

B

D

SIDE

B A

C

D

CASUAL SHOE.

SIDE

B A

C

D

CLOWN'S SHOE NO. 1.

B A

SIDE

C

D

SOLE

B

D

B A

C

D

SOLE

B D

CLOWN'S SHOE NO. 2.

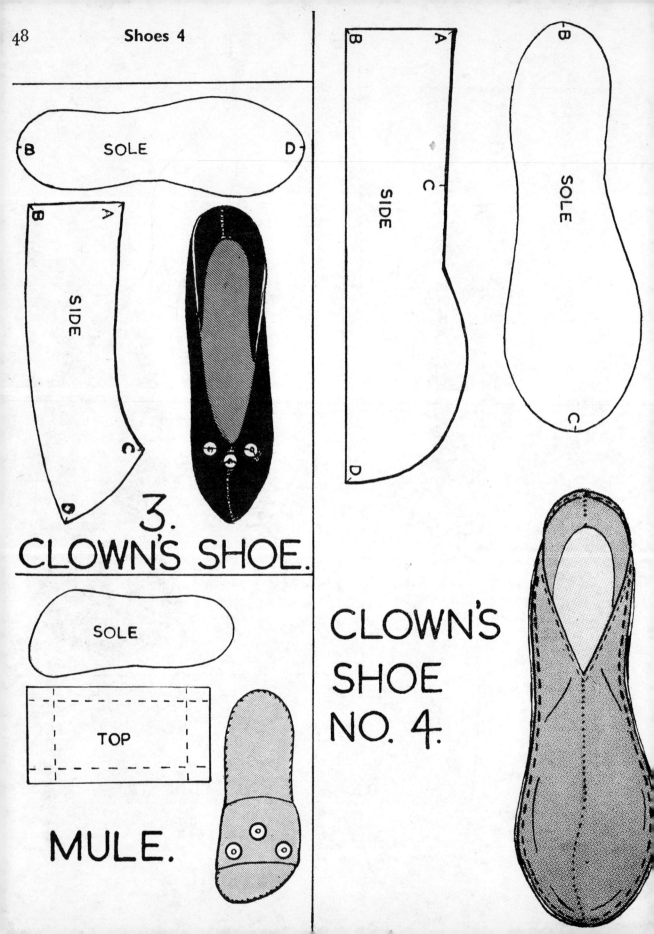

B　SOLE　D

A　B

SIDE

A　B

C

SIDE

D

3.

CLOWN'S SHOE.

SOLE

TOP

MULE.

B

SIDE

C

D

B

SOLE

C

CLOWN'S SHOE NO. 4.

Plate 4. Baby Bunting is giving the Piccaninny a pick-a-back, whilst Toni takes things easy

Plate 5.   Elizabeth is showing off, while "Twinkle" the star fairy and flat based Emily look on disapprovingly

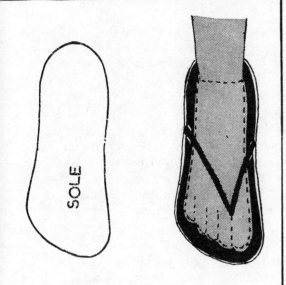

ORIENTAL SANDAL.

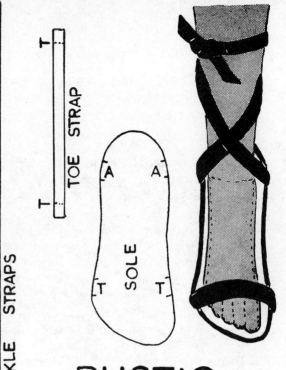

TOE STRAP

ANKLE STRAPS

RUSTIC SANDAL.

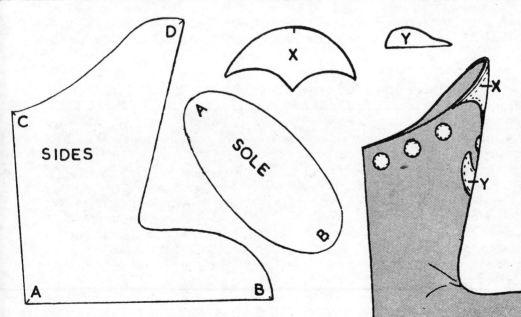

SIDES

SOLE

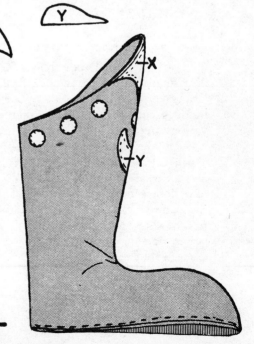

COWBOY'S BOOT.

stick the linings to the stiffeners. Stick the toe strap in place matching T's, and the ankle straps matching A's. Lastly stick on the soles, covering the ends of the straps which were tucked *under* the stiffeners. Allow to dry thoroughly before tying on to doll.

Oriental Sandal (Diagram and pattern page 49)

Prepare two *pairs* of soles (fig. 15 A and B). No linings are needed for these shoes. Place the prepared soles together in pairs and oversew neatly together with the wrong sides inside and using silk or Sylko which exactly matches the top sole. Place on the foot of doll and stitch heel of foot to the heel part of sole of sandal. Make the " strips " by taking two long stitches of thick embroidery cotton, as shown on diagram, stitching right through the foot between the first two toes.

Cowboy's Boot (Diagram and pattern page 49) Illustration plate 7

Prepare soles (fig. 15). Cut two sides for each boot and join back seams A–C and front seams B–D on the wrong side. Turn right side out. Open out boots and place on top of prepared soles matching A's and B's. Stab stitch all round on the right side to form a welt. Decorate by stab stitching circles of yellow felt round the top edges (cut with a leather punch) and shape X shown on pattern to centre front at tops of boots. Sew two shapes cut as Y, meeting diagonally at centre front seam, a little lower down.

Jester's Shoe (Diagram and pattern page 51)

Cut one sole in felt and one very slightly smaller in cardboard and two sides for each shoe. Stick the cardboard (inner) sole to the felt one. Working on the *right* side in stab stitch, join the two sides F–A and B–C–D–E. Place these joined pieces on top of the prepared sole and stab stitch all round A–B–A, with the cardboard inside the shoe. Sew a tiny brass bell securely to each of the three points.

Shoe Box (Diagram and pattern page 51)

Cut out the shapes shown for the base and lid in thin but strong white card. A postcard would be an ideal thickness but is not sufficiently large. The back of a large greeting card can often be utilized or the sheet of cardboard placed by the laundry inside a man's shirt. If neither of these is available, most stationers sell card of various thicknesses for a few pence per large sheet.

On the right side, score the box lightly A–B, B–C, C–D and D–A by running a penknife along the edge of a ruler. Fold the sides and ends upwards so that the W's meet, also the X's, Y's and Z's. Fasten in this position by sticking narrow pieces of Sellotape down each " corner " W–D, X–C, Y–B and Z–A. Make up the lid in the same way. Cut a small label to fit the end of the box, and print on it description of shoe, size and price. This box is designed to fit the sandals, welted ankle straps, dancing pumps, bar shoes, ankle straps, sandal shoes, moccasins and bedroom slippers, but can easily be enlarged to fit any of the other styles.

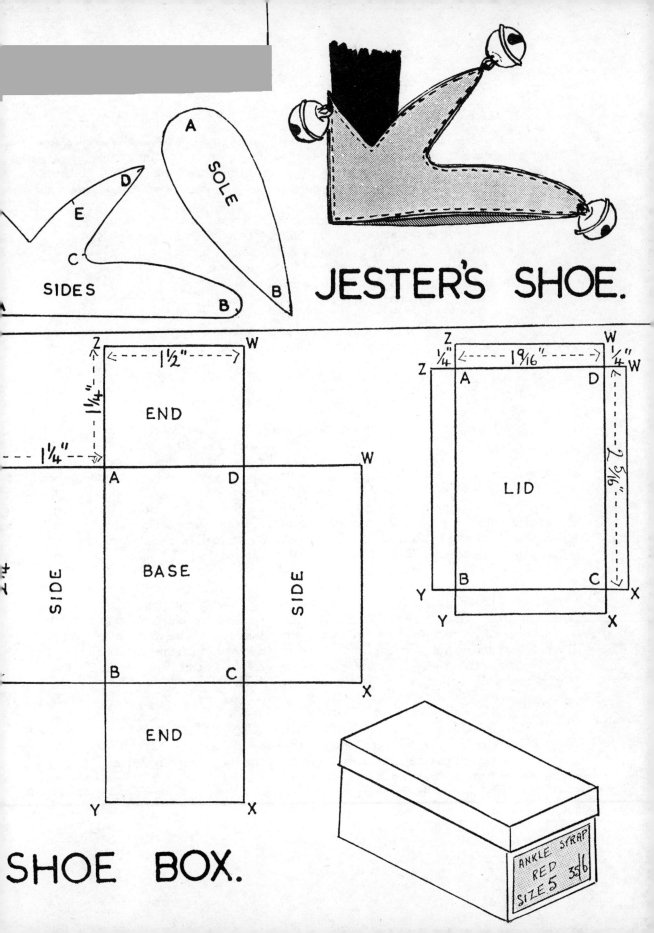

A

D

E

SOLE

C

SIDES

B

B

B

JESTER'S SHOE.

Z ← 1½" → W

1¼"

1¼"

END

A   D

W

SIDE | BASE | SIDE

B   C

X

END

Y   X

Z   ¼" ← 1⁹⁄₁₆" → W ¼"
Z   A   D   W

2⁵⁄₁₆"

LID

B   C
Y   X
Y   X

SHOE BOX.

ANKLE STRAP
RED
SIZE 5   35/6

MAKING HATS AND THE PATTERNS FOR THEM

Felt is the most useful material for hats. Strong cardboard is also needed for stiffening some of the brims, whilst pill boxes form a good foundation for many styles. Don't think you must be perpetually ill in order to acquire these—most chemists will willingly sell them to you for a penny or two and carry a variety of sizes and depths for you to choose from !

The Cowboy's Hat will fit the felt dolls in Section XI.

The Two Clowns' Hats will fit the painted calico dolls in Section IX.

The Witch's Hat will fit the double-ended doll in Section XII.

The Top Hat will fit the snowman in Section VI.

The Boater will fit Wobbly Winnie in Section XII.

The School Cap, Beret, School Hat, Skull Cap, all the hats for the hat shop (also Wobbly Winnie's boater) will all fit the stockinette dolls in Section VIII, although the hats on page 61 with the possible exception of A have not been designed with a little girl character in mind, but merely for the shop.

Cowboy's Hat (Diagram and pattern page 53)

Use a good firm felt in grey or fawn.

Cut two sides and one brim.

Stitch the sides together all around A–B–C on the wrong side. Turn right side out, open out and place on brim. Stitch crown to brim all round A–X–C–X–A. Turn outer edge of brim upwards, tacking in place, so that it makes a " hem " about ¼ inch wide. Hold this edge under a lightly dripping tap to wet it thoroughly, turning the hat round and round and pressing out pleats and wrinkles between your thumb and forefinger. Press all round the rim with a very hot iron over a cloth, until the felt is dry. Remove tacking threads, damp and press again and again until the wrinkles are all " shrunk " out and the hat has a smoothly turned up, outer edge, and is perfectly dry. This all takes a little time and patience, but is very worth while as the finished effect is most professional !

Cut a tiny slit where crown and brim meet, at each of the two X's. Take two pieces of leather thonging each about 7½ in. long. Stitch one piece round base of crown from one X to the other and slip the surplus and remaining length through the slit to the underside of hat. Take the other piece of thonging and stitch from this last X round to the first one, thread the end down through this slit—you should now have a band round the hat and two lengths protruding below. Tie the two ends in a slip knot to fasten under the cowboy's chin.

Witch's Hat (Diagram and pattern page 55)

Use black felt.

Cut one crown in felt and one in stiff paper.

Cut two felt pieces slightly larger than the entire brim pattern, also one " brim " in strong cardboard—i.e. a ½ inch wide circle.

* Place the cardboard brim between the two felt circles. Stab stitch the two

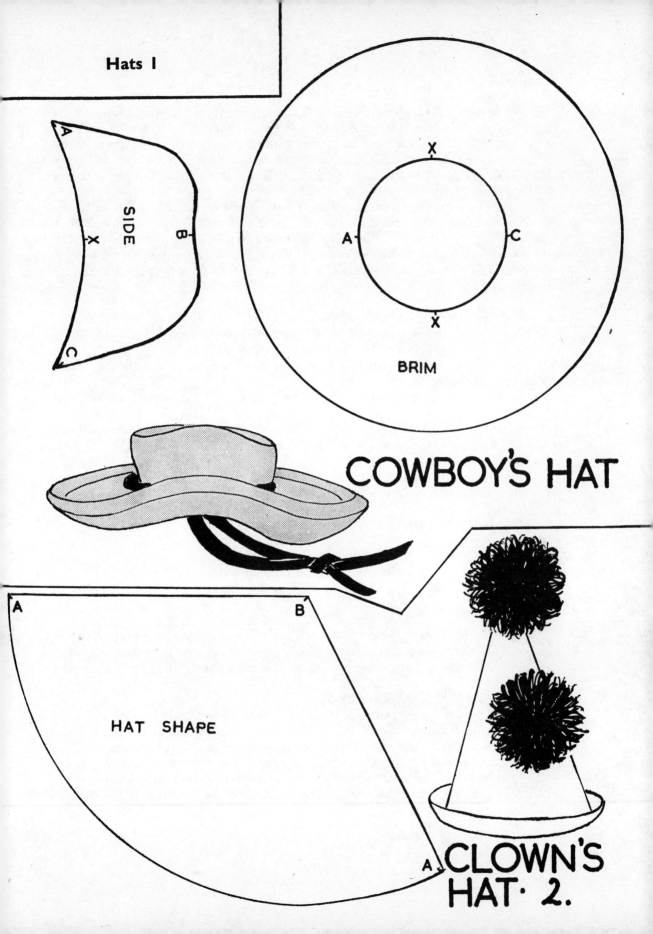

Hats 1

SIDE

BRIM

COWBOY'S HAT

HAT SHAPE

CLOWN'S HAT · 2.

felt pieces together all round outside edge, thus completely enclosing brim. Trim this edge neatly. Stab stitch all round the inner circle of brim, feeling with your needle to get the stitches close in to the cardboard. Now push the point of your scissors through the two thicknesses of felt at X and slash from here to the edge of brim as shown by broken lines on pattern. These felt points will eventually go up inside hat and keep the crown in place.*

Stick the felt crown to the paper one using Gripfix or a similar adhesive. Allow to dry. Roll the piece round so that solid edge A–B rests on broken line A–B and the extension C underlaps. Stick in this position and invisibly slip stitch A–B. †Place the crown on brim and stabbing the needle through from top to under surface of brim stitch the two parts together all round. Fold the slashed points up into hat and stick in place.†

Top Hat (Diagram and pattern page 56)

Cut one top in felt and one in stiff paper, very slightly smaller.

Cut one " side " in felt and one in stiff paper from A–B only.

Cut two felt circles slightly larger than the outer circle of brim, also one " brim " in strong cardboard.

Make up the brim exactly as given for the witch's hat above, working from * to *.

Stick the felt side piece to the paper piece, using Gripfix or similar adhesive. Allow to dry. Roll round so that A's and B's meet and the felt flap overlaps. Stitch invisibly down C–D.

Stick paper top to felt top and place on one end of rolled side piece. Oversew all round neatly. Attach crown to brim as given for witch's hat above, working from † to †.

Press sides up between thumb and finger to give " style ".

Clown's Hat No. 1 (Diagram and pattern page 55)

Fold the piece in half so that the B's meet and stitch A–B on the wrong side. Turn right side out.

Clown's Hat No. 2 (Diagram and pattern page 53)

Fold the piece in half so that the A's meet and on the wrong side stitch seam A–B. Turn right side out. Make two pom-poms (fig. 8) and stitch to front. Press up the lower edge to form a narrow rolled brim, using a damp cloth and hot iron.

Boater (Diagram and pattern page 56)

Cut the brim piece once in strong card and twice in felt, just a fraction larger. Place the card between the felt and stab stitch all the way round the outside edge. Trim if necessary. Take the lid of a 2-inch pill box and cover with felt—a strip round the edge and a circle to cover the top, this is the crown. Place the covered lid in the centre of the brim and ladder stitch the two together all round lower edge of crown. Stitch a narrow piece of ribbon or tape round crown and make a felt

CROWN

A

B

C

B

WITCH'S HAT.

BRIM

HAT SHAPE

B

A

B

CLOWN'S HAT. 1.

BRIM

X

TOP

SIDE

B A

B A
D C

TOP HAT.

BRIM

LID OF

2" PILL BOX

PETAL

LEAF

CENTRE

BOATER.

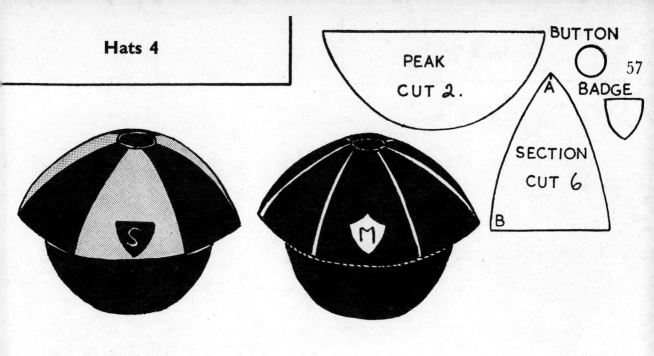

PEAK
CUT 2.

BUTTON

BADGE

57

A

SECTION
CUT 6

B

SCHOOL CAP.

LOWER EDGE.

TOP.

BAND.

BERET.

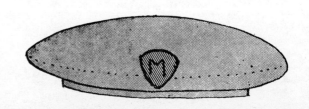

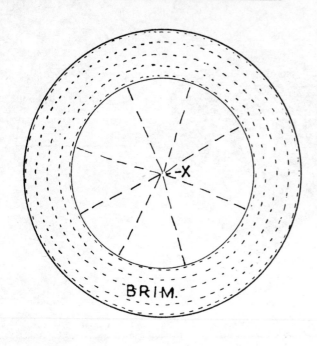

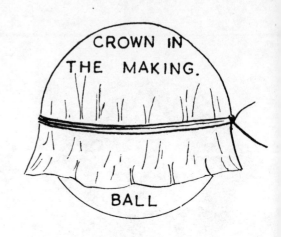

CROWN IN THE MAKING.

BALL

SCHOOL HAT.

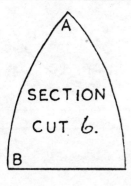

A

SECTION CUT 6.

B

○ LEAF

○ PETAL

SKULL CAP.

flower and leaf at centre front.   Stitch on a piece of round, black elastic, to keep the hat on doll's head.   The flat underside of brim, with no hole for head, will keep the hat sitting right on top of the head at the rather " silly " angle which suits this type of hat.

School Cap (Diagram and pattern page 57)

Cut six sections (three in a light colour felt and three in a dark) and two peaks in one of these colours. Join alternate coloured sections together on the wrong side from A–B. Turn right side out. Sew a small circle of felt where the sections meet at A, for a " button ". Oversew the two peak pieces together round the curved edge on the right side, then slip the cap between these sections along the straight edge and sew on both sides, making sure that one of the sections comes evenly in the centre of peak. Cut a small badge from felt and embroider an initial or initials on it—hem neatly to front of cap.

Alternatively cut all the sections from the same colour felt and sew a very narrow cord down each join.

Beret (Diagram and pattern page 57)

Cut one edge piece and one top in felt. Place the edge on the top and stitch together all the way round the outside. Turn right side out. Stitch a very narrow band of felt all round the inner circle, being careful not to stretch this as you work —or bind this circle with a narrow bias of matching soft cotton material. If intended as a school beret add a badge.

School Hat (Diagram and pattern page 58)

Choose some hard object the same size and shape as the head of the doll who is to wear the hat, e.g. a ball, a small cup, a cardboard Easter egg. Thoroughly soak a piece of felt and press it over the top of the ball, tying it round in the same position as where the hat band will be on the finished article. Put it away for a day or two until thoroughly dry—but take it out from time to time and press and ease the felt to the shape of the ball, trying to make all the " tucks " and " wrinkles " disappear and moulding a smooth crown. If necessary hold in steam and press with your fingers.

Cut two brims, stab stitch together all round the outside edge, then make several rows of stitching round and round to stiffen and add body. Slash from the inner circle to X, following broken lines. When the crown is ready, trim off surplus felt at base and place on brim. Turn the slashed pieces up inside and stitch crown to brim all round, where the stitches will be under ribbon. With a little paste (Grip-fix is good for this), stick the slashed points up inside the crown, cutting the tops off if they seem to be too long. Make a ribbon from a narrow piece of striped cotton material and stitch round hat, turning the raw edges in as you work. Make a mock " bow " in the same way as Bert's tie (page 140 and fig. 52), stitching in place over the join in the ribbon, on one side. Cut out and sew on a small felt badge.

Skull Cap (Pattern and instructions page 58)

Cut six sections in gay coloured felt and, on the wrong side, join them together A–B. Turn right side out and sew a small circle of felt in a contrasting colour where the sections meet at A. Decorate with rows of chain stitch in another colour down each join and round the edge. Cut small circles of felt and hem neatly in place in fives, for flowers. Cut out leaves in green, and hem in place. Work a french knot in the centre of each flower and the stalks in stem stitch using one strand of cotton.

Stocking a Hat Shop (Ideas on page 61)

Every little girl would love a hat shop as a gift. The easiest way to stock it is to use 2-inch pill boxes as a foundation, for on these many " models " can be based. A, B and C are made from the *lids*, in almost the same way as the boater on page 54. These hats will need to go right *on* the head, not rest on the top as Wobbly Winnie's does, so they must have hollow crowns. To achieve this, make the brim as for the top hat or witch's hat (page 54 and 52 respectively) slashing the soft centre part and turning these points up into the crown. A has a simple ribbon trimming with long tails hanging down the back ; B has a large net bow and C a circle of flowers cut from the petal pattern given for the boater on page 56.

D, E and F are made from the *boxes* themselves, which give a deeper crown.

D is made in the same way as A, B and C with a band of spotted material held in place by a watch strap buckle.

E is first covered with soft silk or cotton by cutting a large circle of this material, placing it right over the box, pleating all round and turning the raw edges up inside the box where they are stuck with paste or Seccotine.

The whole hat is then covered by tiny felt flowers and leaves cut from the pattern on page 56 and stitched in place—quite a lengthy process, but a worth while one !

F. For this model the box is covered in the same way as E, and a felt rose and two leaves stitched to one side.

Should you want boxes for your hats, use very large pill or ointment boxes and cover them with gay striped or spotted paper. Stick a tiny label on the side on which is printed the name of the shop—for instance, if the shop is for a little girl called Mary, call it " Mary Hats Ltd." or " Mary the Milliner "—something personal always thrills a small child.

For ideas and instructions for making straw hats see *Modern Soft Toy Making*, Section VI.

SOME GENERAL NOTES TO HELP YOU

Various adhesives are used in the making of the dolls. Which one you use is really a matter of personal choice or what you have by you—those named are only a suggestion. As a general guide :

1. For sticking woolly hair to the sides of the head to give shape and avoid dis-

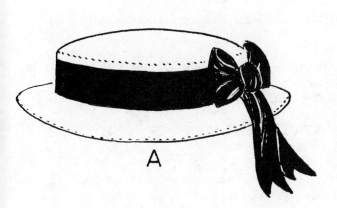

A

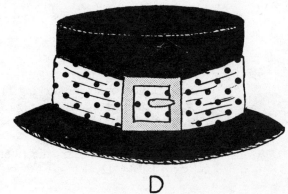

D

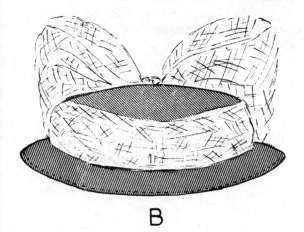

B

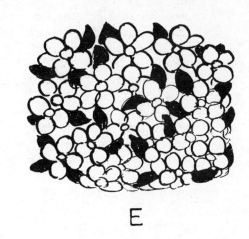

E

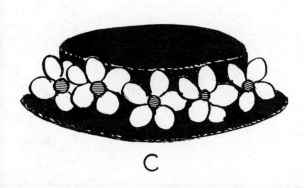

C

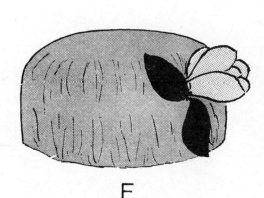

F

USING PILL BOXES TO STOCK A HAT SHOP.

arranging, as in the Witch and " Twinkle ", use something transparent such as gum or Polycell.

2. For making the manger, use the glue pot (if you have one) or Seccotine—the same thing applies to sticking fur fabric to heads (Clowns, Section IX).

3. For making masks use paper hanger's paste—Polycell or flour and water.

4. For sticking felt, Copydex or one of the latex adhesives is good—but use very sparingly.

Gripfix is sometimes effective. NEVER SUBSTITUTE STICKING FOR STITCHING!

Some of the dolls undress and some do not—different age groups have different needs in this respect. When the undressing stage is reached, do remember that small hands find difficulty in putting arms through awkward little armholes—hence the dresses fastening all down the back in Section VIII and simple snap fasteners. Tiny buttons are too difficult for small fingers to fasten. Choose materials which will stand up to repeated " dolls' washing days " and patterns which are small and in proportion to the size of the doll.

As you work through the book you will notice that most of the quantities of materials given are in rectangular or square shaped pieces. This was done on the assumption that most people would have odds and ends in their " bit box " or piece drawer which they would want to use up. However, when it is thought that buying may be necessary, yardage is given as well, and in cases where it is very much more economical to buy sufficient material for more than one doll this has been stated.

*   *   *

Did you know that in 1915 Polish rag dolls were sold in America for the Polish Victims Relief Fund ? Representing children and adults, each doll had a medallion hanging round its neck on which were inscribed the words : " Health and happiness, kind doll lover, who by taking into your heart and home one of my little doll waifs of Poland, have fed a starving mother or child in our sad land.—Helena Paderewski."

Fig. 16. *A clown from a handkerchief*

Section Three

"SPUR OF THE MOMENT" DOLLS

"WHAT CAN I DO NOW, MUMMY?" or "Make me a doll, Mummy!" —every parent must have been faced with these problems and demands. A wet afternoon, a small invalid or convalescent child to amuse, or a grand-child to stay, are all obvious "doll making" occasions. The request usually comes on the spur of the moment, when no suitable material is at hand and time is short.

The three ideas which follow are all made from things most of us can find about the house—a piece of paper, a man's handkerchief, a skein of wool. They are crude but fun, and according to the age of the child mother can do the difficult parts, then sit back and get on with the mending, while small daughter (or son !) adds the trim-mings. These dolls are not intended as permanent members of the toy cupboard —but merely as "something to do".

A CLOWN FROM A FOLDED HANDKERCHIEF (fig. 16)

Take a man's handkerchief or similar sized square of odd cotton material. An old hankie with a frayed hem will do or even a perfectly good one, as it will not be harmed and can be unstitched and returned later.

Fold in half cornerwise (A). Take a small handful of cotton wool from the medicine cupboard and press into a little round ball. Put into the top fold of the handkerchief to make the head, and tie firmly round the neck with strong thread (B). Pull the top corners up to make arms. Tuck the points in and oversew along " edge of sleeves " and down " underarms ". Separate the two lower corners, pulling one to the right and one to the left for legs. Fold these corners so that the edges meet and oversew edges (C). Tie a piece of ribbon round the waist, and a piece of thread round each " wrist ". Stitch a small red button to the centre of face for a nose and with black wool embroider a cross for each eye and V for the mouth. Cut a little bundle of wool 2 in. long and stitch to top of head for hair.

If other buttons or sequins are available even a very young child can amuse herself by sewing these down centre front, or to the wrists and ankles, and decorating her clown as she wishes.

A LITTLE GIRL FROM A SKEIN OF WOOL (fig. 17)

Take an odd skein of wool—any colour. Ideally one ounce of fine knitting wool should be used as this is more " bulky " than one ounce of a coarser wool.

If making a small doll and using darning wool use two skeins put together. (If

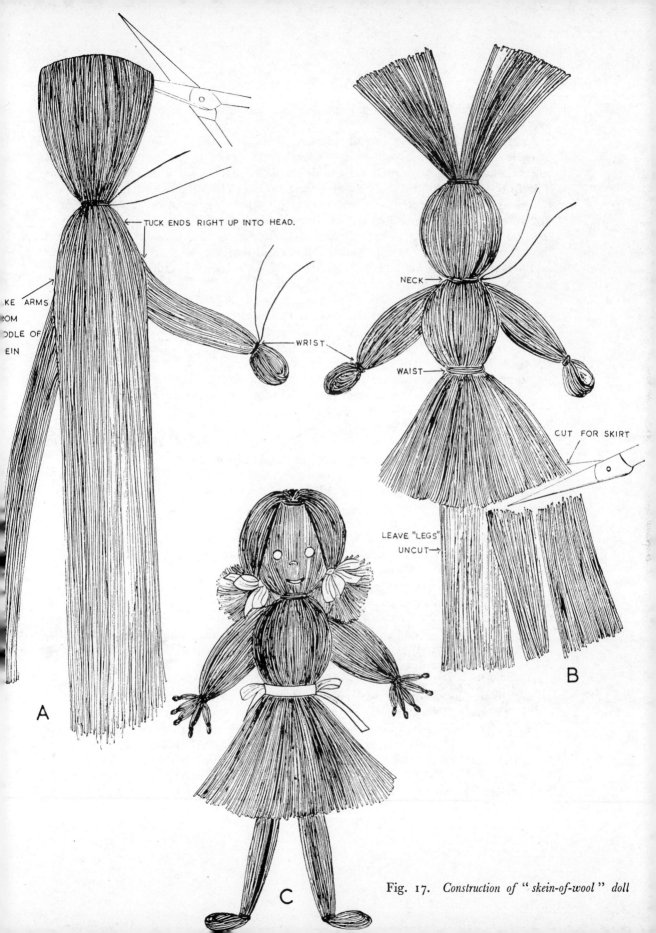

TUCK ENDS RIGHT UP INTO HEAD.

MAKE ARMS
FROM
MIDDLE OF
SKEIN

WRIST

A

NECK →

WAIST

WRIST

CUT FOR SKIRT

LEAVE "LEGS"
UNCUT →

B

C

Fig. 17. *Construction of " skein-of-wool " doll*

no wool is available, raffia or garden bass could be used or even a thick bundle of fine string.)

Open out the skein as though you are going to wind it for knitting, and cut it at each end. Place the two bundles together and hold at the centre with all the cut ends hanging downwards and the doubled end at the top (A). Measure down 3 in. from the top and tie tightly with strong thread. This top section is for the hair. Cut the skein through at top. Now separate a small bundle of the wool from each side of skein ready for the arms. Take this from the " middle " of skein, so that there are strands left at front and back. Double each arm back on itself, pushing the cut ends into the " middle " of the skein and high up, so that when you tie the neck, these ends will be firmly up inside the *head*. Tie a thread tightly round the neck, at each wrist, and at the waist (A and B).

Now separate a bundle of wool coming from the " middle " of the remaining strands, to serve as legs. Cut the strands surrounding this bundle short, to form a skirt, being careful not to cut off the " legs " (B). Separate the leg bundle into two thinner bundles, double back the ends, for feet, and bind round the ankles, enclosing cut ends, and so as to turn the feet outwards (C).

Pull the hair downwards all round the head and tie in two " bundles ", one each side of the head. Tie bows of narrow ribbon over these threads and catch hair to sides of head with a few stitches. Divide each " hand " into five separate little bundles for fingers and tie at ends (C).

Tie a ribbon round waist for a sash. Embroider a small circle in blue wool for each eye and two tiny crescents for nose and mouth in red.

GLIDING PAPER DOLLS (fig. 18)

(Patterns page 249)

These little dolls stand hand in hand in rows, or may be joined into a ring by Sellotaping the two end hands together. If stood on a polished table, they will glide over the surface when gently blown.

Use a good stiff cartridge paper and sharp scissors, and make the dolls colourful characters with long skirts. If a less stiff paper is used, it is a good idea to cut the skirts so that they join at the hem, for added support.

For each line of dolls cut a strip of paper 15 in. long ; make it 4½ in. wide for the Dutch Girls and Angels, 4¾ in. for the Victorian Ladies. This will make four dolls—more folds naturally make more dolls.

Fold the paper in half widthwise, then in half again, and in half again. Trace on the shape, having the straight edge of shape down the last fold to be made.

Cut round outline except for ends of hands and wings, i.e. cut from A–B and from C–D, but *not* from C–B. Open out dolls and following fig. 18 draw in clothes and features. You can either make the dolls all face one way or, as in fig. 18, facing alternately backwards and forwards. In either case draw clothes on both backs and fronts of dolls so that they look nice on both sides. If available use Indian Ink for this job. When dry the children can paint or crayon the dolls in gay colours.

Fig. 18. *Gliding paper dolls*

A. Victorian ladies
B. Little Dutch Girls
C. Angels

The angels look well if a little transparent gum is painted over their haloes, and these are then sprinkled with gold or silver "glitter". A little silver paint touched on the wings is attractive, and these make enchanting Christmas tree or table decorations, especially if joined into a circle.

"Texture" may be added at will in the form of wool for hair, tiny aprons from scraps of cotton materials, pipe cleaners stuck on for "fur", or the dolls may be left just painted.

A glance through the pages of this book should give other ideas for paper dolls and help you to draw the features—monks, wizards, witches, old women, kings and queens, Chinamen—all are suitable !

*   *   *

Have you ever seen a doll with " three " faces ?   There is one in the Luton Museum, with one face asleep, one just awake and one really wide-awake.

*   *   *

Did you know that " Doctor Dolls " were naked, reclining, ivory dolls, owned by Chinese ladies and used by them to point out to their doctors just where their aches and pains were situated, up to the 19th century.   This was an ingenious way to overcome the modesty which forbade these ladies undressing !

Section Four

FLAT BASED DOLLS

T HE DOLLS IN THIS SECTION, whose shape very closely resembles the wooden "stump" dolls manufactured in many European countries during the 17th century, are quick and simple to make; for them the tiniest scraps of almost any sort of material may be used up. They are useful for characterization, for staging "scenes" and "situations", and occasionally in the toy theatre.

Each doll stands on a round base, the size of the bottom of the skirt (no feet or legs are used), so the character chosen must be one that wears a long, full skirt.

The most appealing are, without doubt, little old women. Interesting characters and great variety can be achieved by using different "hair styles", facial expressions and materials for the clothes. Three examples are given below and are aptly named.

THE VILLAGE GOSSIPS (Figs. 19 and 20)

MATILDA

Height 6 in.   Pattern page 248.   Illustration Fig. 20 A and D

This character stands arms folded and with pursed lips.
She has obviously "said her say"!

Materials :

Striped cotton material for body (10 in. × 7 in.).
   „   „   „   „ base (4 in. × 4 in.).
Fine woollen material for shawl (5 in. × 5 in.).
Scraps of pink Winceyette, stockinette or silk for head and hands.
Grey darning wool for hair.
Red and black stranded cotton for features.
2¾-in. diameter circle of cardboard for base.
Kapok for stuffing.
Red water-colour paint.

Method :

Cut out the body and arms (see page 21 for these, as no turning is allowed).

Body (fig. 19) :

Start by making the base. Place the circle of cardboard on the 4-in. square of cotton material and trim the material to a rough circle of 4 in. diameter. Using

69

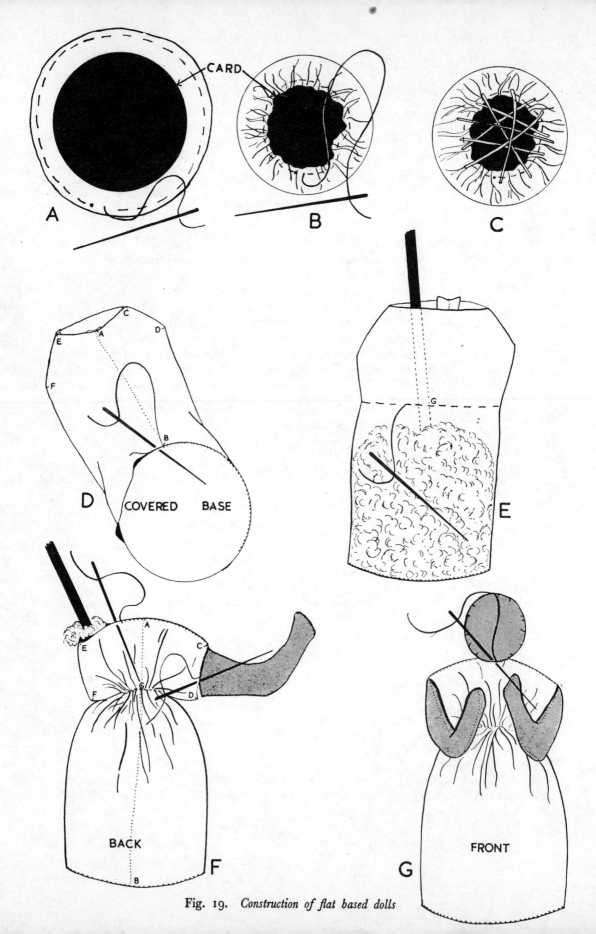

CARD

COVERED BASE

BACK

FRONT

Fig. 19. *Construction of flat based dolls*

strong thread, gather all round the outside edge (A). Having card in centre of circle, pull up gathers tightly (B) and fasten off by lacing securely, backwards and forwards over card, to keep it in place (C).

Place on one side and take body piece.

Fold so that the A's meet and B's meet. Seam A–B. This is the centre back seam. The C's will now meet—seam C–D, and similarly E–F. These are the places where the arms will join. Turn right side out.

Working on the right side, oversew body to base, tucking in a ¼-in. turning all round bottom edge of body (D). Run a gathering thread all round body on broken line at G on pattern. Stuff lower part of body (below this line), packing it firmly round outside edge of base to give skirt a good shape (E). Pull up gathers and fasten off by stitching several times right through the doll at this point—the waist. Stuff the top part of the body very firmly, paying particular attention to the " corners ", and oversew E–A–C (F).

Arms (fig. 19 F and G) :

Place the pieces together in pairs and stitch all round except for the straight side H–I. Trim. Turn right side out and stuff firmly. Turn in and oversew H–I. With back of doll facing you, oversew arms to body between C and D (F).

Head (figs. 8 (1) and 19 G) :

Cut a circle of pink material 3½ in. diameter (a teacup is often this size). Gather all round outside edge, place a *large* knob of stuffing in centre, pull up and fasten off firmly. (The head needs to be *very* firm.)

Sew head to body (G), having the fastening off at centre back, where it will eventually be covered by hair.

Features :

Following fig. 20 A very carefully pencil on, then embroider spectacles and eyes in black, nose and mouth in red cotton, and eyebrows in grey wool.

Hair :

Using a dark grey wool, make the hair, with centre parting and plaited coil at back (fig. 20 A and D). Work as for Elizabeth, fig. 45 (4), but omit the fringe and have the hair longer in order to be able to plait it.

Shawl :

Fringe edges of the piece of woollen material, double it cornerwise and place round Matilda's shoulders, stitching in place. Fold the arms and stitch in position.

Finally, using very weak red water-colours, touch the forehead, cheeks, chin and nose, working the paint well in, to give a natural, healthy appearance (see page 38).

A

MATILDA

"I'VE SAID MY SAY!"

B

ADA

"LET ME THINK."

C

EMILY

"I'M WARNING YOU!"

D

E

F

Fig. 20. *The Village Gossips*

The Schoolgirl Terror in action

Plate 6.

The Rabbit Toothed Queen and Fat King Freddy

The Jester

Plate 7.

The Knave of Hearts

The Cowboy

ADA

Height 6 in. Pattern page 248. Illustration Fig. 20 B and E

This character is made in exactly the same way as Matilda, but her expression clearly says " Let me think ! "

Follow fig. 20 B for features and position of arms. Use a lighter grey wool for hair, arranging it in a braid round the head (fig. 20 E). Pull the head to one side and stitch in this position. Add a small apron.

EMILY

Height 6 in. Pattern page 248. Illustration Plate 5 and Fig. 20 C and F

Make this doll in exactly the same way as the others, consulting fig. 20 C for position of arms and features. Use white wool for the hair, and pull the head round and forward to give her an " I'm warning you ! "—threatening, appearance ; stitch in this position. If available, add some tiny, pearl buttons to front of dress, and make the apron a different size from Ada's.

MORE CHARACTERS TO TRY

MAMMY

Height 6 in. Pattern page 248. Illustration Fig. 21 A and D

Make body exactly as given for Matilda (page 69), using a light-coloured cotton material. Make head and hands in dark brown material. Following fig. 21 A, embroider eyes in black and white, nose and mouth in red cotton. Make the hair by taking looped stitches in black wool, all over the head, and tie a small square of spotted cotton round head, knotting on top to make a bandanna. This doll does not wear a shawl.

MONK

Height 5 in. Pattern page 248. Illustration Fig. 21 B and E

This is one of the few male characters which can be made in this way. He looks well if rather short and fat. Cut out the pieces and make the body as for Matilda (page 69) but increase the circle at base to at least 3 in. and reduce the body length by 1 in. Use brown cotton material for his robes. When joining the head, have the gathered portion at base, where head and body join. The wrinkles will give him a natural, rather " weathered " appearance.

Features :

Embroider spectacles and eyes in black and white, mouth and nose in red cotton and fringe of hair in brown wool (fig. 22, p. 76).

D

Sleeves :

Fold so that the J's and K's meet and seam J–K. Turn a tiny hem in all round lower edge (K), slip a sleeve on to each arm and, turning in the raw edge, oversew in place all round " armhole "—J on sleeve matching D on body.

Girdle :

Make this from smooth, fine string, knotting and fringing each end, and tie round waist. Stitch arms together in front.

Hood :

Join seam L–M (centre back). Turn in $\frac{1}{2}$ in. hem N–O–N (front edge). Turn in a very narrow hem all round neck edge N–M–N, and placing N's on shoulders and consulting fig. 21 B and E, stitch in place, both at neck and at L.

WIZARD

Having made the other dolls consult fig. 21 C and F, and experiment with a wizard. He needs to be tall and thin, so this time make the base circle smaller and the body longer. Make the robes in black silk if available, using the pattern for the monk's sleeve. Make his hair as shown by fig. 23 A, using grey wool. Make beard as shown by fig. 23 B, trimming to a point and stiffening with colourless nail varnish. A green sequin in each eye, as used for witch (page 172), will add much to his general " unpleasantness " ! Make the hat from a cone of thin card or stiff paper, covered with material. Dot him with star-shaped and round sequins and give him a coloured plastic cocktail stick for a wand.

Now experiment with other materials and characters.

1. Make a whole group of " village gossips "—it's a most engrossing occupation ! Some of them can wear hats, hold a basket, bag or stick, or carry a baby.

2. Make kings, queens, princesses or ladies at a ball. Some of the ball gowns can have oval bases and panniered sides, and the hair can be a high powdered wig.

3. Use this method for making figures for a Christmas Crib—it is readily adaptable.

*   *   *

Did you know that in the Middle Ages clay dolls were made with a circular depression in the breast ? It is thought that Godparents put a coin in the hole and gave the doll to their godchild for a first gift when it was baptized.

A   B   C

MAMMY   MONK   WIZARD

D   E   F

Fig. 21.   *More flat based dolls*

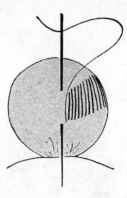

Fig. 22. *Embroidering the monk's hair*

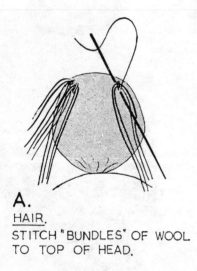

A.

HAIR.
STITCH "BUNDLES" OF WOOL
TO TOP OF HEAD.

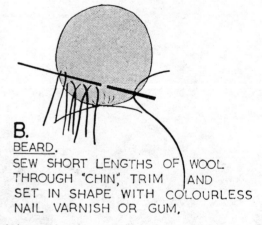

B.

BEARD.
SEW SHORT LENGTHS OF WOOL
THROUGH "CHIN", TRIM AND
SET IN SHAPE WITH COLOURLESS
NAIL VARNISH OR GUM.

Fig. 23. *Wizard's hair and beard*

DOLLS FROM BALLS

BALLS ARE SIMPLICITY itself to make (although not quick !) and in their construction the tiniest of scraps of material, quite unsuitable for anything else, may be used to great advantage. Even such unlikely-looking pieces as narrow hems cut off dresses, and swatches of patterns of the smallest possible size, will come into their own.

Interesting dolls are easily constructed by joining together balls of various sizes. The key to success lies in the choice and placing of the materials. All the originals were made from a family piece bag and the colours given are, of course, only meant to serve as a guide. Each worker will naturally have to substitute what she personally has available, for to *buy* material for this type of doll immediately robs it of its charm and originality. Keep the various " weights " together, using cottons for dolls which need to be simple and are destined for the very young, and silks, satins, brocades and velvets for the more glamorous characters.

CONSTRUCTING A PENTAGON BALL (figs. 24 and 26)

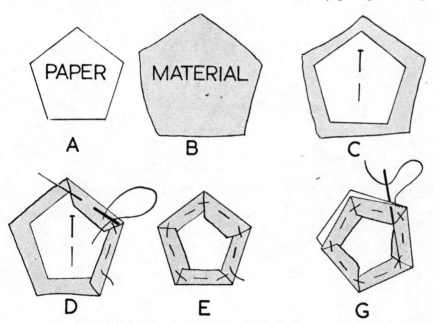

Fig. 24. *Preparation of paper-backed pentagon for ball making*

77

Always use a very fine needle and the finest cotton obtainable in black or white for sewing cotton materials and a pure silk thread for silks and brocades. Sylko is not suitable for this type of work. Aim at 25–30 oversewing stitches to the inch.

Cut twelve pentagons of the required size in stiff paper—old envelopes and letters are excellent for the purpose (fig. 24 A).

Then cut twelve pentagons in the material to be used, about ¼ in. larger all round than the paper shapes (fig. 24 B). Pin, then tack each material pentagon to a paper shape, folding edges neatly (fig. 24 C, D and E).

Next take one central patch and oversew another patch to each side of it (figs. 24 G and 26 A) working on the wrong side. Join these five patches together (fig. 26 B) to make a " cup " (fig. 26 C). Make another cup from the six remaining patches. Stitch these two cups together to form a ball—the points of one fitting into the " recesses " of the other (fig. 26 D). Leave two sides open for turning and stuffing. Remove papers. Turn right side out and stuff **very firmly indeed,** coaxing into a smooth, round shape. Ladder stitch opening (fig. 26 F). Always try to arrange for the opening to appear in an inconspicuous place, e.g. at the base of the head or body, or where some form of trimming will cover it.

When patches need stiffening—back them with cardboard (cereal boxes), lace in position and do not remove (fig. 25).

Whilst making the dolls which follow, refer constantly to the diagrams in question, each of which shows both the front and back of the character, so as to be sure you place the patches correctly when making up the balls.

Fig. 25.   *Prepared " card-backed " pentagon, for stiffened parts of ball dolls*

BABY

Height 5 in.   Pattern page 271.   Illustration Fig. 27

This is simple to make and is an ideal doll for the very young—being small and light it is an excellent pram companion.

Materials :

Scraps of cotton material in pink for face, white for bib and a small patterned print for dress.

Scraps of yellow towelling for hair.

Yellow, red, black and white stranded cotton for features.

Kapok for filling.

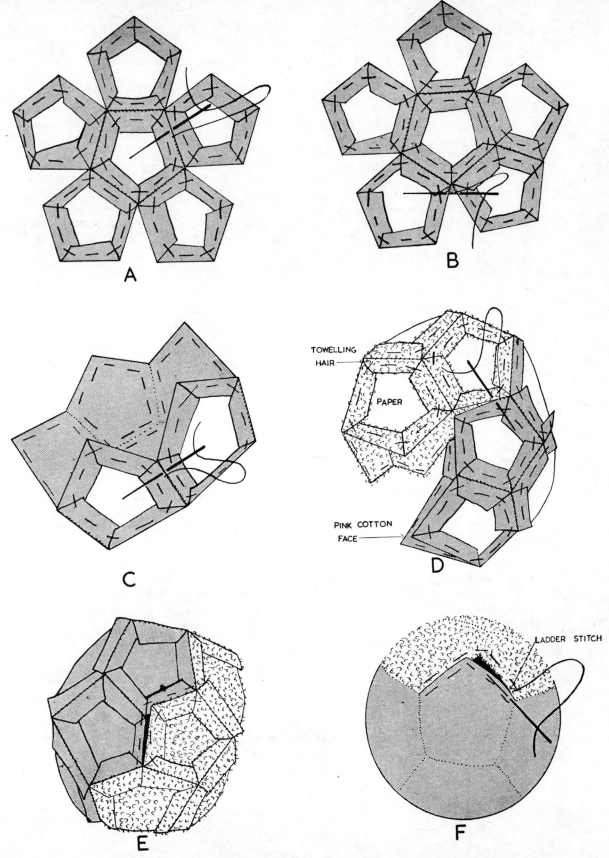

Fig. 26. *Construction of a pentagon ball for doll making—Baby's head*

Method :

Body :

Using pentagon B, prepare eleven patterned print patches and one white (fig. 24 E). Make up into a ball (fig. 26).

Head :

Using pentagon D, prepare six pink cotton and six yellow towelling patches (fig. 24 E). Make up into a ball (fig. 26). Pencil in features lightly and embroider extra curls and brows in yellow, eyes in black and white, nose in red and mouth in red and white. In order to give a "young" expression, take great care to keep the forehead high and features low down on the face. Ladder stitch head to body (fig. 6 B), working round and round several times for absolute security.

MANDARIN
Height 6½ in.   Pattern page 271.   Illustration Fig. 28

Here is a wonderful opportunity for using up tiny pieces of oriental looking brocade and shimmering satin or silk. Having hands and feet, the mandarin takes the worker one step further in making dolls from balls.

Materials :

Scraps of silk in yellow for face, hands and feet.
    ,,   ,, black velvet for hair and sole of sandal.
Bright blue satin for "skirt".
Figured magenta brocade for "tunic".
Black, white and red stranded cotton for features and "cuffs".
Kapok for filling.

Method :

Head :

Using pentagon D, prepare seven yellow and five black patches (fig. 24 E). Make up into a ball (fig. 26). Pencil in and embroider eyes in white, mouth in red and the rest of the lines in black. This time keep the features high on the face to give a "looking down", haughty appearance.

Body :

Using pentagon A, prepare six satin and six brocade patches (fig. 24 E). Make up into a ball (fig. 26). Join head to body (fig. 6 B).

Hands :

Prepare two yellow patches using pentagon D (fig. 24 E). Hem neatly to front of doll. Remove tacks, leaving paper inside. Embroider cuffs in black, using long, straight stitches.

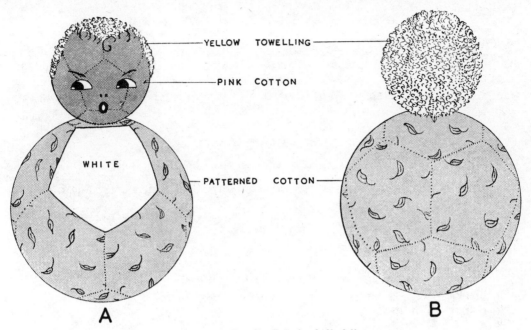

Fig. 27. *Detail of Baby ball doll*

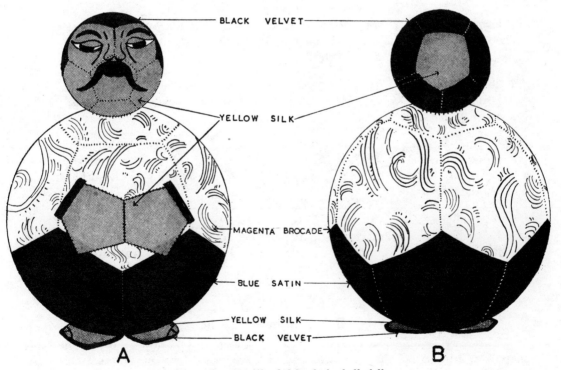

Fig. 28. *Detail of Mandarin ball doll*

Feet :

Using pentagon D, prepare two yellow and two black patches, all cardboard backed (fig. 25). Oversew each black to a yellow on the right side, working all round. Embroider " toe " straps in black and stitch completed feet to base of toy ; yellow sides uppermost.

JAPANESE LADY
Height 9 in.   Pattern page 271.   Illustration Fig. 29

For this doll, three balls are joined together, all of which are made from silks and brocades.

Materials :

Scraps of cream silk for face.
  „ „ black „ „ hair.
Dark blue velvet and orange brocade for clothes.
Black, white and red stranded cotton for features.
Kapok for filling.

Method :

Head :

Using pentagon D, prepare four cream and eight black patches (fig. 24 E). Make up into a ball (fig. 26). Embroider eyes and brows in black and white, nose in red and mouth in red and white.

Top of Body :

Using pentagon C, prepare seven velvet and five brocade patches (fig. 24 E). Make up into a ball (fig. 26).

Skirt :

Using pentagon A, prepare twelve brocade patches (fig. 24 E) and make up into a ball (fig. 26). Stitch the three balls together (fig. 6 B), having the head to one side and bending forward.

Head ornament :

Using pentagon F and extra stiff paper, prepare two patches (fig. 24 E). Oversew these together all round the outside edge. Remove tacks, leaving in paper as stiffener ; stitch to head.

LITTLE OLD WOMAN
Height 8½ in.   Pattern page 271.   Illustration Fig. 30

This very lovable character will use up almost any cotton scraps. The basic shape is still three balls, but a fourth and fifth are added for arms and a sixth for her " bun ".

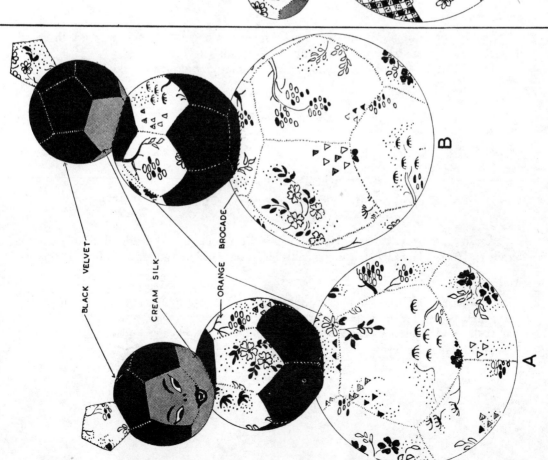

BLACK WHITE STRIPE

PINK

RED GINGHAM

BLACK WHITE PRINT

A

B

Fig. 30. *Detail of Little Old Woman ball doll*

BLACK VELVET

CREAM SILK

ORANGE

BROCADE

A

B

Fig. 29. *Detail of Japanese Lady ball doll*

Materials :

Scraps of pink cotton material for face and " hands ".
"   " black/white striped for hair.
"   " red checked gingham for dress.
"   " black/white print for collar, cuffs and apron.
Black, white, blue and red stranded cotton for features.
Kapok for filling.

Method :

Head :

Using pentagon D, prepare six pink and six striped cotton patches (fig. 24 E). Make up into a ball (fig. 26).

Bun :

Using pentagon F, prepare twelve striped cotton patches (fig. 24 E) and make up into a ball (fig. 26). Sew " bun " to back of head (fig. 6 B). Embroider eyes in blue, black and white, spectacles and brows in black, nostrils and mouth in red.

Top of Body :

Using pentagon C, prepare eleven patches in checked gingham and one in flowered print (fig. 24 E). Make up into a ball (fig. 26).

Skirt :

Using pentagon A, prepare nine patches in checked gingham and three in flowered print (fig. 24 E). Make up into a ball (fig. 26).
Join head to top of body and these completed pieces to " skirt " (fig. 6).

Arms :

Using pentagon F, prepare two patches in pink cotton, ten in flowered print and twelve in checked gingham (fig. 24 E). Make up two balls (fig. 26).
Join arms firmly to sides of body (fig. 6).

RABBIT TOOTHED QUEEN
Height 10 in. Pattern page 271. Illustration Plate 6
(Follow Fig. 31)

Again based on three balls, this gay little queen has the added refinement of hands and feet. Her crown is made from half a ball and her collar from five pentagons.

Materials :

Scraps of pink silk for face and hands.
Black velvet for hair and feet.
Ruby and mauve velvet and bright blue satin for clothes and centre of crown.
Silver lamé for crown.

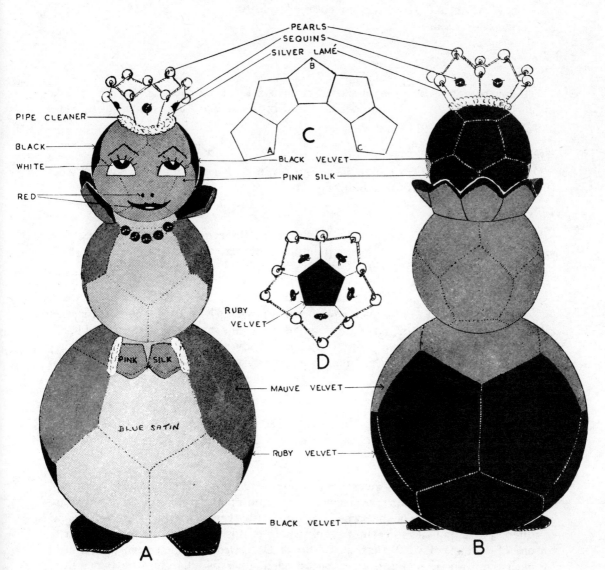

Fig. 31. *Detail of Rabbit Toothed Queen*
   A. Front View
   B. Back View
   C. Position of patches for collar
   D. Top view of crown

Sequins, beads and pipe cleaners for trimmings.
Black, white and red stranded cotton for features.
Kapok for filling.

Method :

Head :

Using pentagon D, prepare six pink and six black patches (fig. 24 E). Make up into a ball (fig. 26). Embroider eyes and brows in black and white, nostrils and mouth in red, teeth in white.

Top of Body :

Using pentagon C, prepare four blue satin and eight mauve velvet patches (fig. 24 E). Make up into a ball (fig. 26).

Skirt :

Using pentagon A, prepare three blue satin, three mauve velvet and six ruby velvet patches (fig. 24 E). Make up into a ball (fig. 26).

Stitch head, body and skirt together (fig. 6 B).

Hands :

Using pentagon E, prepare four pink patches (fig. 24 E). Oversew these together on the wrong side, in pairs, all round four sides. Remove papers, turn right side out and stuff. Oversew opening. Stitch hands to body and to each other where they join at centre front. Sew a short length of pipe cleaner at the top of each, for a fur cuff.

Feet :

Using pentagon D, prepare four card-backed patches (fig. 25) using black velvet. Oversew these together in pairs on the right side. Stitch to base of doll.

Crown :

Using pentagon E and silver lamé, prepare ten card-backed patches (fig. 25). Stitch these together in pairs, oversewing all round on the right side. Now prepare one paper-backed patch of the same size, using ruby velvet (fig. 24 E). Sew a pair of stiffened lamé patches to each of the five sides of this, then join the five together as for one of the cups of a ball (figs. 26 C and 31 D). Decorate the crown with a bead on each point and recess and a sequin on each silver patch. Remove paper from centre piece and stitch to head, at a jaunty, forward angle. Stitch a piece of pipe cleaner all round base of crown for " fur " trimming.

Collar (fig. 31 C)

Using pentagon E, prepare five mauve and five ruby patches (fig. 24 E). Place the mauve together as shown by fig. 31 C and oversew on the wrong side. Place and join the five ruby patches in a similar way. Now place these two joined pieces together, right sides inside, and oversew together all round A–B–C. Remove papers, turn right side out, pushing out points carefully and oversew the remaining edge A–C on the right side. Stitch round the queen's neck and decorate the front of body with sequins.

INTERCHANGEABLE CLOWN
Height 7½ in.   Pattern page 271.   Illustration Fig. 32

Having made up one or two of the preceding ball dolls, it will be easy to see that the scope in this field is almost inexhaustible. With the aid of large press studs, any of these dolls may be "snapped" together, instead of stitched, and the small owner will spend many happy hours popping and un-popping them. As will be seen by fig. 32, this clown, which has four balls and a pair of "feet" as a foundation, can be snapped together in several different ways.

It is essential for easy manipulation that some of the patches have a firm cardboard backing, so that the ball does not "push in" when the fasteners are pressed together—thus causing frustration instead of pleasure !

Materials :

Scraps of white cotton material for face.
    ,,   ,, brown ,,   ,,   ,, hair.
Checked gingham, spotted and large and small patterned print for the "tunic".
Red for the shoes.
Red and black stranded cotton for features.
Six complete large press studs and two halves (knob side only).
Kapok for filling.

Method :
Head :

Using pentagon D, prepare four brown and eight white patches (fig. 24 E). Make up into a ball (fig. 26). Embroider eyes in black and nose and mouth in red. Sew the "knob" half of a press stud to central, lower white patch for joining head to body.

Body :

Using pentagon C, prepare one large patterned print patch and nine spotted (fig. 24 E), also one spotted and one checked gingham of the same size but cardbacked (fig. 25). Make up into a ball, having the gingham card-backed patch at the top and the spotted one at the base (see fig. 32 A for this). Remove papers but leave cardboard in place. Sew the other half of press stud to centre of checked gingham patch and snap on head. Sew the knob half of another press stud to centre of card-backed patch at base of body and two more similar halves to each side of body ready to receive "legs" (see fig. 32 A).

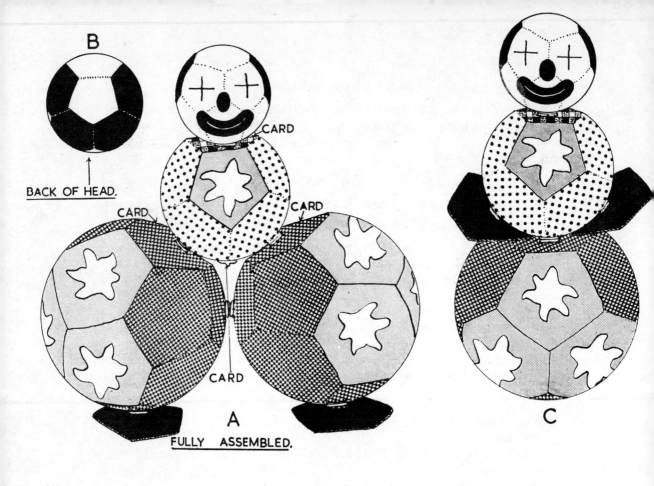

B

BACK OF HEAD.

CARD

CARD   CARD

CARD

A

FULLY ASSEMBLED.

C

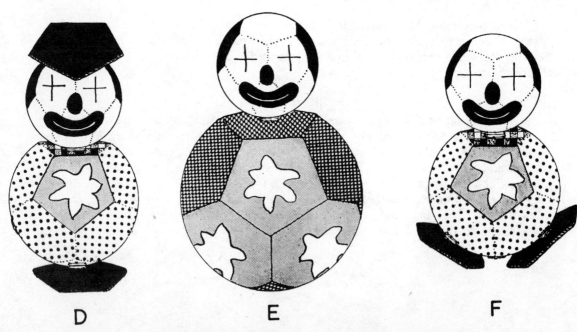

D

E

F

Fig. 32. *Interchangeable clown, showing five change*

Legs :

Using pentagon A, prepare three large patterned print patches and eight small patterned (fig. 24 E). Then prepare one of a similar size in small print with a card backing (fig. 25). Make up a ball consulting fig. 32 A for position of patches.

Make another similar ball for the other leg. Sew the recessed half of two of the press studs to the card-backed patches at top of legs and snap them to body. Take another press stud and sew one half to the inside of each leg and snap them together. Then sew the " knob " half of two more press studs to the base of legs ready to receive feet.

Feet :

Using pentagon A and red cotton material prepare four card-backed patches (fig. 25). Place these together in pairs and oversew together on the right side. Stitch the second halves of the two press studs already on the legs, to the feet, and snap in place.

Should you wish to be able to make up the position shown by fig. 32 D, the " knob " half of a press stud must be sewn to top of head.

FAT KING FREDDY

Height approx. 8½ in. Pattern page 271. Illustration Plate 6
(Follow Figs. 33 and 34)

Having explored some of the possibilities of pentagon ball dolls, a fat and jolly king has been introduced to show that " orange peel " balls may also be used in doll making. He makes an ideal husband for the rabbit toothed queen on page 84. Each ball consists of sections of various coloured silks and velvets. His " orb " is a small pentagon ball and his crown, like the queen's, half a pentagon ball.

Materials :

Scraps of pink silk for face and hands.
Black velvet for hair.
Red velvet, gold corduroy and blue silk for body and " sleeves ".
Brown velvet for feet.
Gold lamé for crown, orb, sceptre and " clasp ".
Sequins, pearls and pipe cleaners for trimming.
Black, white, blue and red stranded cotton for features.
Kapok for filling.
A wooden meat skewer for sceptre.

Method :

Head :

Cut eight paper patches and prepare just as for pentagons (figs. 24 and 33 A), three in pink silk and five in black velvet. Oversew the three pink patches together

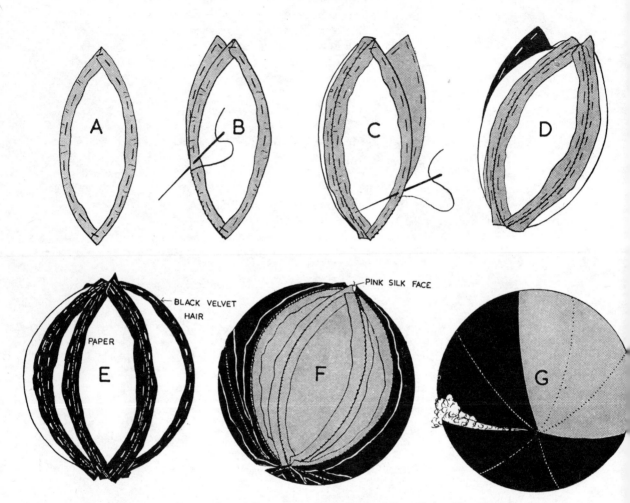

Fig. 33.   *Construction of " orange peel " ball for doll making—King Freddy's head*

on the wrong side, then add a black velvet patch to one side (fig. 33 B, C and D). Now join the remaining four velvet patches (fig. 33 E). Join these two "cups" together all round except for a small section for turning and stuffing (fig. 33 F). Remove papers ; reverse ; stuff firmly and neatly close opening (fig. 33 G).

Embroider eyes in black, blue and white, brows, moustache and stray locks of hair in black, nose, mouth and "wrinkles" in red.

Body :

Follow fig. 34 A for position of patches.

Using larger sized "section" prepare one blue silk, two gold corduroy and five red velvet patches. Make up ball in the same way as for the head. Sew head to body (fig. 6 B), at a rakish angle. Stitch two pipe cleaners down each side of centre front panel for fur trimming.

Clasp :

Using pentagon F, prepare two gold lamé patches, stitch to centre front, under chin, hemming neatly in place. Remove tacking stitches, leaving papers inside. Decorate with gold sequins.

Collar :

Make as for queen (page 86 and fig. 31 C), but use pentagon D and red velvet lined with gold corduroy. Stitch in place.

Crown :

Make as for queen (page 86 and fig. 31 D), but use pentagon D and gold lamé, with red velvet for the centre. Stiffen with stiff paper instead of cardboard so that the points may be curled outwards and give a different effect (fig. 34 A). Decorate with pearls and sequins, stitch in place and finish with a pipe cleaner.

Feet :

Make as for queen (page 86), but use brown velvet and pentagon C.

Arms :

Cut two large sections in paper as for body, then cut each one in half along line marked xxxx. Each arm is made from two halves joined together. Prepare these four patches as shown on pattern—pink at the tip for hands, gold corduroy next for cuffs and red at the top for sleeves. These small pieces should be carefully cut, allowing for turnings, and joined before covering a paper patch. It is a tricky job and needs accuracy and neatness for a good result. Oversew the two prepared patches together on the wrong side. Remove papers ; turn right side out ; stuff firmly and ladder stitch ends. Add a piece of pipe cleaner for fur trimming. With the arms pointing backwards, oversew each one very firmly to the side of body, then bring them forwards so as to hide stitching and catch here and there, to front of body, in positions shown.

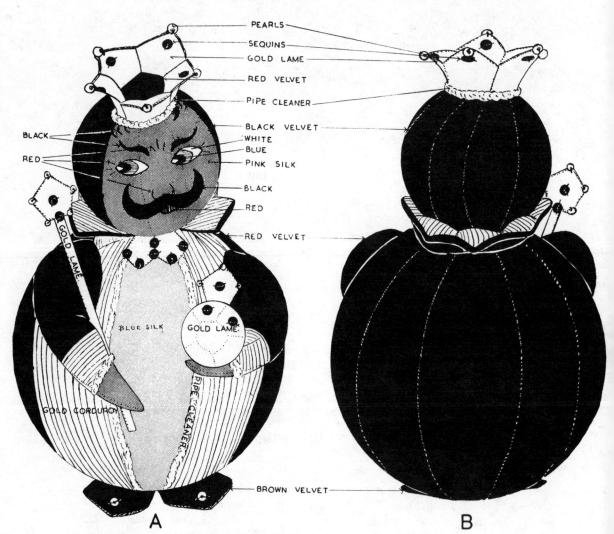

PEARLS
SEQUINS
GOLD LAME
RED VELVET
PIPE CLEANER
BLACK VELVET
WHITE
BLUE
PINK SILK
BLACK
RED
RED VELVET

BLACK
RED

GOLD LAME

BLUE SILK

GOLD LAME

GOLD CORDUROY

PIPE CLEANER

BROWN VELVET

A

B

Fig. 34. *Detail of Fat King Freddy*
    A. Front view
    B. Back view

Orb :

Using pentagon F and gold lamé, prepare twelve patches (fig. 24 E). Make up a ball (fig. 26). Prepare two more patches of the same size but with cardboard backs (fig. 25) and oversew together all round, on the right side. Stitch to top of orb. Decorate with pearls and sequins and stitch orb firmly in place, both to body and hand.

Sceptre :

Cover a wooden meat skewer with gold lamé, hemming neatly across base and down one side. Prepare two card-backed patches using pentagon F and gold lamé (fig. 25). Oversew together on the right side, all round four sides. Slip the covered skewer between the two open sides and stitch in place. Decorate with sequins and pearls. Tuck sceptre under right hand and stitch in place.

VARIATIONS

Having made these ball dolls you should have no difficulty in interchanging the characters and inventing new ideas of your own.

1. Put a small tin containing a few buttons or pebbles inside such simple ones as the baby or little old lady, to make a rattle.

2. Invent a husband for the little old lady and make a family of children based on the baby.

3. Scale down the king and queen, and change their expressions so as to make small princes and princesses—your own Royal Family. Or turn them into the King and Queen of Hearts and make a Knave.

4. Give the mandarin a crown, so as to make him into an oriental king, and invent a black king, so that together with the fat king you have " the Three Kings " for a Christmas decoration.

5. Try making these dolls from scraps of felt. In this case, of course, the patches may be cut direct to size and seamed together, no paper backings are necessary. *N.B.* Felt is not so suitable for the dolls which contain cardboard-backed patches.

For other ideas for pentagon ball dolls see *Patchwork Playthings*, Section III.

For variations based on orange peel ball dolls see *Modern Soft Toy Making*, Section III.

*   *   *

Did you know that at the time of the French Revolution " aristocrat " dolls and toy guillotines were common ? Young patriots used to enjoy bloodthirsty games of beheading aristocrats—the dolls' heads were detachable, so that they could fall realistically to the ground !

Section Six

FLUFFY WASHABLE DOLLS
FOR THE VERY YOUNG

ALTHOUGH VERY YOUNG CHILDREN are more often than not given soft, cuddly animals to play with, there is no reason why they should not own suitably designed dolls; the three in this section have been included with this age group specially in mind. They are made chiefly from fur fabric and stuffed with foam rubber, both of which will wash beautifully. However, the snowman's felt hat must be removed before washing—a very simple task.

Before cutting out fur fabric—see page 21 *about direction of pile, etc., and page* 22 *for stitching.*

BABY SNOWMAN

Height about 9 in. Pattern page 251. Illustration Plate 3 and Fig. 35

Materials :

¼ yd. white fur fabric 48 in. wide (this will be sufficient for this doll and for the Eskimo Boy).
Scraps of black felt for the hat.
  ,,   ,,   ,, Vynide for the features.
A few yards of red and white wool for the scarf.
Foam rubber for stuffing (see page 26 for use of this).

Method :

Cut out the pieces as given, also eyes, nose and mouth in black Vynide, which you may have over from the dolls' shoes. (Alternatively the features may be embroidered.)

Head :

Join the four pieces together, just as the eight pieces were joined for the King's head in fig. 33, matching A's and B's. Leave a small opening on one side. Turn right side out, stuff lightly and close opening with ladder stitch (fig. 6 A).

Body :

Join the three pieces together all down the three seams C–D. Open out at the bottom and insert the base circle, stitching all round except for a small section. Turn right side out, stuff lightly and close opening. Ladder stitch head to top of body, working round the neck several times for strength (fig. 6 B).

94

←BLACK FELT (REMOVE FOR WASHING.)

BLACK VYNIDE

←RED/WHITE KNITTED

←WHITE FUR FABRIC

Fig. 35. *Washable baby Snowman*

Limbs :

Fold each of the four pieces in half widthwise and join seams E–F. Open out one end of each and insert a base circle, stitching all round. Turn right side out. Stuff the limbs lightly and ladder stitch to body in the position shown on fig. 35, turning in the raw edges as you work.

Features :

Hem the eyes, nose and mouth neatly in place, or embroider them in thick, close satin stitch, using two strands of embroidery cotton. (Do not use felt, it does not wash very well.)

Scarf :

Using an oddment of 3-ply red wool, and size 12 knitting needles, cast on twelve stitches and knit 14 in. in K2, P2 rib, introducing a narrow white stripe at the ends, if the wool is available. Cast off. Make a tasselled fringe, by knotting red and white wool alternately along each end. Tie round the snowman's neck.

Hat (Pattern and instructions pages 54, 56) :

Make up a top hat using black felt. Fill with a little stuffing and ladder stitch firmly to snowman's head, placing it a little on one side, and stitching round several times.

Remove hat before washing the doll.

ESKIMO BOY

Height about 13 in. Pattern page 250. Illustration Plate 3 and Fig. 36

Materials :

White fur fabric for clothes ($\frac{1}{4}$ yd. 48 in. wide will make both this doll and the snowman).

Odd scraps of chamois leather for gloves, breeches and boots (or a piece $14\frac{1}{2}$ in. × 9 in.).

Top of a nylon stocking for face.

Brown and red stranded cotton for features.

About 18 in. white string for lacing.

One stockinette body, made as given on page 112, but stuffed with foam rubber (see page 26 for use of this).

A little extra foam rubber.

Method :

Cut out the pieces as given.

Face :

Take the stockinette body (on which it is not necessary to make knees and elbows). Cut the top (the thick part) off an old nylon stocking, preferably in a dark beige shade. Using this double, just as it comes off the stocking, stretch it tightly round the face, fastening it securely with rows of stitching down the back of the head. This gives a lovely dusky, " weather-beaten " texture to the skin. Embroider hair (so that it will come well under hood) in brown stranded cotton using the full thickness and working in long, straight stitches, and brows using stem stitch and one strand of brown cotton. Embroider nose and mouth in red.

Hood :

Join the two darts A–B, then join centre back seam A–C. Turn right side out. Put on to doll so that the D's meet under chin and the front of hood fits snugly round face. The front edge will be raw—this will be dealt with later.

Plate 8.   The Corset Lace family pose by a teacup to show how small they are !

Plate 9. Deborah and her dancing partner clown

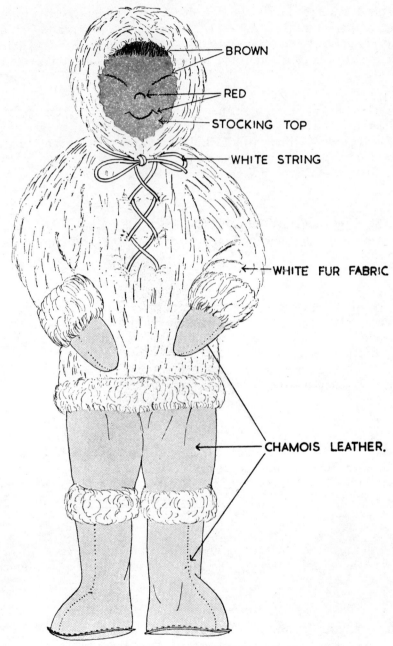

BROWN

RED

STOCKING TOP

WHITE STRING

WHITE FUR FABRIC

CHAMOIS LEATHER.

Fig. 36. *Washable Eskimo boy*

E

Breeches :

Open the two pieces and place flat, one on top of the other. Join inner leg seam E–F–E and two outside seams G–H. Turn right side out and pull on to doll, stitching all round waist and pleating to fit. Run a gathering thread round base of legs G–E–G, pull up to fit and stitch to legs of doll at about knee level.

Boots :

Fold each piece in half and stitch front seam H–I–J. Turn right side out. Open out base and stab stitch sole in place, matching H's and K's ; work on the right side to make a " welt ". Push a little stuffing into toe of the boot and pull one on to each foot. Add more stuffing round ankles, to give a good shape, and stitch tops of boots to the legs, so that they meet the breeches.

Gloves :

Place the pieces together in pairs and stitch all round S–T–U, leaving S–U open. Turn right side out and pull one on to each hand ; stitch to arm, all round top of glove.

Tunic :

Open out the two pieces flat and slit one of them from L–M. This is the centre front opening. Place the two pieces together and join side and underarm seams P–Q–R, and top of sleeve seams O–N. Turn right side out, and put on to doll. Gather edge of sleeves to fit wrists and stitch to arms, so that they meet gloves. Ladder stitch round neck and down centre front opening, turning in the raw edges as you work. Stitch to body all round lower edge.

Fur Trimming :

From the remainder of your fur fabric cut strips $1\frac{1}{4}$ in. wide, having the pile running across the width if possible. Measure round the edge of hood, wrists, tops of boots and lower edge of tunic, cutting off lengths to fit each one, with about $\frac{1}{2}$ in. extra for turnings. Stitch these strips in place, to cover raw edges, hemming along both edges and turning in $\frac{1}{4}$ in. so that the finished trimming is about $\frac{3}{4}$ in. wide.

Lacing :

Thread the string into a packing needle and stitch criss-cross down centre front and up again, to resemble lacing. Tie the ends in a double bow under chin.

BABY BUNTING
Height approx. 12 in.   Pattern pages 252–3.   Illustration Plate 4

Materials :

$\frac{1}{4}$ yd. extra long pile white fur fabric 48 in. wide.

Scraps of pink stockinette over from the dolls in Section VIII for face and ear linings.

Blue, white, black and red stranded cotton for features.

Handful of rayon strands.

Foam rubber for stuffing (see page 26 for use of this).

Method :

Cut out the pieces as given, remembering that when cutting " pairs " the pattern should be reversed for one of the pieces, so that the two bodies, outer and inner arms, and inner legs are in fact pairs and face in opposite directions.

Ears :

Place each stockinette piece on top of a fur fabric piece and stitch together all round except straight edge A–B–A. Turn right side out and oversew A–B–A. Fold so that the two A's meet B and stitch in this position. Put on one side.

Arms :

On the outer arms join darts C–D–C and E–F–E. Place each inner arm on top of an outer arm and stitch all round C–G–E. Turn right side out and put on one side.

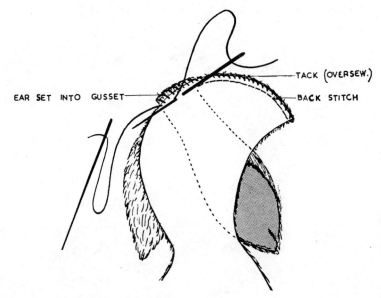

TACK (OVERSEW.)

EAR SET INTO GUSSET

BACK STITCH

Fig. 37. *Including ear, when sewing in gusset on Baby Bunting's head*

Body :

Take the inner leg pieces and join one to each side of body gusset H–I. Now join this piece to one of the body sides J–H–K and from L–I. Join on the other body side in the same way. Insert base of feet, matching letters and stitching all round K–L–K. Join back I–M. Take the head gusset and stitch to one side of body O–P ; now insert prepared ear between P and Q, so that the lining will face outwards when the doll is reversed. Stitch right through the gusset, ear and side of body (fig. 37). This will make for a stronger doll, and the ears will be very much more secure than if they were sewn on afterwards. Continue stitching from Q–R. Attach the other side of body to the gusset and insert the other ear in the same way. Stitch down back R–N.

Face :

Take the two pieces and use them together so that the face is made of double material. Place in " hole " on body and stitch all round O–J–O.

Stuffing :

Turn the doll right side out and stuff, using rayon strands for the part behind face and foam rubber for the rest of the doll, if you intend to " model " the face. If not, foam rubber will be suitable throughout. Close opening N–M. Stuff the arms and place the open ends flat against the side of body ; ladder stitch in place, working several times round the top of each arm. Try to vary the position of the arms, so that they are not both the same—having one curving downwards and one upwards in a natural " baby " position (see Plate 4).

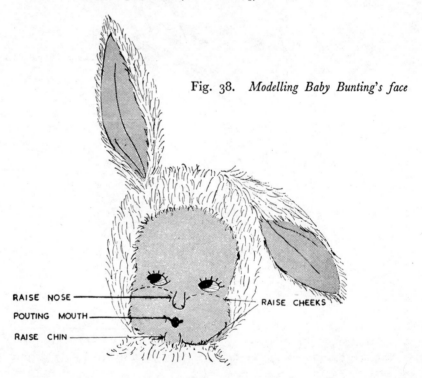

Fig. 38.   *Modelling Baby Bunting's face*

RAISE NOSE

POUTING MOUTH

RAISE CHIN

RAISE CHEEKS

Tail :

Place the two pieces together and join all round the curved edge S–U–S.   Turn right side out, stuff lightly and turn in and ladder stitch S–S.   Stitch firmly to base of toy at I, and catch to the back so that it " sticks " up in a saucy way.

Features (fig. 38) :

Using one strand of cotton, embroider eyes in blue and white, lashes in black and a small circle in red for the mouth.   Now model mouth into a pout (page 37 and fig. 14).   Raise a little nose, and embroider two tiny red nostrils.   Raise a tiny chin and raise the cheeks by stitching from under the eyes to the edge of the fur hood and pulling tightly.   Sink the eyes a little if you think it necessary.   This is a " baby " face, so above all keep the features *low* on it.   Although it is tempting to add some rosy cheeks with water colour, this would run in the wash, so resist the temptation.

If you want a quicker and simpler face, make plain features as for the dolls in Section VIII following fig. 38, but omitting any modelling.

Finally pull the head a little over to one side and stitch in this position—see Plate 4.

*   *   *

Did you know that crocheted woollen dolls existed in A.D. *600—they have been found in graves at Akhmin Panapolis.*

Section Seven

JUMPING JACKS

No one who has visited Southern Germany, Austria or Switzerland can have failed to find among the many fascinating wooden dolls which fill the shops, modern examples of " Jumping Jacks " in various guises. These animated, lively little characters, which are often gaily painted boys and girls in national costume, appear to jump for joy when a string is pulled. Among the earliest examples of this type of doll are a pair of 12th-Century knights engaged in a fight, and probably made in Nuremberg.

Experiments have shown that these dolls need not be of wood, but that the needlewoman, too, can make them.

The examples which follow are made from felt-covered cardboard, with paper fastener " joints ". Woollen hair, fur busbies, sequined haloes, etc., all give them a certain depth and texture which the wooden dolls lack.

Care must, however, be taken to follow the directions for assembling exactly, or the limbs, which naturally do not possess the weight of their wooden counterparts, will " stick " in an upright position when the string is pulled, instead of falling easily back into place.

GENERAL INSTRUCTIONS FOR JUMPING JACKS

Materials for each doll :

Four *long* brass paper fasteners (for the Angel only two) (at least size S.5-6)
One small brass ring.
Approx. 1½ yd. red or fancy string (fine).
One large bead.
Stiff cardboard, such as the back of a pad of notepaper.
Four small trouser buttons.
A tiny piece of cotton wool.
And the items mentioned under each separate doll.

Preparing the pieces :

Using the pattern concerned, cut two bodies, two arms, two legs and one head from thick card.

Consulting the diagrams which illustrate the doll you are making, place each cardboard shape on a piece of felt of the appropriate colour (e.g. the cossack's head on flesh felt) and with a soft pencil draw all round twice (fig. 39 A). Cut these felt pieces out *very* slightly larger than the cardboard shape. Where two colours are

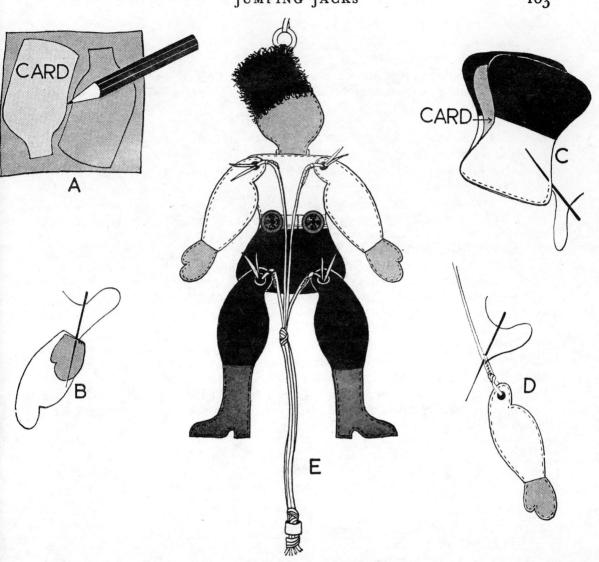

Fig. 39. *Construction of a Jumping Jack*

needed (e.g. the cossack's arm) join the felt pieces together neatly on the wrong side (fig. 39 B), remembering to make the seams on opposite sides, so as to make a " pair ". Place the cardboard shape between the two felt pieces, with the pencil marks inside, and, using matching Sylko and a small needle, stab stitch neatly all round the outside edge (fig. 39 C). When making the heads, embroider features *before* inserting the card, then push a little cotton wool between face and card to raise the face slightly.

Assembling the pieces :

Having prepared the pieces as given above and under the instructions for each individual doll, assemble them as follows :

With a leather punch make a small hole in the four corners of both front and back of body, and the top of each limb, punching right through the card and both layers of felt.

Take 10–11 in. of string, thread through hole at top of arm, tie one flat knot, then stitch the end to the long length of string (fig. 39 D). The object is not to have a bulky knot or the limbs will not work smoothly, but will be " caught " by the knot. Fix a similar length of string to the other arm and about 8 in. to each leg.

Take two trouser buttons and stitch them at the " waist " on the *back* of back of body, as far apart as they will go without showing on the right side. Sew two more to the back of front of body (fig. 39 E). Now keeping arm strings *between* the buttons, push a paper fastener through each hole in front of body, through the hole at top of appropriate limb and through hole at back of body. With a small pair of pliers (or nimble fingers), twist the tips of the paper clips round so that they turn inwards and firmly " dig into " the back of the doll. *The whole object is to keep the front and back of the doll as far apart as possible, so as to leave plenty of room between them for the limbs to move up and down.* It will be seen that the two buttons, touching, will help to achieve this and it will now also be clear why the paper fasteners must be long.

With the doll's limbs relaxed, knot the four strings about one inch from the point where they protrude from the two body pieces, and again near their ends. Slip a large bead on to the end and knot in place. Sew a small ring to top of head and knot on to it about four inches of string to make a hanging loop. Stitch head to body just *behind* centre of front of body, unless otherwise stated under each individual doll.

COSSACK

Height 9 in.   Pattern pages 254–5.   Illustration Fig. 40 A and B

Materials :

Scraps of flesh felt for face and hands.
White felt for blouse.
Navy blue felt for trousers.
Red felt for boots.
Scrap of black fur for hat.
Red ribbon for sash.
Stranded cotton in red, black and white.
Oddments as quoted on page 102 for all dolls.

Method :

Prepare the pieces as given on page 102, embroidering the eyes in black and white, brows and moustache in black, nostrils and mouth in red.

Fig. 40. *Detail of Cossack and Schoolgirl Terror*

Stitch head to *front* of body. Cover this join with a narrow strip of white felt, stitched neatly in place to make a typical Russian collar. Stitch a strip of black fur fabric in place for hat and a piece of red ribbon round each separate section of the body for a sash. Assemble the pieces as given on page 104.

SCHOOLGIRL TERROR

Height 8½ in. Pattern page 255. Illustration Plate 6 and Fig. 40 C and D

Materials :

> Scraps of flesh felt for face, hands and legs.
> Navy blue felt for tunic.
> White felt for blouse and socks.
> Black felt for shoes.
> Wine ribbon for girdle and bows.
> Yellow wool for hair.
> Black, white, blue and red stranded cotton.
> Oddments as quoted for all dolls on page 102.
> Copydex.

Method :

Prepare the pieces as given on page 102, embroidering the eyes in black, blue and white, spectacles in black, mouth and nose in red and brows in yellow wool.

To make the pigtails, take about eighteen strands of yellow darning wool and plait a sufficient length to cover the cardboard base. Bind the ends and cut off to leave a loose bunch of hair at one end. Make four plaits like this and, with Copydex, stick one to the back and one to the front of the two cardboard bases so as to cover them completely. Following the diagrams and using long, straight stitches embroider the hair on front and back of head, giving the effect of a centre parting and completely covering top of head.

Assemble the pieces as given on page 104, and finally tie bows to end of pigtails and girdle round waist.

DRUMMER BOY

Height 9½ in. Pattern page 255. Illustration Fig. 41 A and B

Materials :

> Scraps of red felt for tunic and drum.
> White felt for gloves.
> Flesh felt for face.
> Navy blue felt for trousers.
> Black felt for shoes.
> Yellow felt for drum-sticks and drum.

Fig. 41. *Detail of Drummer Boy and Clown*

Black fur for busby.
Red and yellow cord for drum.
One 2-in. pill box for drum.
8 in. stiff wire.
Black, white, blue, brown and red stranded cotton.
4½ in. narrow white tape for belt.
Oddments as quoted for all dolls on page 102.

Method :

Prepare pieces as given on page 102, embroidering the eyes in blue, white and brown, brows and moustache in brown, mouth and nostrils in red.

Make up the busby separately with the pile of the fur running downwards, slip on head and stitch.

Assemble the pieces as given on page 104. Cover the pill box with felt—a red strip round the edge and a yellow circle each side to make a drum. Edge with red cord and decorate with yellow ric-rac braid or zig-zag stitches in thick yellow stranded cotton. Stitch a belt of narrow, white tape round the soldier's waist and stitch the drum in place at centre front. Add a length of red cord round neck to " hold " it.

Cut the wire into two pieces and bend each one double, pressing tightly with pliers, so as to have two lengths 2 in. long. These are the foundation for the drum-sticks and their weight will help to make the hands fall smartly and quickly to the sides of the doll, after being raised. Fold a strip of yellow felt round each piece of wire, stitching across ends and down one side. Stitch to hands.

CLOWN
Height 9½ in.   Pattern pages 254–5.   Illustration Fig. 41 C and D

Materials :

Scraps of pink felt for tunic.
White felt for face and hands.
Pale green felt for shoes and hat.
Black wool for hair.
Black and red stranded cotton.
Sequins for decoration.
Green ribbon for ruff.
Four small bells.
Oddments as quoted for all dolls on page 102.

Method :

Prepare the pieces as given on page 102, embroidering the eyes in black, mouth and nose in red, and the hair in black wool. Join the hat to face before inserting cardboard. Decorate with sequins.

Assemble as given on page 104. Make the ruff by gathering a short length of green ribbon along one edge, pull up to fit neck and stitch round neck with seam at centre back. Sew a small bell to each hand and toe.

FATHER CHRISTMAS
Height 9 in. Pattern pages 255. Illustration Fig. 42 A and B

Materials :

    Scraps of red felt for tunic.
    Black felt for boots.
    Flesh felt for face and hands.
    Blue and green felt for parcels.
    White fur fabric or bouclé wool for trimming and beard.
    Red ribbon for belt.
    Black, white and red stranded cotton.
    Oddments as quoted for all dolls on page 102.

Method :

    Prepare the pieces as given on page 102, embroidering the eyes in black and white, mouth and " wrinkles " in red.

    Assemble as given on page 104. Bind a piece of red ribbon round waist for a belt and stitch in place. Stitch fur trimming round lower edge of tunic on both front and back and round wrists and front edge of " cap ". Stick tiny pieces in place for moustache and brows or embroider in white wool. Cut a $1\frac{1}{4}$ in. square and a rectangle $1\frac{3}{4}$ in. × 1 in. in cardboard, and cover one with blue and one with green felt to make the parcels. Tie a thread round each (silver was used for the original) and finish with a bow. Stitch one to each hand. Add a beard.

CHRISTMAS ANGEL
Height $9\frac{1}{2}$ in. Pattern page 254. Illustration Fig. 42 C and D

Materials :

    Flesh felt for face and hands.
    White felt for robes and wings.
    Yellow felt for halo.
    Yellow wool for hair.
    White wool for wings.
    Brown and red stranded cotton.
    Gold sequins for halo.
    Copydex.
    Oddments as quoted for all dolls on page 102.

Method :

    Prepare the pieces as given on page 102, embroidering the eyes in brown and

Fig. 42. *Detail of Father Christmas and Christmas Angel*

mouth and nostrils in red. Embroider a few long stitches in white wool on the tips of the wings.

Assemble the pieces as given on page 104, reading " wings " for arms. There will be no legs. Stitch the head to the *front* of body front, and with a little Copydex, stick the two collar pieces, so as to cover the stitching. Take about twenty-five strands of yellow darning wool 6 in. long and stitch to centre front top, and a little way down back of head to make a centre parting. Take each side over to the back and down behind head to each shoulder. Stick in place (to shoulder) with Copydex. Decorate halo with gold sequins and stick to back of head. Stick hand to centre front of body and tips of sleeves where shown on diagram. Fold each sleeve at " elbow " and stick over end of hand.

A great many uses will be found for these enchanting creatures. The schoolgirl, for instance, is a most original " good luck " mascot at exam. time, whilst Father Christmas and the Angel look wonderful hanging on the tree, or make an exciting and very special " Christmas Card ". They could be joined by the three kings, and footballers, boxers, tennis players, and jockeys can easily be designed for the special occasions which crop up in every family.

If you experience trouble in making the arms fall easily, add a " prop " of some sort appropriate to the character, such as Father Christmas's parcels, the Drummer Boy's sticks, or small bells as for the Clown—these act as a weight and solve the problem.

*   *   *

Did you know that at one time live birds were put into the hollow bodies of dolls instead of stuffing ? The frantic efforts of these helpless and terrified little creatures to free themselves gave the doll the appearance of being alive or driven by clockwork and was a disgusting form of entertainment which amused adults and children alike.

Section Eight

STOCKINETTE DOLLS

THESE DOLLS ARE specially designed for the very young. They are soft and cuddly with very simple features consisting mainly of embroidered squares, circles and straight lines worked in cotton. Their hair is wool or Coton à Broder, and as they will have such young owners, they are dressed in a simple cotton frock which opens all down the back for easy dressing, and cotton knickers to match. If the future owner is *very* young, these are probably the only clothes she will be able to manage, but a pattern is included for a plain knitted vest which slips easily on and off without any fastenings to hamper small fingers and for shoes and socks, if you would like to make them.

Great care should be taken when working the features to keep them in exactly the same positions as shown on sketches, if you want to achieve the same character and expression. Before working them read page 36 on faces.

Colours and materials for frocks are, of course, only an approximate guide ; you will naturally use whatever scraps you have available. Above all keep the dresses *very short* to give the dolls a young appearance. When the doll is standing, the dress should be no longer than one inch *above* the knee (see Angel, fig. 47).

N.B. It will be found economical to cut several of these dolls at once. 1 yd. of tubular stockinette 36 in. wide will make five, and ½ yd. only two. One doll needs two pieces 16½ in. × 7 in.

MAKING THE BODIES
Height 12 in. Pattern pages 256–7. Weight undressed 4 oz.

The body for all the dolls is made in the same way. Use a cotton stockinette available from good handicraft shops specially for doll making (see page 28).

Materials :

Two pieces of flesh pink stockinette 16½ in. × 7 in. " grain " running lengthwise.
About 2 oz. kapok.
Thin piece of wood 2½ in. long (about the thickness of a wooden meat skewer).
A strip of old rag about 1 in. wide.

Method (fig. 43) :

Lay the cardboard pattern template for the body on top of the two pieces of stockinette and draw accurately all round with a soft pencil. Now machine twice all round the pencil mark (with a fairly large stitch and loose tension) leaving opening,

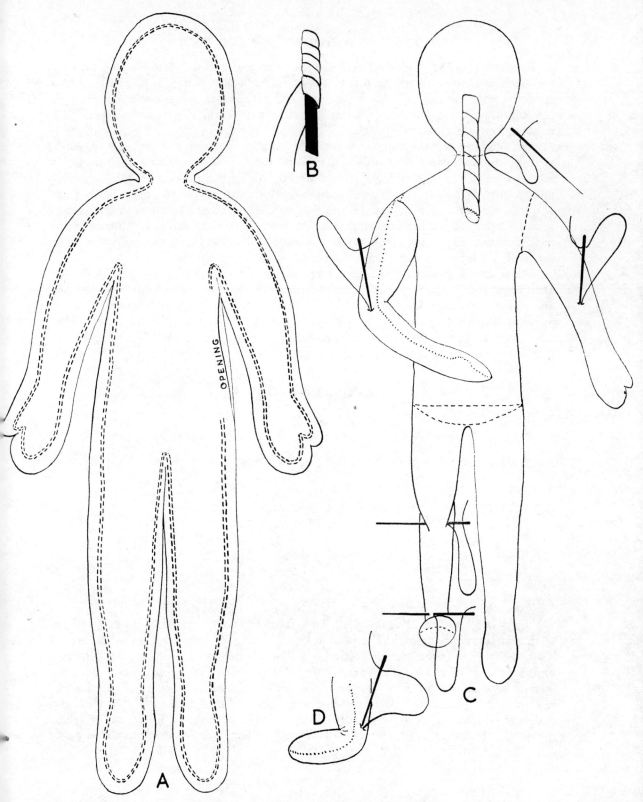

Fig. 43. *Making body of stockinette dolls*

as shown, for turning and stuffing. Cut out the shape of the doll about ¼ in. from the machined edge. Turn right side out and do not be worried by the rather extra-ordinary appearance. The doll shortens and fattens out when stuffed. Stuff the legs carefully, using only tiny pieces at a time and working slowly and thoroughly to avoid lumps in the wrong place. When you reach the top of the legs, machine two rows of stitching across base of body in order to allow the doll to " sit " (as shown by broken lines on pattern). Stuff the arms, and stitch across top of each (as shown on pattern). Stuff head, pushing the front well out to form a chin and shaping carefully into an oval or round according to which doll you are making (consult figs. 44 and 45). Bind the stick firmly with the rag (fig. 43 B) to soften it, and push one end up into the head, leaving the other protruding into the body. This will ensure a firm neck that does not " wobble ". Stuff all round the stick, being careful not to make the neck *too* fat. Stuff the body and sew up the side opening.

Now run a gathering thread all round the neck and pull up tightly to help accentuate the " chin ". Take a few stitches halfway down arm from front to back, and then from side to side on the back of arm (fig. 43 C) to form an " elbow ". Turn up approximately 1½ in. of leg to make a foot, and ladder stitch in place. Then take a few stitches from side to side at back of foot to make an " ankle ". Finally take a few stitches from side to side, halfway down leg, to make a " knee " (fig. 43 C).

SIX LITTLE GIRLS

JUDY

Pattern page 256. Illustration Plate 11 and Fig. 44 (1)

Judy has short straight auburn hair and a perpetually surprised expression.

Materials :

Completed body as described on page 112.
One skein " auburn " darning wool for hair.
Brown, red and white stranded cotton for features.
7 in. white ribbon, ½ in. wide for hair.

Method :

Hair (fig. 44 (1 A and B)) :

Cut two " bundles " about 3 in. long from the wool and stitch to top of head so that it covers the back. Then cut two bundles 7 in. long and lay across top of head so that they cover first lot of stitching. Back stitch neatly in place using double pink Sylko—so as to form a side parting. Using a length of auburn wool stitch the hair to head where the bow will be. Tie the bow in place, then stitch the hair to head just below the bow. With a soft brush, smooth the wool neatly down all round and trim with sharp scissors to a fairly long " bob ". Smooth a little gum or trans-parent adhesive over head and smooth hair on to it so that it clings neatly to head. Give a final trim.

Features :

Read page 36 and follow fig. 44 (1 C). Embroider mouth and nostrils in red, eyes and brows in brown, highlights in white. Give her rosy cheeks with a little weak water-colour—if necessary repeat when dry.

Vest :

See page 125.

Dress and Knickers :

Judy's dress is yellow/white striped cotton, with the stripes running *round* as she has straight lanky hair.

Make as given on page 126, following fig. 44 (1 C) for treatment of top. Make three rows of gathers round the neck, and pull up to form a yoke; bind the neck and " sleeves " with yellow bias binding. For Knickers see page 126.

Socks :

See page 125. Judy's are yellow.

Shoes :

Make a pair of brown felt ankle straps with chamois leather soles as shown on page 44, diagram and pattern page 45.

SALLY
Pattern page 256. Illustration Plate 11 and Fig. 44 (2)

Sally is younger than Judy and has " bunched ", straight yellow hair of rather thick wool. You may have seen her on television, as she has been demonstrated in the B.B.C.'s " Home at 1.30 " programme.

Materials :

Completed body as described on page 112.

Small quantity of yellow wool for hair (4-ply if available, failing this, skeins of darning wool).

Blue, white, red and brown stranded cotton for features.

About 14 in. red ribbon, ½ in. wide, for hair.

Method :

Hair (fig. 44 (2 A and B)) :

Take a bundle of wool about 2 in. long and stitch along top of head. (This will be the fringe.) Then take several bundles about 7 in. long, place across top of head and back stitch down centre, using double pink Sylko to make a parting. Tie very tightly in a bunch at each side of head, with a length of yellow wool. Then tie on the ribbons, pulling the bows tightly so that the hair sticks out in an appealing way. Trim to required length with sharp scissors.

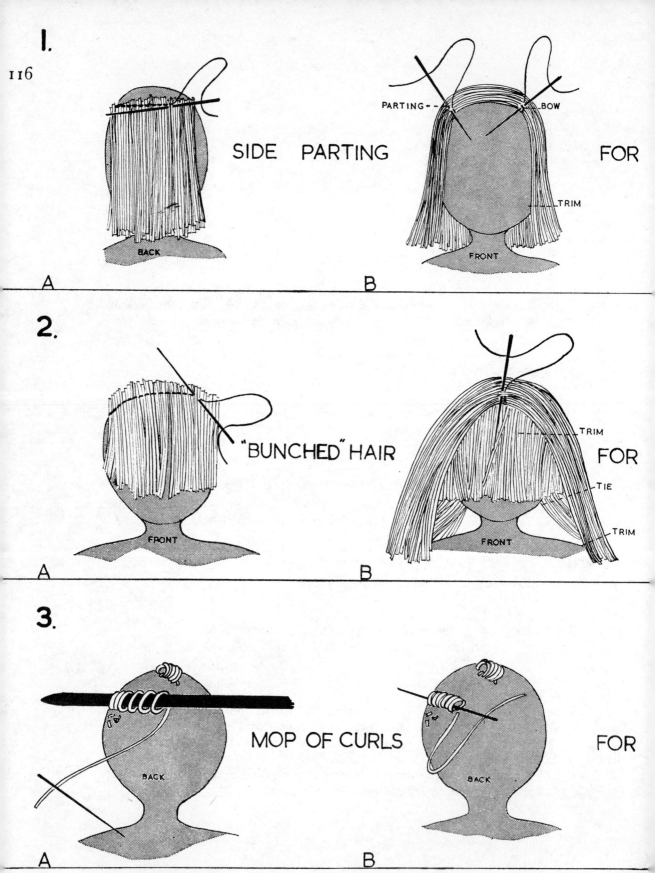

1. SIDE PARTING FOR

A   B

BACK

PARTING — — BOW

TRIM

FRONT

2. "BUNCHED" HAIR FOR

A   B

FRONT

TRIM

TIE

TRIM

FRONT

3. MOP OF CURLS FOR

A   B

BACK

BACK

Fig. 44. *Suggestions for heads of . . .*

JUDY.

SALLY.

SUE.

. . . little girl stockinette dolls

Features :

Read page 36, and follow fig. 44 (2 C).

Embroider mouth and nostrils in red. Eyes in blue. Highlights in white. Brows in brown. Give her rosy cheeks with a little weak water-colour—if necessary repeat when dry.

Vest :

See page 125.

Dress and Knickers :

Sally's dress is red/white striped cotton. Because she has " bunchy " hair, the stripes run downwards. Make as given on page 126 following fig. 44 (2 C) for treat- ment of the top. Make two rows of gathers round the neck to form a yoke, then sew a piece of yellow bias binding flat, on both the front and back of this, and give three rows of stitching as a trimming. Bind the sleeves with similar binding, but use it in the normal way. Make a tiny pocket on the frock, $1\frac{1}{4}$ in. square, with the stripes running horizontally and the top bound with yellow bias. Sally's hand will just fit into this. For Knickers see page 126.

Socks :

See page 125. Sally's are white.

Shoes :

Make a pair of sandals from red Vynide with brown suède soles as described on page 44, diagram and pattern page 43.

SUE
Pattern page 256. Fig. 44 (3)

Sue is rather a surprised little girl, with a mop of golden curls and an open mouth.

Materials :

Completed body as described on page 112.
A small ball of yellow wool (preferably 3-ply) for hair.
Blue, white, red and black stranded cotton for features.
7 in. of green ribbon, $\frac{1}{4}$ in. wide, for hair.

Method :

Hair (fig. 44 (3 A and B)) :

Thread as long a length of yellow wool as you feel you can comfortably work with into a slim darning needle. Anchor the wool to the head with one or two stitches, then take a knitting needle about size 4 or 5 and, placing it against the head, wind the wool six or seven times round it. Slip your threaded needle along between wool and knitting needle, pull away knitting needle and stitch the loops to head. Repeat this all over head until it is well covered with curls. It is rather a long job, but worth while, as the resulting " hair-do " is most effective. Stitch the green ribbon to one side of head and tie in a small bow.

Features :

Embroider the lips and nostrils in red, inside of mouth in black, teeth in white and eyes in blue and white.

Give her a healthy colour, with weak red water-colour. Her character rather calls for a slightly stronger colour than her sisters, but do not overdo it !

Vest :

See page 125.

Dress and Knickers :

Sue's dress is green/white checked gingham. Make as given on page 126 following fig. 44 (3 C) for treatment of top. Make three rows of gathers round the neck and pull up to form a yoke. Bind neck and " sleeves " with a narrow piece of the gingham cut on the bias. For Knickers see page 126.

Socks :

See page 125. Sue's are white.

Shoes :

Make a pair of green felt sandal shoes with chamois leather soles, as shown on page 44, diagram and pattern page 45.

ELIZABETH

Pattern page 256. Illustration Plate 5 and Fig. 45 (4)

Elizabeth has the appearance of being a little older than the first three dolls. Her cotton hair can be really brushed and combed and her neat white collar gives her a particularly fresh look.

Materials :

Completed body as described on page 112.
Two skeins of brown Coton à Broder (if unobtainable use darning wool).
About 9 in. yellow ribbon, $\frac{1}{2}$ in. wide, for " Alice band ".
Brown, white and red stranded cotton for features.

Method :

Hair (fig. 45 (4 A and B)) :

Open out one skein of cotton and cut off a bundle about $1\frac{1}{2}$ in. long. Stitch this across top of head for a fringe. Divide the rest of the skeins into lengths $6\frac{1}{2}$ in.

Fig. 45. *More suggestions for heads of . . .*

ELIZABETH.

JANE.

PAM.

. . . little girl stockinette dolls

long.   Lay across head so as to cover first stitching and extend for about $1\frac{1}{2}$ in. back —have the cotton particularly thick at the back, where it will have the whole of the back of the head to cover.   Back stitch hair to head, down the $1\frac{1}{2}$ in. centre parting, using double pink Sylko.   Tie the ribbon round head to form a neat Alice band, with the knot under the long back hair.   Comb the hair and trim to shoulder length with sharp scissors.   Tidy up fringe so that it is *very* slightly longer at centre front than at the sides.

Features :

Read page 36 and follow fig. 45 (4 C).
Embroider mouth and nostrils in red, eyes and brows in brown, highlights in white.   Give her rosy cheeks with weak water-colour paint.

Vest :

See page 125.

Dress and Knickers :

(Material needed for dress : scraps, or $\frac{1}{4}$ yd. 36 in. wide cotton.)
Using blue/white spotted cotton material cut out the front, backs and sleeves as given on pages 256–7, and the collar pieces in plain white cotton.   Also cut a piece 26 in. $\times$ $5\frac{1}{2}$ in. in the spotted material for the skirt.
Join backs to front A–B and C–D.   Gather skirt piece all along one long side and join to " bodice ", turn back a narrow hem all down both sides of back—bodice and skirt all in one, so that the dress will open all down the centre back.   On the sleeves, fold each one in half and join underarm seam A–F.   Make a very narrow hem all round lower edge of sleeve F–G–F.   Run a strong gathering thread round top of sleeve A–D–A, pull up to fit armhole and stitch into bodice matching letters.   Gather round lower edge of sleeve and pull up to fit the doll's arm, making a little frilled edge (see plate 5).   Join collar pieces together in pairs H–I–J–K.   Turn right side out, press carefully and stitch each one to neck of dress, from centre front of body to the back opening—stitching first one thickness of collar on the right side of dress, then on the wrong side, turning in the raw edge and slip stitching the second thickness.   Press flat.   Try the dress on to doll and turn up lower hem of skirt at just above knee level.   Sew small press studs all down centre back to fasten.
For the Knickers see page 126.

Socks :

See page 125.   Elizabeth's are white.

Shoes :

Make a pair of black kid dancing pumps with brown suède soles as shown on page 44, diagram and pattern page 43.

JANE

Pattern page 256. Illustration Plate 2 and Fig. 45 (5)

Jane is perhaps the plainest of the dolls, with her black woollen pigtails.

Materials :

Completed body as described on page 112.

Small ball of black wool for hair (original was 2-ply but darning wool may be used).

About 14 in. yellow ribbon, ¼ in. wide, for bows.

Red, white, black and blue stranded cotton for features.

Method :

Hair (fig. 45 (5 A and B)) :

Cut a bundle of wool about 1½ in. long, stitch along top of head for fringe. Cut several bundles about 12 in. long and lay across top of head, to cover first lot of stitching. Back stitch across top of head and right down back using double pink Sylko to make a centre parting. Divide into two and plait, binding the ends with black wool. Tie on bows. Trim fringe and ends of pigtails.

Features :

See page 36 and follow fig. 45 (5 C).

Embroider mouth and nostrils in red, eyes in blue, teeth and highlights in white, brows and lids in black. Give her just a *little* colour with weak red paint—but she should look a little paler than her sisters.

Vest :

See page 125.

Dress and Knickers :

Jane's dress is acid yellow poplin, trimmed with red and white braid. Make as given on page 126 following fig. 42 (5 C) for treatment of top. Make one row of gathers round the neck and bind this and the sleeves with a narrow piece of the self material cut on the bias. Stitch a piece of ½ in. wide braid right round edge of " yoke " and sleeves, all round lower edge of dress and across the top of two little pockets which are 1¼ in. wide by 1½ in. long. Make a tiny hankie for one pocket, by hemming a square of white cotton material. For Knickers see page 126.

Socks :

See page 125. Jane's are yellow.

Shoes :

Make a pair of black felt bar shoes with fawn felt soles as described on page 44. Diagram and pattern page 43.

PAM

Pattern pages 256–7.   Illustration Plate 11 and Fig. 45 (6)

Pam's short fair pony tail and tiny mouth give her a suspiciously innocent appearance.

Materials :

Completed body as described on page 112.
A small ball of very pale yellow 2-ply wool for hair.
About 7 in. of red ribbon, ½ in. wide.
Blue, white and red stranded cotton for features.

Method :

Hair (fig. 45 (6 A and B)) :

Cut the wool into about 5 in. lengths and use a small bundle of these lengths at a time.   With a soft pencil draw all round head just above where the eventual hair line will be.   Stitch the bundles of wool to the head just below the pencil line, with the long ends hanging downwards, and short ends to top of head.   Spread it evenly all round head and stitch firmly.   With a soft brush gather wool up evenly all round and bind with a short length of wool at top of head to form a pony tail. Tie on bow so that it stands up crisply on top of head, and trim wool neatly, graduating the ends a little so that the " tail " is shorter at the sides and dips at the back.   Thread a slim darning needle with a long length of wool and work a few long, straight stitches from the face on to the hair—this breaks up the hairline and gives the effect of stray wispy hairs which the possessor of a pony tail always has !   At the same time embroider eyebrows.

Features :

See page 36 and follow fig. 42 (6 C).
Embroider mouth and nostrils in red, eyes in blue, highlights in white.

Vest :

See page 125.

Dress and Knickers :

(Material needed for dress : scraps, or ¼ yd. 36 in. wide cotton.)
Cut out front and backs as given on pages 256–7 and a piece 26 in. × 5½ in. for skirt.
Make this dress exactly as for Elizabeth but make darts as indicated by X–Y and broken lines on front pattern—two on the front and two on the back to give a shaped and more fitted front.   Omit the collar and sleeves and bind these with a narrow bias cut from matching material.
For Knickers see page 126.

Socks :

See page 125.   Pam's are yellow.

Shoes :

Make a pair of red felt ankle strap shoes with broad felt soles as shown on page 44.   Diagrams and pattern page 43.

A SIMPLE VEST FOR ALL DOLLS

This is merely two pieces of K3, P1 rib, which will slip easily on and off and stay neatly in place without any fastenings.

Materials :

A very small ball of 2-ply white wool (1 oz. would make about twelve vests).
A pair of knitting needles size 12.

Method :

Cast on 27 sts.   Work one row into the back of sts.
1st row : K1, P1, (K3, P1) 6 times.   K1.
2nd row : K2, (P3, K1) 6 times.   K1.
Repeat these 2 rows 15 times.
33rd row : Cast off 4 sts., rib to end.
34th row : Cast off 4 sts., rib to end.
Work 20 rows in rib pattern.
Cast off *very* loosely in rib.
Knit another piece in exactly the same way.   Press lightly and place the two pieces one on top of the other with the top straight edges overlapping (the front over the back) for ½ in.   Oversew this ½ in. on top of each armhole (not along shoulder seam), then seam the sides.

SOCKS

Pattern page 256

The ideal material for these is found in the finely ribbed tops of children's socks. (The feet usually wear out first, leaving the tops in good condition.)   Cotton or nylon are best, but fine wool may be used.

Cut out two socks, having the top selvedge edge of sock running along straight edge A–C of pattern and the ribbing running in direction of arrow.   Fold each piece in half so that A meets A and oversew all down the centre back seam A–B.   Oversew back again for extra strength.   Turn right side out.   If insufficient tops are available use the leg part of the sock, but in this case cut slightly longer so that a tiny rolled hem may be made all round top.

SIMPLE ONE PIECE DRESS FOR
JUDY, SALLY, SUE AND JANE

The whole secret of making a doll young-looking instead of old-fashioned and dowdy is to keep the clothes very short and very full. This little dress is quickly and simply made from one piece of material and opens all down the back so that the dolls can be easily dressed by even the youngest of owners.

How to make it (fig. 46) :

Cut a piece of material as shown by fig. 46, 24 in. long and 7 in. wide. Cut two curved slits for armholes where shown and bind these all round with bias binding. (Do this by hand for real success.) These slits make enchanting little " epaulettes " on the finished dress. Now gather along top edge of dress A–C—you may need one, two, or three rows of gathers according to which doll you are dressing. See instructions under each separate doll for this. Pull up gathers very tightly. Turn a narrow hem back all down back openings A–B and C–D. The neck of dress should fit snugly round neck of doll (see figs. 44 and 45). Bind top edge as given under each separate doll and turn up a narrow hem all round bottom edge. Add pockets if required. Fasten the back with either small press studs or buttons and button-holes.

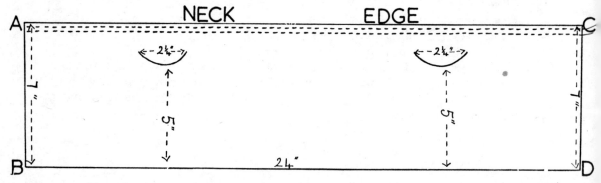

Fig. 46.   *Measurements for cutting a simple one-piece dress for the stockinette dolls*

KNICKERS FOR ALL DOLLS
Pattern page 271

(Material needed : one piece 10 in. × 5¼ in., or two pieces 5 in. × 5¾ in.)
These may be cut in one piece as given on pattern with a fold between the legs, or if insufficient material is available cut in two pieces and joined between the legs.

How to make them :

Turn up a tiny rolled hem all round legs. Join side seams. Turn down a hem $\frac{1}{2}$ in. wide all round top edge leaving a small opening. Thread in elastic (see page 24) to fit waist of doll and stitch ends together. Close opening.

BABY ANGEL FOR THE CHRISTMAS TREE
Pattern pages 256–7. Illustration Fig. 47

This appealing small person makes a pleasant change from the traditional fairy on top of the Christmas Tree, and an exciting present for the youngest member of the family. After Christmas her halo and wings can very easily be removed, thus turning her into a cuddly little girl doll.

Materials :

Completed body as described on page 112.
Yellow wool for hair.
Scrap of yellow cotton material for halo.
Red, blue and white stranded cotton for features.
White cotton material for dress and knickers (24 in. × 7 in. and 10 in. × 5¼ in.).
White felt for wings (10 in. × 5½ in.).
Cardboard for stiffening wings and halo.

Method :

Follow fig. 47.

Hair :

Using very pale yellow wool (2-ply), make the hair exactly as for Elizabeth (fig. 45 (4 A and B)) but cut it shorter and do not make an Alice band.

Features :

See page 36 and follow fig. 47.
Embroider mouth and nostrils in red, eyes in blue, highlights in white and brows in yellow wool.

Halo :

Cut two circles of cardboard and cover them with brilliant yellow material or gold lamé, as shown by fig. 19 A, B and C. Place the two covered circles together and oversew all round the outside edge. Stitch to top of head.

Dress :

Make as described on page 126 and fig. 46 in crisp, white cotton material. Edge top of sleeve slits and hem with gathered up lace. (Allow 2½ times the length to be

Fig. 47. *A Baby Angel for the Christmas Tree*

trimmed to get a really full frill.) Finish neck with a neat binding of self material cut on the bias.

Knickers :

Make as given on page 126 in material to match the dress. Edge legs with frilled lace.

Wings :

Cut two from stiff cardboard and four from white felt just very slightly larger. Place each cardboard stiffener between two of the felt pieces and stab stitch all round the outside edges. Consulting fig. 47 embroider a few long, straight stitches in white wool to give a feathered effect. Fold end portion of wing forward at A–B and hem firmly to back all round A–B–C–D so that the two edges A–B meet at centre back (fig. 47 C and B).

Put on dress and fasten so that one press stud is at neck edge and the next one immediately underneath wings (fig. 47 B).

Holly :

Cut leaves from emerald and bottle green felt and small round berries from red felt. Stitch to head to form a wreath and to one hand. If available, a silver sequin under each berry adds an attractive sparkle.

" TWINKLE "—THE LITTLE STAR FAIRY
Pattern pages 256–7. Illustration Plate 5

Twinkle is a cuddly, little girl fairy, who brings to life the well-known nursery rhyme. To give her the necessary glitter and shine, to live up to her name, silver lamé or brocade is used for the star which forms her wings, and " jewels " or silver sequins are scattered liberally about her dress and sewn to her wand and headdress. She is therefore not suitable for the *very* young. However, she is such a typical " little girl " that after some special occasion, such as Christmas, her stars and lace dress can be removed and she can be put into an ordinary cotton frock.

Her face, unlike the other stockinette dolls, is slightly modelled, but may of course be left flat if preferred.

Materials :

One completed body as described on page 112.
Yellow wool for hair.
Red, blue, white and brown stranded cotton for features.
White lace for dress (24 in. × 7 in.).
White cotton material for slip and knickers (24 in. × 7 in. and 10 in. × $5\frac{1}{4}$ in.).
Scraps of silver lamé for star and wand (or $\frac{1}{8}$th yd.).
One wooden meat skewer.
One white postcard.

Some cardboard (cereal box).

Diamond-like " jewels " or silver sequins.

Method :

Follow fig. 48.

Features :

See page 36 and follow fig. 48.

Embroider mouth and nostrils in red, eyes in blue and white, lashes in brown, using one strand of cotton. With a long slim needle and Sylko or silk that exactly matches the face, raise a tiny nose, sink the eyes (fig. 83 K, L, M, and N), and raise the cheeks.

Hair :

Using pale yellow wool (2-ply) make the hair exactly as for Elizabeth (fig. 45 (4 A and B)) but cut it short and do not make an Alice band. Using Polycell cellulose adhesive and a large brush, soak the hair at the front edges and twist it round slightly so that it curls towards the face and sticks to the cheek. Very lightly touch the cheeks with a little weak, red paint. Leave this and the paste to dry overnight.

Dress :

Make as shown on page 126 and fig. 46, using white lace or net. Do not bind the neck, but turn the raw edge inwards and run two or three rows of gathers along here. Edge top of sleeve slits, and hem of dress with $\frac{1}{2}$ in. wide lace, gathered up *very* fully. (Allow $2\frac{1}{2}$ times the length to be trimmed to get a really full frill.) Make a little lace frill and stitch round neck about $\frac{1}{2}$ in. from top. Decorate the dress with silver sequins or jewels. Make a similar dress in fine white cotton material to act as a slip, underneath the transparent lace top. Omit the lace edging if you wish, although this does add to the charm of the doll.

Knickers :

Make as given on page 126 in fine white cotton material. Edge legs with frilled lace.

Star for Wings (Pattern page 285) :

Cut twelve diamonds in stiff card, and twelve in silver lamé about $\frac{1}{4}$ in. larger all round (if the material frays very badly, cut these pieces larger still). Cover the card diamonds with the lamé, lacing the material firmly across the back (fig. 25). On the wrong side, oversew the diamonds together to form two stars. The easiest way to do this is to sew three together, then another three, then sew these two threes together all along the straight edge. Place the two stars together, wrong sides inside, and, leaving the cardboard stiffeners in place, oversew the two together all round the outside edge. Bend the star in half along one of the joins to form " wings ", so that each half will stand slightly away from the body. With strong thread and a

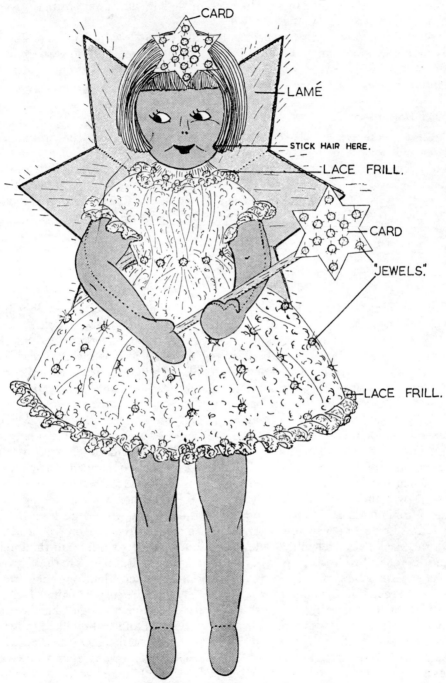

CARD

LAMÉ

STICK HAIR HERE.

LACE FRILL.

CARD

"JEWELS."

LACE FRILL.

Fig. 48. *"Twinkle"*, *the little star fairy*

tough needle, sew the centre of star to back of doll in the same position as angel's wings (fig. 47). Do this very securely.

Try on dress, and run a gathering thread round " waist " at a position just under where star joins body. Pull up to fit waist and fasten off. Sew snap fasteners to back of dress, at neck and waist, so that one fastens above and one under where star joins body, just as the angel's dress fastens round the wings (fig. 47).

Wand and Headdress :

Cover a wooden meat skewer with silver lamé by rolling a strip round it and oversewing all down the tucked-in raw edge, also along top and bottom end. Cut two stars from a white postcard (pattern page 284). If available, paint these with silver paint—but they look almost as nice left white. Decorate them both with silver sequins or " jewels ". Stitch one to the top of the head, at a forward angle, and the other to the top of the wand. Stitch the wand into the fairy's hands.

VARIATIONS
Using other colour stockinette remnants

You may find that you have a piece of coloured stockinette—possibly from a cotton cardigan or sun-top, which is just large enough to make a doll.

1. With a piece of white, try making a clown. So many clowns' faces and clothes are given in other sections of the book that no special idea is given here. Merely make up the doll in white instead of flesh material and adapt the features and garments from Section IX to suit him, embroidering them instead of painting, or you can adapt the ideas on pages 107 or 182, or, better still, invent your own.

2. With a piece of brown, try making a piccaninny (see plate 4). Make the body exactly as for the other dolls (page 112). An idea for her features is given in fig. 49. For the hair use fine black wool and cover the head closely with a series of loops as shown for the clown in fig. 68 B, but make the loops much longer—at least 2½ in. When the head is covered, cut the loops and make a series of short stubby pigtails all over the head, binding them after the first inch with matching wool to keep them firmly plaited. Thread a needle with double wool and go over the head, taking long stitches to cover any " gaps " in the wool so that no brown head shows through the black hair. Then take a few stitches from the hair line on to the forehead, to form a pointed " widow's peak ", thus giving a more natural look to the " growth " of the hair. Tie a bow of very narrow red ribbon to each plait, one inch from the head. Stitch each bow to its plait for safety, then cut off the surplus hair. Embroider the features as shown by fig. 49 and make a gay cotton dress and knickers as for the other dolls (page 126) and a pair of sandals (page 44) and socks if liked (page 125).

An alternative piccaninny " hair-do " can be made exactly as for Sue (fig. 44 (3 C)) but using black wool instead of yellow. If you particularly want to make a coloured doll but have no brown material, have a piece of flesh stockinette dyed. Any reputable firm of cleaners will do this for about two shillings. Do remember, however, to allow

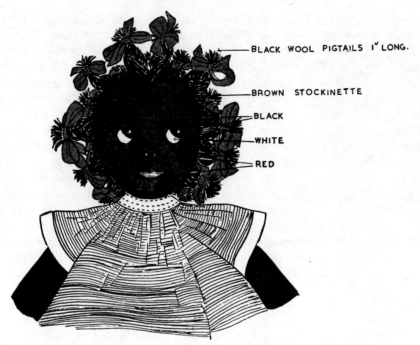

Fig. 49. *An idea for the face of a Piccaninny stockinette doll*

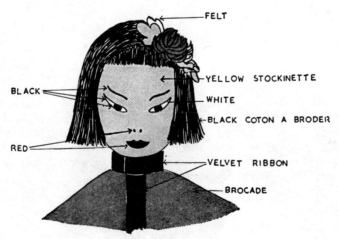

Fig. 50. *An idea for the face of an oriental child stockinette doll*

for shrinkage and send a length of 21–22 in. in order to be able to use the pattern on page 256. The usual amount of shrinkage is 3 in.

Black stockinette *is* very readily available, but although this makes an excellent " Mammy " (page 177), it does not look so well on a child doll, because it seems to give it rather a " Golliwogish " appearance, whilst brown looks quite natural.

3. With a piece of fawn, such as a thick stocking top, make the Eskimo Boy in Section VI. Only his face will show, so you only need quite a small piece.

4. With a piece of yellow or cream—try making an oriental child.

Make up the body exactly as given for the other dolls on page 112, using the yellow stockinette. Fig. 50 gives an idea for her features. Make her hair from fine black wool, or better still cotton or silk, working exactly as given for Elizabeth, fig. 45 (4 A and B) and page 119, but omit the Alice band and cut the hair shorter. She may be dressed in an ordinary cotton frock like the other dolls if she is, perhaps, to go to school with them, or if you prefer Eastern clothes make a tunic and trousers. A pattern for these is given on page 258. Make them in silk or brocade if possible, and edge the front of tunic with velvet ribbon, making a high collar to match. Give her two chrysanthemums and some leaves in her hair, in colours to blend with her clothes.

To make each flower, cut three circles in felt and slash inwards as shown by broken lines. Place the three together, stitching together at the centre ; then, with a needle, ruffle up the petals, and take a few stitches through one or two of them to make the flower stand up, instead of lying flat. Stitch them firmly to the head. Either leave the doll barefooted or make her a pair of " strip " or oriental sandals, adjusting the pattern (pages 45, 49) to fit her feet.

*   *   *

Did you know that Jane Taylor, who wrote " Twinkle Twinkle Little Star " (as a hymn—not a nursery rhyme) was one of the talented family of a Congregational Minister ? Part of her childhood was spent in the house which stands next door to the author's present home, and Jane spent many hours " sailing " on the moat which separates the two gardens, " in an old brewing tub propelled with a coal shovel ".

Section Nine

PAINTED CALICO DOLLS

UNTIL QUITE RECENTLY and for the past century or so, "COBO DOLLS" have been the loved companions of many little girls on the delightful Island of Guernsey. As their name suggests, they originated in the little village of Cobo, having been made there for several generations by members of the Le Huray and Guille families, and sold not only in the village post-office but in shops in St. Peter Port.

Unfortunately, their popularity has recently declined—probably due to their hardness and to their many commercially made rivals now so readily available. However, Mrs. Beatrice Le Huray was able to tell of the unbleached calico purchased by herself at 3d. per yard, for making these dolls, and of how she sold them at 10d. each after the first world war and made them from sugar and flour bags when evacuated to the mainland during the second.

The little girl figures (see plate 2), some 15 in. high, which were rather on the crude side, were made from strong unbleached calico and stuffed very hard, with sawdust—each one weighing about 1½ lb. So hard were they, in fact, that they constituted a considerable menace if used as a " weapon " ! The feet, face and hands were depicted with ordinary household paint—the features being marked with a matchstick dipped in paint. They were usually named after the original two women who made them—Cobo Alice or Judy, and were sold without clothes. Most families dressed them in a simple cotton frock and knickers using pieces over from home dressmaking, and put a " scoop " (a kind of sun bonnet stiffened with cane) on their heads, like those traditionally worn by Guernsey women working in the fields.

A modern version of this type of doll is fun to make and gives scope to those who prefer painting features to embroidering them. They also have the advantage of being to a certain extent washable—all grimy marks on the face being easily sponged away with a damp cloth. Clowns and Augusts seem ideal subjects for painted features, so patterns are included for four of these. Instructions are also given for a little girl —Meg, who somewhat resembles the old wooden Dutch dolls in shape.

GENERAL INSTRUCTIONS FOR MAKING THE DOLLS' BODIES
Pattern page 260. Height approx. 13 in.

Materials :

¼ yd. unbleached calico 36 in. wide.
Very dry sawdust. (This should have been dried in a tin in a hot cupboard for

at least three weeks before using or it will gradually dry and shrink inside the doll, causing the calico to become loose and the paint to crack.)
Size, undercoat and gloss paints in pink or white.

Method (fig. 51) :

Cut out the pieces as given, using either the large or small head and round or oval nose, as directed under the instructions for each separate doll.

Body :

Place the two body pieces together and machine all round about ¼ in. from edge, except across small neck opening.

Legs :

Place the pieces together in pairs and machine all round except across straight top edges.

Arms :

Make just as for legs.

Head :

Close each small dart and machine. Then place the two pieces together and machine all round on the wrong side, except between A and B.

Assembling :

Turn all the pieces the right way out. Stuff the body and the head VERY, VERY hard with dry sawdust. This is a lengthy job as every corner must be packed tightly and the sawdust rammed down again and again with a blunt piece of wood. If the slightest corner is left empty the paint will eventually crack, so the finished parts must resemble solid wood as regards hardness. Now take a piece of wood, about meat skewer thickness, and 2½ in. long—ram one end into the head and the other into the body leaving about ⅜ in. gap between the two. Wrap a piece of calico several times round the stick to make the neck, turning the raw edges in as you work. (It is simpler to press these edges back before you begin.) Fasten the end securely with a few stitches and ladder stitch the top of neck to head and lower edge to body—working all round. Stuff the lower part of arms, then stitch twice across at " elbow ", to allow for bending. Finish stuffing arms. Work a row of stitching across top about ½ in. from end, then oversew top. (This makes a " hinge ".) Stuff and stitch the legs in the same way, then oversew all four limbs to body.

Nose :

Run a gathering thread round outer edge of nose, about ¼ in. from edge. Stuff this very firmly and pull up gathers to form a hard " knob " (as shown in fig. 8 (1)). Consult the sketch of the features of the doll you are making for position and ladder stitch in place—working round several times.

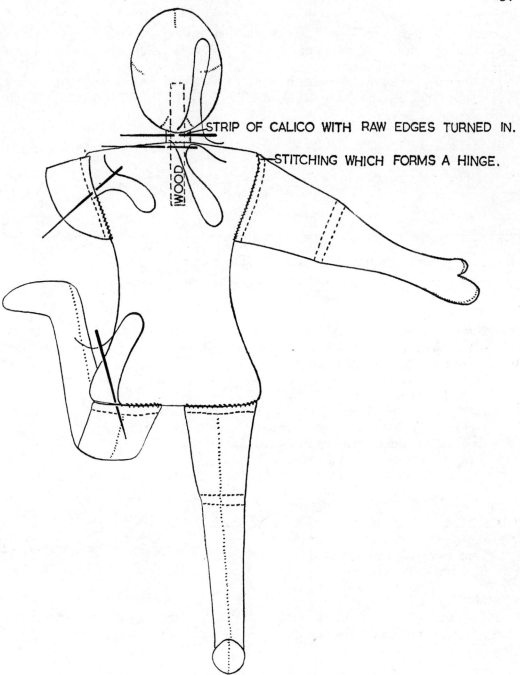

STRIP OF CALICO WITH RAW EDGES TURNED IN.

STITCHING WHICH FORMS A HINGE.

WOOD

Fig. 51. *Construction of painted calico doll's body*

Painting :

Paint the doll all over with a generous coat of size, or Polycell paste. Hang up to dry by a string tied round one ankle, either on the clothes line or in a warm room. Leave overnight.

Paint all over with undercoat in white or very pale pink according to which doll you are making. Leave to dry thoroughly. Paint all over with gloss paint in pink or white.

N.B. Make sure you do not use a " lead " paint as this is for a child's plaything —but in any case this is a doll for the older child, not one at the sucking, chewing stage !

If preferred, the hands, face and legs only can be painted.

FOUR CLOWNS

BERT

Pattern pages 260–4.   Illustration Plate 11

Bert is the typical " nincompoop " August, with trousers and hat too small and large, bulbous, turned in shoes.

Materials :

A completed body, prepared as given on page 136, using the large head and oval nose and painted white.

Small piece of brown fur or fur fabric (4¼ in. square) for hair.

Cork from a medicine bottle for hat.

Odd piece of cotton material in large black/white check and bright yellow for coat (or ¼ yd. of each 36 in. wide).

Grey flannel for trousers (7 in. × 14½ in.).

Scrap of red check cotton material for tie.

„   „   black felt for hat.

„   „   orange „   „   shirt.

„   „   white „   „   waistcoat.

Ribbed cuffs of old blue jersey for stockings.

Brown Vynide and suède for shoes.

Four medium pearl buttons.

One black coat button.

Method :

Cut out the pieces as given, making sure that on the hair the pile on the fur fabric runs in the same direction as arrow on pattern, i.e. *up* the head at back (fig. 52 B).

Hair :

Gather along curved edge (broken line on pattern) turning in a small hem as

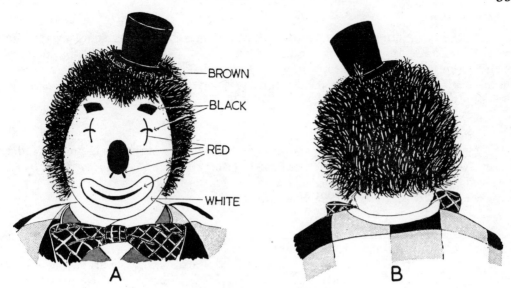

Fig. 52. *Details of Bert's features*

you work. Pull up gathers so that the curved edge fits round back of head. Using Copydex, stick hair to head (point to centre front), turning in a small hem all down two straight edges.

Hat :

Cut a circle of stiff cardboard $1\frac{1}{2}$ in. in diameter and two circles of black felt very slightly larger. Place the cardboard between the two felt pieces and oversew all round the edge. This is the brim. Cover the medicine bottle cork with black felt—a circle at each end and strip all round edge, oversewing in place. This is the crown. Place the covered cork upside down on brim, so that the largest end is at the top, and ladder stitch crown to brim. Stitch hat to head, as it will not otherwise stay in place, or, if preferred, make removable like the rest of the clothes by stitching a length of round, black elastic to the brim. This can pass round back of head and be "lost" among the hair.

Features (fig. 52) :

Paint these, using a fine brush and ordinary high-gloss paint. If you have no "remnants" in your household, buy tiny tins from the ironmonger, for about one shilling or less.

The nose, mouth and vertical eye slits are red, eyebrows, nostrils and horizontal eye slits are black.

" Dicky " Shirt :

On the back join A–B–C to form a dart and make the collar stand away from body. Join back to front along shoulder seams D–E. Make two small buttonholes as shown on pattern on right front and sew two small buttons in place to correspond. Put on to clown, buttoning in place and turning down the " collar " all round, pressing into place with your fingers (fig. 52 A and B).

Waistcoat :

On the wrong side join fronts to back by sewing side seams C–D and shoulder seams A–B. Make two small buttonholes on the left front, as shown on pattern, and sew on two small buttons to correspond. Place on clown and button in place, with the shirt collar overlapping it at the top.

Trousers :

Join each leg seam A–B, then join the two legs together C–A–C. Make a $\frac{3}{4}$ in. hem all round top and thread with elastic to fit clown's waist. Turn up a similar hem round bottom of legs and herringbone in place. The finished trousers should be *much* too short, to give the ridiculous effect aimed at—i.e. about $5\frac{1}{4}$ in. long. Put on to doll, tucking under waistcoat.

Coat :

Use an enormous check material for this—one that is out of all proportion to the size of the doll.

Take the check pieces and join fronts to backs all down side seams A–B and top of sleeve seams C–D. Then do the same with the yellow lining pieces. Now place these two pieces together right sides towards each other and stitch together all round outside edges, D–E–B–F–B–E–D. Leave a gap between the two D's at back of neck, and through this turn the coat right way out. Press edges neatly and slip stitch opening. Slip stitch lining to sleeve all round lower edge of arm. Sew a large, black coat button to the right front and make a buttonhole to correspond. Put on to clown.

Tie :

Cut a strip of red check cotton material on the cross, $1\frac{1}{4}$ in. wide and 6 in. long. Make a narrow hem all along each edge. Fold the two ends so that they meet at centre, and stitch. Wrap another narrow strip of the material round this piece, at the centre, to form a mock bow (fig. 52 A), stitch in place at back and at the same time sew on a small gilt safety pin. Pin tie in position.

Stockings :

Cut the stockings from the ribbed cuffs of an old jersey. Royal blue was used for original. Oversew twice on the wrong side from A–B. This will be the centre back seam. Turn a narrow hem all round tops. Pull on to doll.

Shoes :

Using brown Vynide with brown suède soles, make up Clown's shoe No. 1, as shown on pages 46-7.   Stuff the bulbous toes with cotton wool to keep them in shape and put on to doll.

ALGY
Pattern pages 260, 266.   Illustration Plate 11

Algy is Bert's " mate ".   He wears a long raglan style check shirt, trousers with enormous braces, and a rather outsize tie.

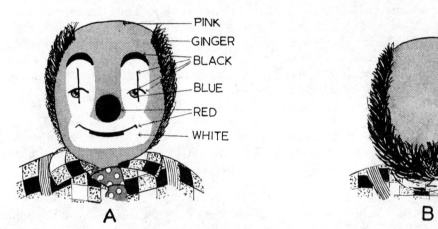

Fig. 53.   *Details of Algy's features*

Materials :

A completed body, prepared as given on page 136 and using the large head and
   round nose, and painted pink.
Scrap of gingery fur fabric for hair.
   ,,   ,,   fawn felt for braces.
About one foot of $\frac{1}{4}$ in. wide white elastic.
Black/white stripe cotton material for trousers (18 in. × 9 in.).
Red/white check gingham for shirt (27 in. × 7 in.).
Grey/white spotted cotton for tie ($3\frac{1}{2}$ in. × 13 in.).
Scrap of red Vynide and brown leather for shoes.
Six small buttons.

Method :

Cut out the pieces as given.

Hair :

Consulting fig. 53 B cut two strips of fur fabric about ¾ in. wide. Glue to head so that they meet at centre back and the pile sweeps upwards each side.

Features (fig. 53) :

Using high-gloss paint and a small brush, paint the white patches behind eyes and mouth. Allow to dry thoroughly, then paint nose and mouth red, eye " crosses ", pupils and brows black, and eyes blue. Don't forget to leave a tiny white highlight on each pupil, to bring it to life.

Shirt :

Cut one of the pieces down centre A–B. This will be the front. Join front to back down side seams C–D and top of sleeve seams E–F. Turn back a tiny hem down front edges, edge of sleeves and all round bottom. Make a straight collar by folding a piece of gingham 4½ in. × 2¼ in. in half widthwise and stitching short ends together on the wrong side, with ¼ in. turnings. Turn right side out, pushing out points. Slip neck edge of shirt between open edge of collar and slip stitch in place. Fasten front with tiny press studs and put on doll.

Tie :

Make a very narrow hem across A–B–C and D–E–F. Then fold together so that D meets F and A meets C ; stitch this seam on the wrong side. Turn right side out and press flat with seam down centre back. Put on doll and knot in front.

Trousers :

Fold each piece so that A's meet and join the two leg seams A–B. Then join the two legs together C–A–C. Turn right side out. Face the top edge with a piece of bias material ¾ in. wide and with red Sylko sew on the six white buttons, in a position to hold the braces, two at each side of front and two at the back. Try on doll and turn up a hem all round lower edge of legs, keeping trousers long.

Braces (fig. 54) :

Place the button tabs together in pairs and stab stitch all round outer edge except for top ends. Reinforce the buttonholes. Cut and stitch the elastic together as shown in fig. 54. Place one of the " back " tabs on each side of the elastic where it crosses at centre back, stab stitch the two tabs together all round outer edge. Push the ends of the elastic into the tops of the button tabs and stab stitch in place. Fasten to trousers and put on to doll.

Shoes :

Using red Vynide with brown leather soles, make up Clown's shoe No. 4 (pattern and instructions pages 46, 48). Stuff long fronts with cotton wool to keep in shape and put on to doll. The original wore no socks or stockings but these may be made as for Bert or Meg, if required.

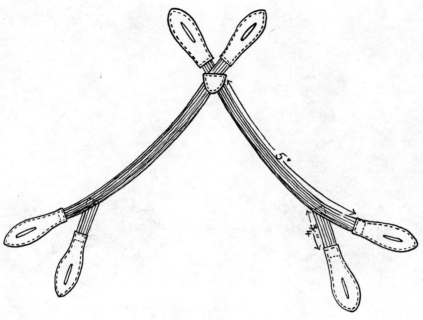

Fig. 54. *Algy's braces*

JOEY
Pattern pages 260, 268

In his spotted tunic, crisp ruffs and white felt hat Joey is somewhat reminiscent of a Pierrot, but he is the young child's idea of a " proper " clown.

Materials :

A completed body, prepared as given on page 136, using the small head and either round or oval nose and painted white.

⅜ yd. red/white spotted cotton 36 in. wide for tunic (or a piece 12½ in. × 30 in.).
Red wool or fur fabric for pom-poms.
White organdie and green bias binding for ruffs (6 in. × 15 in.).
Scrap of white felt for hat.
Scrap of black leather cloth or Vynide and fawn felt for shoes.
White stockinette (old sock tops) for socks.
Six small press studs (ooo).

Method :

Cut out the pieces as given.

Features (fig. 55) :

Using high-gloss paint and a small brush, paint nose and mouth red, and the rest of the lines in black.

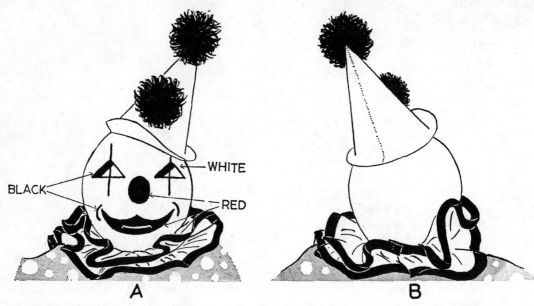

Fig. 55. *Details of Joey's features*

Hat :

Pattern and diagrams page 53. Make in white felt with red pom-poms. Stuff with a little cotton wool to keep the shape and stitch at a rakish angle to the clown's head. (See also page 54.)

Tunic :

On each piece slit A–B for leg seams and on *the back only* D–C for opening. Place the pieces together and stitch shoulder seams E–F, underarm and side seams G–H–I–J, and leg seams A–B–A. Make a narrow hem round base of legs and sleeves and run in very narrow or round elastic to fit the wrists and ankles tightly (see page 24). Face back opening and round neck, with ½ in. matching facing. Sew three small press studs to back, and three pom-poms to match those on hat, to the front.

Ruffs :

Cut a strip of white organdie or similar material 2¼ in. × 15 in. for the neck and two 1¾ in. × 12 in. for the arms. Make a narrow hem at each short end and bind the long edges with bright green bias binding. Run a *strong* gathering thread down centre of each piece and pull up the large one to fit neck and the two smaller ones to fit arms. Fasten off gathers and sew a small press stud to each end of all the ruffs. These will then be completely detachable and snap on and off the doll for easy washing and ironing.

Socks :

Make up the socks exactly as given for Meg on page 148.

Shoes :

Using black Vynide with fawn felt soles make up Clown's shoe No. 2 (pattern and diagram page 47). Add a large red pom-pom to the toe of each like those on tunic and hat.

TONI
Pattern pages 260, 270. Illustration Plate 4

Toni is the spangled clown. Although not essential, a material with a small all over spot design is useful, for the spots can conveniently be used as a guide for sewing on the sequins. The original had pale blue, mauve and magenta sequins on blue/white spotted material. .

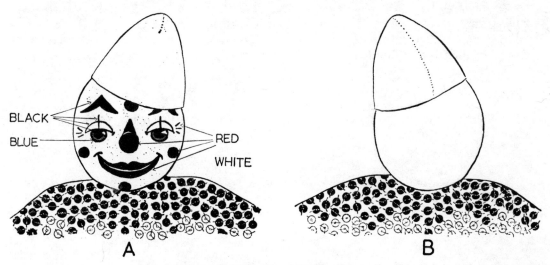

Fig. 56. *Details of Toni's features*

Materials :

A completed body, prepared as given on page 136, using the small head, round nose and painted white.
Blue/white spotted cotton material for the tunic (2 pieces, $9\frac{1}{2}$ in. × $13\frac{1}{2}$ in.).
A large quantity of sequins for the tunic.
Scrap of white felt for the hat.
White stockinette (ribbed tops from worn socks) for the stockings.
Scraps of black and fawn felt for shoes.
Four small press studs.

G

Method :

Cut out the pieces as given.

Features (fig. 56) :

Using gloss paint and a fine brush, paint the nose, mouth, eye " wrinkles ", and spots in red, eyes in blue, pupils, eyelids, brows and " crosses " on eyes in black.

Hat :

Pattern and instructions pages 54–5. Make in white felt ; stuff with a little cotton wool to retain the shape and stitch to top of head with a forwards and sideways tilt.

Tunic :

Make as given for Joey, but this time do not slit down the back but have the opening on shoulder E–O. This is so that a smooth pattern of sequins can be kept on the back. Run elastic round neck, sleeves and knees, so that they fit the doll neatly and tightly, and sew four small press studs to opening. Using the spots as a guide, sew sequins all over the tunic so that it is really well covered. This is a long job, but makes a lovely spangled garment. Try to arrange the colours so that the darker sequins form a pointed " collar " round neck, and broad pointed bands round wrists and legs of tunic.

Stockings :

Make exactly as given for Bert (page 140), but use fine ribbed tops of worn socks, or white stockinette.

Shoes :

Using black felt with fawn felt soles make up Clown's shoe No. 3 (pattern and instructions pages 46, 48). If you have trouble in keeping the shoes on, sew a short piece of round, black elastic to each one and cross over instep as a dancing pump.

MEG
Pattern pages 260, 265. Illustration Plate 10

Meg is very much the same style as the old wooden Dutch dolls—no protruding nose and with painted hair and features.

Materials :

A completed body, prepared as given on page 136, with no nose, a large head and painted pink.

¼ yd. pale blue cotton material 36 in. wide for dress.

Fine white cotton material for slip and knickers (24 in. × 4½ in. and 6 in. × 4½ in.).

White stockinette or fine ribbing from top of old socks for socks.

Scraps of black felt and fawn suède for shoes. Three small press studs.

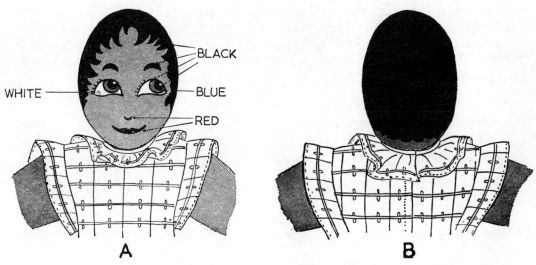

Fig. 57. *Details of Meg's features*

Method :

Cut out the pieces as given.

Features (fig. 57) :

Using gloss paint and a fine brush, paint mouth and nose in red, eyes in blue, whites of eyes and highlights in white, edges of eyes, lashes, pupils, brows and hair in black.

Knickers :

Open out flat, place the two pieces together and join side seams C–B and between leg seams A–A. Turn a tiny rolled hem all round legs and $\frac{1}{2}$ in. hem round top. Insert narrow elastic in waist hem to fit body.

Waist Slip :

Cut a strip of white cotton material 24 in. × 4$\frac{1}{2}$ in. Join short ends to make a centre back seam. Turn a $\frac{1}{2}$ in. hem all round top and a slightly wider hem all round bottom edge. Decorate this edge with rows of stitching or lace. Run elastic into top hem to fit doll's waist.

Dress :

Make up in the normal way as for Elizabeth (see page 122) with a back opening fastened with press studs. The skirt is two pieces, 13 in. × 5 in., gathered on to bodice. Stitch a tiny frill all round neck. To make this cut a piece of material 10 in. × 1$\frac{1}{4}$ in. Turn a narrow hem all round one edge and along two short ends. Run a gathering thread along the other edge, pull up to fit neck, and stitch all round neck edge before binding this with a very narrow piece of the material cut on the cross.   The epaulette sleeve is a flat, curved piece.   Turn back a narrow rolled hem along curved edge between X's.   Join tiny seams X–B.   Stitch into armhole matching A's and B's.   If liked, add a sash of self material which ties at the back so as to ensure the dress fits snugly.

Socks :

With the ribbing running down the length of socks, join back seams A–B.   Turn in a narrow hem all round tops.

Shoes :

Using black felt with fawn suède soles, make up a pair of casual shoes.   (Pattern and instructions pages 46–7.)

VARIATIONS

You will find you can interchange these dolls endlessly—especially the clowns.
1. Try giving Bert, Algy's head, and Toni, Joey's, or invent different features of your own.
2. Make a midget and " stilt-man " to complete the troupe.
3. Make the dolls soft.   Stuff them with kapok and embroider the features. These will be real old-fashioned " rag " dolls, and of course should be unpainted.
4. If sawdust is not available try bran.

*   *   *

Do you know why a clown is so often called Joey ?

This name has been handed down from Joseph Grimaldi, probably the greatest of all clowns—not of the circus but of an old theatre Harlequinade, quite unknown to modern children.   When only 58 years old this strange little man died and was buried in 1837 in the Churchyard of St. James's, Pentonville.   Although this is now a children's playground (and what could be more appropriate ?) a memorial to him still stands, and each January clowns from all over the British Isles assemble in this church for a special service at which they honour " Joey "—king of them all.

Section Ten

THE GOLLIWOG FAMILY

GOLLIWOGS (Plate 10)

ALTHOUGH ONE OF THE most popular dolls in the nursery at the beginning of this century, the Golliwog seems recently to have declined in popularity, probably partly due to the fact that he has often been depicted as somewhat grotesque and ugly and partly to the usual rise and fall in fashion which occurs in dolls as well as everything else.

He was made famous by Florence Upton in her delightful stories about the Dutch Dolls and the Golliwog, and it has been interesting during the course of the preparation of this book to come into contact with Mrs. Phyllis M. Robinson, at one time receptionist to Miss Upton. She tells of seeing the Golliwog, which appeared in the books bearing his name, acting as a plaything for children coming to the Upton Studio to have their portraits painted—for Florence was a talented artist in this field, as well as that of toyland. The Dutch Dolls were, of course, made of wood, and a very similar doll is available again in London today—made in the Dolomites— but the quality is not in the same category as the originals, the wood being so brittle that arms and legs are easily broken.

Meg, the painted calico doll on page 147, would make a good substitute for a wooden model.

It is interesting to note the variations in spelling which crop up in different places. Florence Upton uses GOLLIWOGG—in other books we find GOLIWOGG, GOLLYWOG and GOLLYWOGG, but for the purpose of this book we chose GOLLIWOG which seems to be the most commonly used version today.

Our doll has been slightly modernized, in that he has been given a happy face and a " Girliwog " wife. They have a " Golliwoglet " son and a " Girliwoglet " daughter, dressed in jerseys and dungarees, who in their turn have a toy golliwog and girliwog with which to play, and these toys own even smaller models—four generations.

The four largest (fig. 58) are made on cotton body bases, with felt heads, and a little knitting has been introduced in the form of jerseys and stockings—just to please the many knitters among us.

BASIC BODIES FOR ALL THE GOLLIWOG FAMILY

Height: Golliwog and Girliwog 16½ in.: Golliwoglet and Girliwoglet 10½ in.
Pattern pages 272–7

Materials :

Odd pieces of black felt for head (or ¼ yd. 36 in. wide makes all four golliwogs).

Odd pieces of black sateen for body and limbs (or ½ yd. 36 in. wide makes all
four golliwogs).

Kapok for stuffing.

Scraps of red and white felt for features.

Method :

Cut out the pieces as given, noting that the arms are shorter than the legs.

Body :

Make up and stuff the body with limbs attached exactly as described for the
felt dolls on page 159 and illustrated by fig. 59.

Head :

On both pieces and on the wrong side, join the dart A–B–A and the three other
similar darts. Place the two pieces together and stitch all round the outside edge
except for C–D. Turn right side out and stuff very firmly.

Take a piece of wood about 4 in. long for the two large dolls and 2½ in. for the
smaller size, and bind it with rag as described for the stockinette dolls on page 114
and illustrated by fig. 43 B. Push one end down into the body and the other up
into the head, leaving about ½ in. " gap " for neck on the large sizes and ¼ in. on
the small. Ladder stitch head to rag which binds the wood, also the top of body.
Take a strip of black felt ½ in. wide for the large sizes and ¼ in. wide for the small
and roll it round the wood between head and body to form a neck, as described on
page 136 for the painted calico dolls and illustrated in fig. 51. Stitch end of strip at
centre back and ladder stitch top of " roll " to head and base of roll to top of body.

MAKING THE FACES

Golliwogs may have the features merely sewn in place and their faces left flat
—this is usual. However, much interest and character is added by a little modelling
in the form of added " patches " raised by padding.

Features of Golliwog and Girliwog :

Follow fig. 58 :

Cut out the pieces as given.

On the nose, join the small dart M–N–M and the corresponding dart on the
other side. Turn right side out. Stitch nose to centre of face, O at the top, stuffing
it very firmly as you work and pushing it well into a " point "—not spreading it
out too much. Embroider two tiny red nostrils at base.

Sew a pupil to each eye and add a highlight either cut from white felt and stitched
in place or satin stitched in white stranded cotton. Sew the completed eyes to head.
Take a few invisible stitches all round each eye, working right through the head
and pulling tightly to slightly sink the eyes.

Stitch the mouth to face, working in back stitch all along centre broken line

GOLLIWOG.

GIRLIWOGLET.

GOLLIWOGLET.

GIRLIWOG.

Fig. 58. *Details of features of the Golliwog family*

P–Q. Now hem all round outside edge of mouth, stuffing each lip as you work by pushing in tiny pieces of kapok with a cocktail stick. This will raise the lips and give the mouth shape. Sew the patches for cheeks and chin in place, stuffing each one in the same way as the lips and hemming neatly all round.

Features of Golliwoglet and Girliwoglet :

Follow fig. 58 :

Raise a little nose by needle modelling as described on page 37 and illustrated by fig. 83 K, L and M. Hem the mouth neatly all round. Make up and attach the eyes just as described for the larger sizes on page 150. No chin or cheek patches are used. Hem red nose piece in place.

Hair :

How you make a golliwog's hair depends of course on what material is available. Black fur is the ideal material. If sufficiently large pieces are available, make up like a little cap. A pattern for the smaller sizes is given on page 276. The straight edge should be stitched round edge of face, then the gathers at back pulled up to fit neatly round back of head and the remaining free edges stitched in place. (Always remember to cut fur with a razor blade—cutting only the skin at the back and never the fur pile.)

Should you have to buy fur, it is often easier to obtain (and cheaper) in strips, by the yard. For the original larger sizes a fur trimming about 1 in. wide was used. This was stitched round the edge of face and head in a circle, then continued round and round the head in the form of a spiral until the back of head was completely covered.

If fur is not available, or if you want your dolls to work out a little cheaper, use thick black wool in loops, as described for Sue on page 118 and illustrated by fig. 44 (3 A and B).

DRESSING THE GOLLIWOG FAMILY

DRESSING THE GOLLIWOG

Pattern pages 272–5. Illustration Plate 10

Materials :

One large size body complete with head.
A piece of blue felt for the jacket (16 in. × 9 in.).
  „   „   „ red   „   „   „ trousers (8 in. × 14 in.).
Scraps   „ black „   „   „ shoes.
A piece of white   „   „   „ gloves and collar (8½ in. × 6 in.).
Oddment of red/white spotted cotton material for the tie.
Five white buttons (about shirt size).
A packet of pipe cleaners for stiffening fingers.

Method :

Cut out the pieces as given.

Trousers :

On the wrong side join inner leg seam B–C, on both legs, then join the two legs together A–B–A. Turn right side out, pull on to Golliwog ; make two pleats at the front and two at the back, so that the top of trousers fits the body, and stitch to body all round waist.

Boots :

Place the two card soles on to black felt and cut out two pieces, about $\frac{1}{4}$ in. larger all round than the card pieces. Prepare soles as described on page 42 and illustrated by fig. 15 A and B ; do not put in a lining. Join the two boot pieces D–E on the wrong side. Turn right side out. Place on prepared soles and stitch all round F–E, stab stitching on the right side to form a welt. Roll the trousers up a little way, stuff foot part of boot, then pull each one on to the end of a leg and stitch boot to leg all round the top. Roll down trousers.

Coat :

On the wrong side join shoulder seams G–H and side seams I–J. Shape the back by stitching the two darts L–K–M. Slit coat up centre back O–N to form " tails ". Fold each sleeve in half and join underarm seam P–I. Insert into armholes, matching letters, and stitching all round I–H–I. Turn coat right side out and put on to golliwog, stitching in place all down centre front and along the lower edge of coat fronts.

Collar :

Place this piece round the neck so that the Q's meet at centre front. Stitch all round Q–Q with the collar standing upright and covering neck, then turn it neatly down to cover stitching, so that the two points (R) hang down in the front.

Tie :

Take a strip of red/white spotted cotton material $2\frac{3}{4}$ in. $\times$ 9 in. Make a narrow hem along the two long edges. Bring the two ends together and fold flat, so that the tie is $4\frac{1}{2}$ in. long with the ends meeting at the centre. Cut a little piece of matching cotton material $\frac{3}{4}$ in. wide and $1\frac{1}{4}$ in. long. Fold the $\frac{3}{4}$ in. raw edges under, pressing between your finger and thumb, and stitch this piece round centre of the larger prepared piece, pulling it in at the middle to make a mock bow (see fig. 58). Stitch this to golliwog's coat at centre front underneath collar, and catch the outside edges to front of coat at shoulders. Sew three buttons evenly down front of jacket and two at centre back at top of division for tails, using red Sylko for added decoration.

Gloves :

Roll back the sleeves as far as elbows. Make up the gloves exactly as given for the felt doll's hands on page 160.   Use black Sylko for the stitching and add three black " nips " on the back on each glove.   Push two doubled pipe cleaners into each finger as they are rather large.   After attaching to arms and taping, roll down the sleeves and stitch sleeve to glove, covering the join.   If you would like a permanent " bend " in the arm, ladder stitch in the desired position at the elbows ; curl fingers as wanted.

DRESSING THE GIRLIWOG
Pattern pages 272–5.   Illustration Plate 10

Materials :

One large size body, complete with head.
A piece of red felt for the jacket (15½ in. × 9 in.).
„   „   „ blue „   „   „ skirt and trousers (26 in. × 4½ in.).
Scraps of black „   „   „ shoes.
A piece of white „   „   „ gloves and collar (8½ in. × 6 in.).
Oddments of red/white spotted cotton material for the bow.
20 in. red ric-rac braid for trimming skirt.
Three white buttons about shirt size.
A very small quantity of 3-ply red wool for the stockings.
A packet of pipe cleaners for stiffening fingers.

(Abbreviations : K = knit ; P = purl ; tog. = together ; sl. = slip ; p.s.s.o. = pass slip stitch over.)

Method :

The Stockings :

With a set of 4 needles size 12 and 3-ply red wool, cast on 24 sts. 8 on each needle. Work 5 rounds in K1, P1 rib.
6th Round : K to last st.   Repeat this round 14 times.
21st Round : K1, K2 tog., K to last 2 sts., sl. 1, K1, p.s.s.o.
22nd Round : K.   Repeat this round 4 times.   Repeat 21st to 26th rounds 5 times.
58th Round : K.   Repeat this round 4 times.
63rd Round : K2 tog. all round.
64th Round : K.   Break off wool and thread into a needle, slip through remaining stitches, pull up and fasten off securely.
Make another stocking in the same way.
Pull stockings on to legs, stitch to body all round top of each stocking.

Knickers :

Place the two pieces together and on the wrong side join seams A–B and C–D. Turn right side out and pull on to Girliwog, with these seams at centre front and back.   With a few stitches join front to back between the legs.   Stitch base of knickers to top of stockings.   Run a gathering thread round top of knickers, pull up to fit body and stitch in place, working all round the waist.

Shoes :

Make these exactly as given for the Golliwog's boots on page 153, stuff the foot firmly, pull on to end of stockinged leg and stitch in place, working all round the top of each shoe.

Skirt :

Cut a strip of blue felt 4½ in. wide and 20 in. long.   Join the ends and turn up a narrow hem all round the bottom edge.   Decorate hem with a piece of red ric-rac braid, machined over the stitches.   Run *two* rows of gathers all round the top edge.   Place on Girliwog with the seam at centre back and pull up gathers to fit body.   Stitch in place working all round the waist.

Jacket :

Make this just as given for the Golliwog's coat on page 153, but this has a short, shaped back and no tails.   Put on to the doll and stitch down centre front as far as X only.   X–Y on each side should separate in opposite directions, forming two " points ".   Stitch three buttons evenly down centre front—using blue Sylko, the lowest one at X, and the top one at top of jacket under " chin ".

Collar :

Stitch to doll just as for Golliwog, page 153.

Gloves :

Make up and stitch to doll just as for Golliwog, page 153.

Bow :

Make exactly as given for Golliwog's tie, page 153, but stitch to top of Girliwog's head.

DRESSING THE GOLLIWOGLET
Pattern pages 276–7.   Illustration Plate 10

Materials :

One small size body complete with head.
A small quantity of 2-ply red wool for jersey.
One 9 in. square blue felt for dungarees.
Scrap of black felt for shoes.
  „   „ white „   „ collar.
  „   „ red/white spotted cotton material for tie.
Four tiny pearl buttons.

Method :

Jersey :

Work with size 12 needles and 2-ply wool.

BACK : Cast on 24 sts.

1st row : K2, P2, repeat to end of row.   Repeat this row 19 times.

21st row : Cast off 3, rib to end.

22nd row : Cast off 3, rib to end.

23rd row : Work in rib for 18 rows.
          Cast off in rib.

FRONT : Make exactly as for back.

SLEEVES : Cast on 20 sts.

1st row : K2, P2, repeat to end of row.

2nd–27th row : Repeat 1st row 26 times.   Cast off in rib.   Make another sleeve in the same way.

To make up :

Place the front and back together and join shoulder seams for $\frac{1}{4}$ in. only.   Insert sleeves and sew up sleeve seams and down side seams.   Turn right side out and put on to doll.   Catch the remainder of the shoulder seams together with a neat lacing stitch, so that the jersey fits tightly round the neck.

Dungarees :

Fold each leg in half and join the inner leg seams B–C.   Then place the two legs together and join centre back and front seam A–B.   Turn right side out and try on to doll, making two small pleats at front to fit waist neatly.   Stitch these pleats.   Stitch bib to top front of dungarees matching A's.   Cross " braces " at back of doll, tuck ends inside back of trousers and stitch two tiny pearl buttons, where braces meet trousers.   Stitch waist of trousers to doll's body through the jersey—all round except for bib.

Collar :

Stitch to doll as given for large Golliwog on page 153.

Tie :

Make just as given for large Golliwog on page 153, but have a smaller piece of material—5 in. × 1 in. is a good size.

Shoes :

Make and attach exactly as for large Golliwog on page 153.   Sew a tiny pearl button to the top of each shoe, using red Sylko.   (Notice that these shoes are slightly shaped, so remember to make " a pair ".)

DRESSING THE GIRLIWOGLET
Pattern pages 276–7.   Illustration Plate 10

Materials :

One small size body complete with head.
A small quantity of 2-ply blue wool for the jersey.
A piece 12 in. × 6 in. of red felt for the skirt and knickers.
Scrap of black felt for the shoes.
   „   „ white „   „   „ collar.
Red/white spotted cotton material for the bow.
13 in. blue ric-rac braid for trimming the skirt.
Four small pearl buttons.

Method :

Jersey :

Knit this and put on to doll, exactly as given for the Golliwoglet on page 156, but use blue wool.

Stockings :

Knit these exactly as given for the large size Girliwog on page 154, but use blue wool and size 14 needles.
Instead of knitting 15 rounds before the decreasing knit only 10.
Put on to doll and stitch in place all round top of leg.

Knickers :

Make and put on to doll just as given for larger size Girliwog on page 154.

Shoes :

Make and attach just as for Golliwog's boots on page 153 ; stitch a small pearl button to the top of each one, using red Sylko.

Collar :

Sew to doll as given for Golliwog on page 153.

Skirt :

Stitch the bib to the doll along X–A–Y at front.   Cross braces at back and stitch to doll.   Cut a strip of red felt 12 in. × 3½ in.   Make up and put on to doll just as given for larger Girliwog on page 155—decorating hem with blue ric-rac.   Stitch to doll all round waist, covering edges of bib at front and braces at back.   Stitch a small pearl button to skirt, where each end of the braces tucks under the top of skirt.

Bow :

Make as for Golliwoglet's tie, page 156, and stitch to top of head.

N.B. Neither the Golliwoglet nor Girliwoglet wears gloves, but it would be quite easy to cut a pair and add them if you wish.

VARIATIONS

It is a simple matter to switch round the colours on these dolls—red and emerald green make lovely Golliwog clothes—or be very modern and use lemon and shocking pink.

Should you want to make toy Golliwogs for this family to play with, instructions for an enchanting pair made of shoe laces will be found on page 213, and they in turn have their own *very* miniature Golliwogs, made from millinery wire bound with embroidery cotton. On plate 11 Judy is holding one of these.

* * *

Did you know that the name " Golliwog " probably (but not definitely) dates from the time at the end of the 19th century when Alexandria in Egypt was occupied by the British?

Native workers, called GHULS, then wore armbands bearing the letters W.O.G.S. (working on government service). Our troops quickly turned GHUL and WOGS into " Golliwogs ", and when small dolls representing these workers started to appear (probably brought home by our soldiers as souvenirs for their children), the name naturally clung to them as well.

SWING LEGGED FELT DOLLS

FELT IS A "SOOTHING" MATERIAL with which to work and presents few problems as it does not stretch or fray. Small character dolls look well in this material and are particularly suitable for the toddler age child who has not yet arrived at the age of dressing and undressing his toys. The clothes are stitched to and become part of the doll.

Many felt dolls are made by stuffing the felt itself, but this makes the finished article rather " wooden " in appearance and unyielding when the small owner tries to bend the arms or sit the doll down.

The dolls given here are therefore made on a simple, stuffed, cotton body, with felt head and hands added, and felt clothes stitched on to this basic shape. So many characters present themselves when deciding which dolls to make, that it is a temptation to choose those which appeal to yourself and to forget the young recipient.

Children of an age to appreciate these dolls are usually found to prefer well-known nursery rhyme or fairy tale characters, such as Little Boy Blue, Old Mother Hubbard or The Knave of Hearts. Small boys will love policemen, soldiers, sailors, cowboys, Indians or any figure in a costume or uniform well known to them, as well as gay, colourful and imaginative people such as clowns and jesters.

MAKING THE BODIES
Height approx. 11½ in. Pattern page 279

Materials :

Unbleached calico or any strong cotton material (¼ yd. 36 in. wide makes 4 dolls).
Flesh felt for hands and head (one 9 in. square makes two dolls).
4 in. of wire (about 14 gauge).
Few inches of adhesive tape (½ in. wide).
Small quantity of kapok for stuffing.
Five pipe cleaners.

Method (fig. 59) :
Cut out the pieces as given.

Limbs :
Place the limbs together in pairs and machine all round A–B–C, about ¼ in. from outside edge, leaving top A–C open. Turn right side out and stuff lower half.

Machine twice across D–E.   Stuff top half and stitch across X–X, and turn in and oversew A–C.

Body :

Machine all round F–G–H–I–J–K, leaving the neck F–K open.   Turn right side out and stuff firmly, still leaving neck open.   Oversew the arms and legs in position.

Head :

* Join the dart A–B–A and all the others round the edge of face, stab stitching on the wrong side.

Join the curved edge of backs of heads together on the wrong side B–C, then join the straight edges of backs to the face A–B–A, still working on the wrong side. Turn right side out, easing carefully through the neck opening with the blunt end of a pencil, and stuff the head very firmly indeed, shaping a good firm " chin ".*

Double the piece of wire so that it is 2 in. long and bind it tightly with adhesive tape, covering the sharp ends carefully.   Then bind with a narrow strip of rag and stitch this in place (fig. 43 B).   Push one end up into the head and stitch A–O–A just as shown for the wired figures in fig. 83 H and I.   Stitch head to the rag which binds the wire, to keep it firm.   Push the other end of wire down into body and stitch all round neck of body, attaching the body to base of neck (fig. 59).

Hands :

Place these together in pairs and make up exactly as given for the hands of the wired figures on page 216 and fig. 83 A, B and C, except that these hands will be short, with no arms attached.   Use half a pipe cleaner, doubled like a hairpin and pinched tightly together, for stiffening each finger and thumb.   Place a very small quantity of stuffing into each hand—a little at each side of the pipe cleaners—and pull the hands over ends of arms, thumbs uppermost.   Stitch hands to arms, working round once or twice, and finally stick a small piece of adhesive tape, round arm, to cover any sharp ends of pipe cleaners (fig. 59).

Nose :

On the wrong side fold the piece so that the A at centre meets one of the side A's and stitch this little " dart " using a very fine needle and working very neatly in tiny oversewing stitches.   Join the other dart in the same way, so that the three A's almost meet.   Consulting the diagram of the face of the doll you have decided to make, place the nose in the appropriate place—(above all, avoid putting it too high up) and hem very neatly to face, pushing a little stuffing inside with a cocktail stick, just before you complete the stitching.   The best way is to start stitching at A, work up to B and work down the other side.   The nose should be a nice, protruding, rather pointed shape.

Now follow the separate instructions given for each doll.

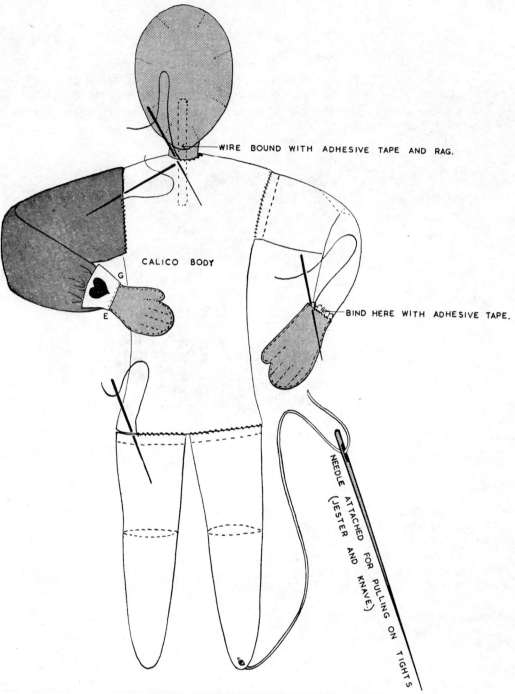

WIRE BOUND WITH ADHESIVE TAPE AND RAG.

CALICO BODY

BIND HERE WITH ADHESIVE TAPE.

NEEDLE ATTACHED FOR PULLING ON TIGHTS (JESTER AND KNAVE.)

Fig. 59. *Basic construction of felt dolls*

JESTER

Pattern pages 278-9.   Illustration Plate 7

This is a gay, jolly fellow with his jingling bells and a wonderful playmate, but be sure the recipient is beyond the " sucking " stage because of the danger of the bells being swallowed.   Use any gay felts you have by you—the original was emerald green and a rather mauvy pink.

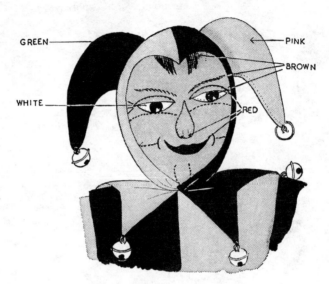

Fig. 60.   *Detail of Jester's face*

Materials :

A basic body made as given on page 159.
Piece 12 in. × 9 in. of green felt⎱for clothes.
  „   „   „   „   „ pink   „ ⎰
Twenty-one very small brass bells (from the toy shop).
Scraps of red, brown, white and flesh felt⎱for features.
Red, brown and white stranded cotton   ⎰

Method :

Cut out the pieces as given.

Face (fig. 60) :

Sink two eye sockets, one each side of bridge of nose as given for wired figures on page 38 and fig. 83 N.   Hem whites of eyes, then pupils (cut in brown), in place and embroider each tiny white highlight.   Hem lids in place, working across top, curved edge. Stitch on mouth. Embroider nostrils (two tiny stitches on base of nose) and smile and eye wrinkles in red ; brows in brown. If you are not very sure of yourself leave flat like this, but for a really professional finish, needle model cheeks and chin. To do this take a long, *very* slim needle and exactly matching silk or Sylko, and work a series of invisible stitches from under the eye to a point level with the mouth, pulling them tightly to raise the cheeks, and across from side to side to raise a little chin. Work slowly and experimentally, making sure you are achieving a good expression. On the diagram for each doll, small dotted lines are shown as a guide as to where to stitch. It cannot be emphasized too strongly, however, that this is a matter for individual and personal taste and no two faces will be the same when finished, each one depending on how hard the head is stuffed, how tightly the modelling stitches are pulled and exactly where the features are placed.

For all the clothes, work in a tiny stab stitch on the wrong side except where otherwise stated.

Tights :

Fold each piece in half lengthwise and stitch from A to B. Now place the two pieces together with tops opened out and stitch down front from C–B (crutch) and up back to other C. Turn right side out and ease on to doll, having the green leg on the left. In order to get the ends of legs right down into the tips of " stockings ", take two pieces of fine string and two packing needles. Make a large knot in end of string and push needle through " tip " of leg, thus attaching a string to each leg (fig. 59). Drop each needle down a " stocking ", emerging through the " tip ", and pull. The legs will slide easily into the tights. Cut off the string closely, leaving the knots inside. Stitch tights to body all round waist.

Sleeves :

Fold each sleeve in half and join underarm seam D–E. Turn right side out. Place on to doll, green one on the left, pulling well on, and stitch to body all round D–F–D. Gather round extreme edge of wrist G–E–G, pull up to fit doll tightly and stitch firmly to hand, covering the join between hand and arm.

Tunic :

To make the front, join a green and pink top H–I, having green on the right of doll. Join a green and pink skirt I–J, having green on the left of the doll. Now join the two pieces along waist line, with the I's matching in the centre. Make the back in the same way but reverse the colours, so that when you join the side seams, the skirt will be pink on both front and back above the green right leg, and the top pink at both front and back round the green left arm, and vice versa. Check this before joining ! Join side seam K–L–M on one side and shoulder seam N–O on the same side. On the other side join side seam from K to the waist, leaving the rest, also the shoulder seam open. Turn right side out and ease on to doll ; the " overhanging " shoulders will cover the tops of sleeves. Neatly ladder stitch from waist to underarm and along shoulder seam on the open side.

Hood :

On the main pieces join parts P–Q, R–S and T–U. Then join the two pieces together down curved centre seam V–W, this time having green on the left side of face. Join collar pieces W–X, and join completed collar to main part all round neck Y–W–Y. (The green of the collar is also on the left.) Turn right side out. Place on to head, mark in lightly with pencil a few strands of hair which will protrude on to forehead. Remove hood, embroider hair using the full thickness of brown stranded cotton and working in long straight stitches. Replace hood and stretching tightly round face stitch firmly in place, under chin. Place the two green " points " together and stitch all round except for straight edge Z–Z. Do the same with the pink. Turn right side out and stuff very firmly indeed. Consulting fig. 60, sew to head, opening out the ends wide and ladder stitching all round the " circle " two or three times. Sew a bell firmly to tip of each of these points, also to the five points of collar and eight round bottom of tunic.

Take an invisible stitch through each knee as shown for the stockinette dolls, fig. 43. This gives a nice finish.

Shoes (Pattern and instructions pages 50, 51) :

Make one in green and one in pink felt. Stuff the entire shoe firmly. Slip each end of a leg into a shoe, green shoe on pink stocking and vice versa and stitch shoe to leg, working neatly and invisibly round top edge.

The wire in the neck will enable you to bend the head to an interesting, sideways angle. The fingers may also be curled, and if you wish the arms to remain in a curved attitude, ladder stitch them in this position at the elbows. The legs will swing freely and allow the doll to sit down.

THE KNAVE OF HEARTS
Pattern pages 278–80. Illustration Plate 7

This sly-looking Knave has been chosen to represent the nursery rhyme characters. He is dressed in black, white, yellow and red felt and carries one of the tarts he has stolen.

Materials :

A basic body made as given on page 159.
Scraps of red   felt ⎫
    „   „ black „ ⎬for clothes (or 9 in. square of each).
    „   „ white „
    „   „ yellow „ ⎭
Black darning wool for hair and brows.
Scraps of flesh, white, black and red felt ⎫for the
Red and white stranded cotton   ⎭features.
One coat button about 1 in. diameter for the tart.

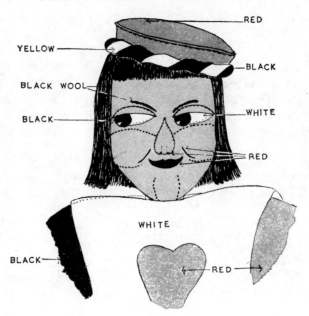

Fig. 61. *Detail of Knave's face*

Method :

Cut out the pieces as given, having the cuffs yellow.

Face (fig. 61) :

Make this exactly as given for the Jester on page 162 but follow fig. 61 for positions of pupils, which are black, and use the different pattern for mouth. This time there are no " eye " wrinkles.

Hair :

Make exactly as given for Elizabeth, page 119 and fig. 45 (4), but cut a little shorter and omit Alice band. Use black darning wool or Coton à Broder.

Tights :

Make up and attach to doll exactly as given for Jester, page 163, having the red stocking on the right leg.

Sleeves :

Make up and attach to doll exactly as given for Jester, page 163, having the red sleeve on the left arm.

Cuffs :

Stitch the cuffs round edge of sleeve, leaving the tops and ends free (fig. 59).

Cut a red and black heart, using pattern No. 2, and hem the red one to right cuff and black one to left cuff.

Tunic :

Cut out the pattern running along base of tunic in yellow felt and appliqué this to front of tunic, stab stitching or hemming neatly all round ; decorate the back of tunic in the same way. Cut out two red hearts, using pattern No. 1, and appliqué one each to the centre of front and back. Pad these with a little kapok to raise slightly.

Join one side seam A–B and the shoulder seam on the same side C–D. Join the other side seam A–E and leave the shoulder seam open. Turn right side out and place on doll. Neatly ladder stitch open side seam E–B and remaining shoulder seam.

Shoes (Pattern and instructions pages 50, 51) :

Make exactly as for Jester, page 164, but have one red and one black and omit bells. Stitch red shoe to black stocking and vice versa. Decorate with two small hearts (pattern No. 2) as on cuff, a red heart sewn to the top of the black shoe and vice versa.

Hat (fig. 61) :

Place the two sides together and on the *wrong* side join the small seams E–F and G–F. Open this jointed piece out and on the *right* side join to top of hat all round circle F–F. The finished effect is that of a sort of " pancake beret ". Put a little stuffing inside and place on head at a jaunty angle, stitching all round.

Trimming :

Cut two strips of felt, one yellow and one black, each about $\frac{1}{4}$ in. wide and long enough to stretch round the head and a little to spare. Place one on top of the other and stitch ends together, then stitch these to centre back of lower edge of hat. Twist the felt so that it forms a colourful " cord " (fig. 61) and pull tightly round head, stitching the other end at centre back. Stitch securely here and there all round " cord ".

The Tart :

A tart may, if liked, be stitched to one hand, but for a very young child it may be superfluous. To make it, cut two circles of yellow felt by drawing round a coat button—this is the pastry. Then cut one slightly smaller circle in red felt for the jam. Stab stitch this red circle to one of the yellow ones, then stab stitch the two yellow circles together with the button between them.

On the original Knave, the tart was stitched to one hand and to the mouth as though being eaten, whilst the other hand was apparently rubbing his tummy, but you may prefer to leave both hands free.

COWBOY

Pattern pages 279, 280.   Illustration Plate 7

This will undoubtedly be the favourite of a very small boy.   The original had a somewhat quizzical expression, achieved by sewing on the mouth piece at an angle.

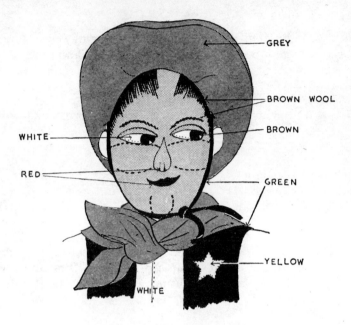

Fig. 62.   *Detail of Cowboy's face*

Materials :

A basic body made as given on page 159.
Scraps of white felt for shirt (or 9 in. square).
 „   „ grey   „   „ hat and boots (or 9 in. square).
9 in. square of fawn felt for trousers and soles of boots.
Scrap of red felt for scarf and mouth.
 „   „ green felt for bolero.
Scraps of yellow, brown, flesh and white felt for trimmings and features.
Red and yellow stranded cotton for nostrils and buckle.
About 15 in. leather thonging for hat strap.
 „   ¾ yd. picture cord for lasso.
Brown darning wool for hair.

Method :

Cut out the pieces as given.

Face (fig. 62) :

Make exactly as given for Jester on page 162, but use the different pattern for the mouth and sew it on at a slight angle. Consult fig. 62 for position of pupils, which are brown. Embroider brows in brown darning wool and sew an ear to each side of head. There are no " eye " wrinkles or smile markings.

Trousers :

Fold each piece in half lengthwise and join inner seams A–B. Open these pieces out and join together from top of front down to " crutch " and to top of back C–B–C. Turn right side out and put on to doll but do not stitch round waist yet.

Sleeves :

Make these and attach to doll just as given for jester on page 163, giving him white cuffs.

Shirt :

Slit *one* of the pieces right up the centre fold, this is the front. Join shoulder seams D–E and side seams F–G. Turn right side out and put on to doll. Stitch down centre front. Tuck inside trousers and stitch these all round the waist.

Belt :

Cut a strip of brown felt 7 in. long and ½ in. wide. Stitch all round waist, overlapping at front. Embroider a buckle at centre front, using the full thickness of yellow stranded cotton. (Alternatively using a narrow leather watch strap for a belt.)

Bolero :

Join fronts of bolero to the back, along shoulder seams H–I and side seams J–K. Turn right side out and put on to doll. If liked, cut a Sheriff's star from yellow felt and appliqué to one of the fronts.

Neck Scarf :

Cut a triangle of red felt, having each side approximately 6½ in. Knot round the cowboy's neck, having a loose " twist " on the front of right shoulder (fig. 62). Stitch firmly in place.

Boots (Pattern and diagram pages 49, 50) :

Make these in grey felt with fawn felt soles and yellow felt decorations. Wrap the base of trousers tightly round end of leg and stitch in place. Stuff the foot part of each boot very firmly, then slip one on to each leg and stitch in place at top of centre back seam and through the ankle.

Hair :

Cover head with long, straight stitches using brown wool and coming to a point at centre back. Have the front a little " straggly " over the forehead.

Plate 10.   Meg and the golliwogs seem amused at seeing a picture of themselves in one of Florence Upton's enchanting old books

Hat (Pattern and instructions pages 52, 53) :

Make this in grey (or fawn) felt with a strap of leather thonging—the original was green. If thonging is not available, cut strips of leather from old gloves or use a good strong felt. (This is really not very practical as it is inclined to break in play.) Tie the ends of chin strap together in a slip knot. Put hat on to *back* of head (fig. 62). Stitch in position and catch the strap here and there to keep it in place round " edge " of face.

Lasso :

Pass the cord through the right-hand side of belt two or three times, so that it hangs in a coil at the waist. Bind the two ends to avoid fraying and catch them together to keep the lasso in place.

If you prefer your doll to be throwing or " twirling " a rope, thread a length of stout wire (about 14 gauge) into the picture cord (which is always hollow). He can then hold the " rope " in one hand and the wired cord can be bent into any circles and loops that you wish—with the realistic effect of standing up in the air. Although this looks effective, it may be found to get in the way a little when the doll is played with, and the simple coil hanging from the waist to be more practical.

*   *   *

Did you know that before the days of fashion books, dolls were used to show would-be customers the fashions of the day ? In 1391 the Queen of England had a set of dolls sent from France, to show her the fashions being worn at the French Court, in order that her dressmakers could copy those that she liked. This practice continued until well into the 18th century, and the dolls were given to the small daughters of the household to play with, after their mothers had finished with them.

H

Section Twelve

NOVELTY DOLLS

DOUBLE ENDED DOLLS

A GREAT FAVOURITE with the Victorians was the double ended doll. Old examples which occasionally turn up in attics and other unexpected places are very often made with a black doll one end and white doll the other. Full and long skirted characters are necessary, as the skirt must reverse right over the head, so as to conceal each end of the doll in turn. The arms must be very loosely attached, so that they hinge easily up and down and do not hinder the pulling up and down of the skirt.

To extract the fullest " meaning " from the dolls, two completely opposite characters should be chosen. The example given here has a Fairy Princess at one end and " Wicked Witch " at the other. The body and heads are made from felt, with silhouette type faces.

WITCH AND FAIRY PRINCESS
Pattern pages 282–3. Illustration Figs. 64 and 65

Materials :

$\frac{1}{4}$ yd. of flesh felt for body, heads and arms (or three 9 in. squares).
One 9 in. square black felt for Witch's hat and bolero.
$\frac{1}{4}$ yd. white cotton material for Witch's blouse (or two pieces 13 in. × 7$\frac{1}{4}$ in.).
$\frac{3}{8}$ yd. 36 in. wide red sateen for Witch's skirt.
$\frac{1}{2}$ yd. 36 in. wide cream or white taffeta for Princess's dress.
Oddments of yellow and grey wool (3-ply or darning) for hair.
Silver or gold lamé, beads and sequins for Princess's crown.
Stranded cotton in blue, white, black and red for features.
Scrap of white felt⎫
Two green sequins⎭for Witch's eyes.
A piece of wood—$\frac{1}{2}$ in. dowelling or similar, 12 in. long.

Method :

Cut out the pieces as given.

Body (fig. 63) :

Place the two pieces together and stitch all round A–B–C–D–E and then F–G–H–I–J leaving A–K–J and E–K–F open for the necks. Turn right side out and stuff the body firmly. Bind the wood with a strip of rag as shown on fig. 43 B and push and " wriggle " it in one neck, right through centre of body and out of the other

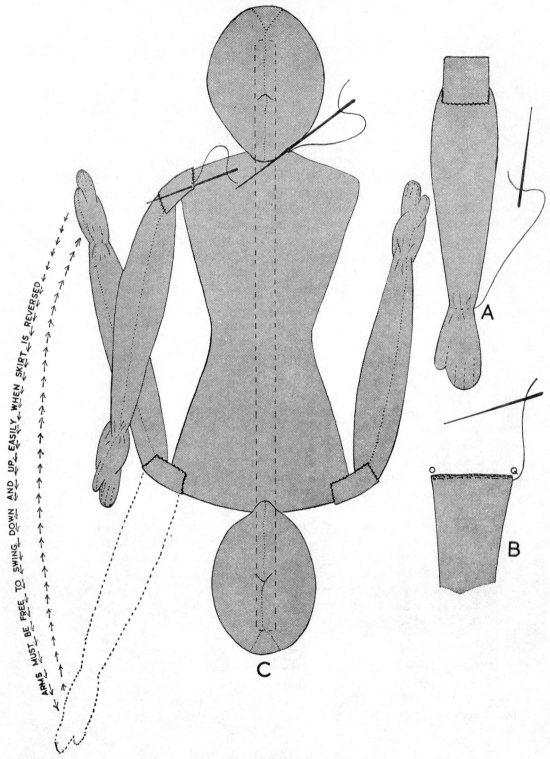

ARMS MUST BE FREE TO SWING DOWN AND UP EASILY WHEN SKIRT IS REVERSED

A

B

C

Fig. 63. *Construction of body of double ended doll*

neck, leaving an equal length protruding at each end. Now add any more stuffing which may be necessary for complete rigidity and make sure the wood is firmly embedded.

Heads :

Take the Witch's head pieces and join them together from K–L ; insert the head gusset from L–M, matching letters (this gives width to the head), then join the two head pieces together M–N. Turn right side out, carefully pushing out the nose and chin with a blunt orange stick. Make the Princess's head in the same way. Stuff both heads very firmly, taking particular care over the noses. Try to get the Witch's head long and thin, but the Princess's more plump by careful modelling.

Ease one head on to each end of body, working the protruding wood up into the heads until the base of each head touches the neck opening. Both heads can face the same way or, if you want to make the doll more complicated, one head can be facing the opposite way, so that when the skirt is reversed the doll must also be turned round ! Ladder stitch heads to body, working all round several times and using a *long* slim needle to make this rather awkward job easier.

Arms :

Place the pieces together in pairs and stitch all round from O–P–Q, leaving top end O–Q open. Turn right side out and push a little stuffing into fingers and thumbs (only a *very* little !). Indicate fingers by stab stitching as shown by broken lines on pattern. Complete stuffing of hand and arm and oversew O–Q. Run an invisible gathering thread round wrist and pull up slightly to give a good shape (see fig. 63 A). Fasten off. Cut four small pieces of flesh felt 1 in. square to act as arm " hinges ". Oversew one end to top of each arm and the other to top of shoulder, having gathered along O–Q (fig. 63 B) and pulled up to fit, so that the arms are firmly attached, but will swing loosely up and down as the doll is reversed. Make sure the " thumbs " are forwards—according to which way the head in question is facing.

Witch's Face (fig. 64) :

With one strand of cotton embroider mouth opening in black, lips and nostrils in red, teeth in white. Sink eye sockets (see page 38 and fig. 83 N) and sew on whites of eyes. Sew a bright green sequin to each eye, using white cotton to make a highlight. If this does not appear to be large enough to look sinister add another sequin to each eye, overlapping the first one a little, but sew this on invisibly with matching green Sylko. Stitch on lids. Embroider wrinkles and a tiny " dot " in the inner corner of each eye in red cotton and the brows in grey wool.

Witch's Hair :

Using grey wool make the hair as for Jane, page 123, and omit the fringe. Do not trim off evenly, but cut the ends in an uneven and " straggly " arrangement. Catch the hair to sides and back of head here and there, using matching wool, so that it does not get too badly disarranged when the skirt is pulled over it.

Fig. 64. Double ended doll showing Witch with Fairy Princess reversed

GREY WOOL

GREEN SEQUINS

WHITE FELT

RED

BLACK

VERY LOOSE RAGLAN

STYLE BLOUSE

31" ALL ROUND

Witch's Hat (Pattern and instructions pages 52, 55) :

Using black felt make up the hat. Push a little stuffing into the pointed crown to keep it a good firm shape and stitch a little to one side of Witch's head, working round several times for security.

Witch's Blouse :

On the wrong side join underarm and side seams R–S–T and one top of arm and shoulder seam U–V. Join the other top of arm seam from U–W. Turn right side out, slip on to Witch. Ladder stitch blouse to neck of doll all round, tucking in the raw edge as you work, then ladder stitch remainder of shoulder and top of arm seam V–W. Run a gathering thread round wrists and base of blouse, turning in a small hem as you work, to get rid of the raw edges. Pull up gathers and stitch sleeves to wrists, working round several times, and stitch base of blouse to waist of doll all round C–H–C on body. The finished garment will be very large and loose, but this is necessary to allow the arms to swing up and down and it will look very much more attractive when the bolero is eventually added.

Witch's Bolero :

Fold the piece so that the " fold " on pattern comes at centre back and stitch shoulder seams Y–Z on the wrong side. Turn right side out and place on one side for the present.

Princess's Face (fig. 65) :

Sink eye sockets (page 38 and fig. 83 N) and embroider the whites, then the blue iris and black pupil, using one strand of cotton and working in a thick close satin stitch. (If preferred these pieces may be cut from felt and appliquéd.) Add a tiny white highlight to each, also lashes, using black cotton. Embroider the mouth in red cotton and brows in yellow wool.

Princess's Hair (fig. 65) :

Make the hair as given for Elizabeth, page 119, but make it very thick and a little longer, including the fringe. Roll the fringe up, round a pencil, to make a long " sausage curl " along forehead, and stitch this firmly in place slipping a long, slim needle along between wool and pencil, and drawing the pencil out when the curl is completed, in a way very similar to that used for Sue's mop of curls (fig. 44 (3)). Smooth the rest of the hair down evenly all round head, and stitch wool to head, working all round at the level indicated by X on fig. 65. Now divide the hair into two " layers " and dress it in two " rolls " all round head. Make two long sausage curls (one above the other) at each side and along the back, working in the same way as you did for the top front curl and making sure that the three separate curls in each " layer " join into one long " roll ".

Princess's Crown :

Using silver or gold lamé if available, or if not any strong, bright yellow material,

PEARLS.

SEQUINS.

YELLOW WOOL.

Fig. 65. *Double ended doll showing Fairy Princess with Witch reversed*

X

WHITE
BLUE
BLACK

RED

SEQUINS
O

"10"

31" ALL ROUND

make the crown exactly as given for The Rabbit Toothed Queen on page 86, but use pentagon D (page 271) for your pattern. Decorate as you wish with pearls, beads and sequins, and stitch firmly to the top of doll's head.

Top of Princess's Dress :

From the cream taffeta, cut two strips each $8\frac{1}{2}$ in. long and $3\frac{1}{2}$ in. wide. Turn back and stitch a narrow hem along the four long edges. Place a strip over each shoulder, and join together at centre front and centre back, to form a V neck at both front and back. Join the two pieces from the base of V downwards. Gather all round waist, turning in a small hem as you work, pull up and stitch to doll, exactly meeting base of Witch's blouse. Do not join the two pieces together under arms, so that the arms can swing up and down. Catch the top of shoulder of dress at O, on fig. 65, to top of arm with one or two stitches. If liked, decorate neck and sleeve lines with a few sequins with a tiny bead in the centre of each (fig. 7 (2)).

Double Skirt :

Cut a piece of the cream taffeta and a piece of red sateen each 11 in. wide and 32 in. long. (Several smaller pieces may be used and joined widthwise if necessary.) Machine the short ends of each of these strips together (centre back seam). Then place the two " tubes " together, right sides inside, and stitch all round the lower edge ($\frac{1}{2}$ in. turning). Turn right side out and press the skirt very carefully so that the lower edge is quite even, no red showing on the cream side and vice versa. Run a very strong gathering thread all round the very edge of top joining the two colours together and turning in $\frac{1}{2}$ in. on each as you work. Put the skirt on to the doll, red on the Witch's side, cream on the Princess's ; pull up gathers to fit waist tightly and fasten off. Hem all round the Witch's waist, then turn and work all round the Princess's waist. This *is* an awkward job as there are so many thicknesses to work through, but it *can* be done !

Finally put on the Witch's bolero and " lace " with strong thread down centre front.

VARIATIONS

1. Red Riding Hood and her grandmother would make a good double ended doll, but the little girl is bound to look a little old-fashioned as she must have long skirts.

2. You might like to be really enterprising and make a doll that is not only double ended but two faced as well. You could make a coal black mammy one end, and little old lady the other, each one with a smiling and a miserable face (see page 177).

TWO FACED DOLLS

When making rag dolls for their children, our Victorian ancestors often contrived to give them two faces—one on each side of the head, so that when the dolls were

Fig. 66. *Two Faced Coal Black Mammy*

A. Happy face
B. With bandanna reversed, showing miserable face
C. Side view of head

turned round a different expression presented itself. The most usual was a long-skirted little girl doll crying on one side and laughing on the other.

In deciding what characters to use when making this type of doll, several factors must be borne in mind. (1) The head-gear must cover the back of the head so that it hides one face and can be removed when the doll is turned round and placed over the other face. (2) The doll must not have " feet " or shoes or they will be facing the wrong way round when the doll is reversed. (3) It is therefore necessary to have a long-skirted figure, which will hide the lack of " feet ".

Modern " little girl dolls " look old-fashioned in long skirts, it is therefore better to choose a character which the child of today accepts as being dressed in this way. A " Coal Black Mammy " makes a good example.

TWO FACED COAL BLACK MAMMY
Pattern pages 256–7. Illustration Fig. 66

Materials :

> Two pieces of black stockinette 16½ in. × 7 in. (see note on page 28 for buying this material).
> About 2 oz. kapok.
> Thin piece of wood 2½ in. long (about the thickness of a wooden meat skewer).
> A strip of old rag about 1 in. wide.
> A scrap of spotted cotton material for the bandanna.
> „   „   „ white   „   „   „   „ apron.
> ¼ yd. striped cotton material 36 in. wide for the dress and knickers.
> Two small brass rings for earrings.
> Black, white and red stranded cotton for features.

Method :

Body :

> Make up a stockinette doll exactly as given on page 112, but use black (or brown) material, and work only as far as the making of the " chin ", i.e. do not turn up feet or indicate knees or elbows, so that the doll is completely reversible.

Features :

> Following fig. 66 A and B, embroider the two faces, happy on one side and miserable on the other. Use one strand of cotton and a fine needle, making the eyes black and white and nostrils and mouth red. Stitch a small ring securely to each side of head, on the seam between the two faces.

Dress :

> Make the dress and knickers exactly like that given for " Pam " on page 124, but make the dress to fasten along both shoulder seams with small press studs—

instead of down the back. In this way the appearance will be almost the same on both sides.

Make the skirt long, so that the tips of legs just show (fig. 66 A).

Apron :

Make a small white apron, gathered into a band, with narrow strings tied in a bow at the back. This can be twisted round to the other side of doll when the face on the opposite side is used.

Bandanna :

Cut a triangle of spotted cotton material, with a long side of 16 in. and two short sides each 10 in. Make a very narrow hem all round. Tie on to the doll having the long side at nape of neck and fasten with a reef knot on top of head ; then bring the loose " point " forward over the knot and tuck underneath.

You can now use either face at will by changing the apron and bandanna.

OTHER IDEAS FOR TWO FACED DOLLS

1. A Victorian Lady, with bonnet and fichu that will reverse.
2. Red Riding Hood's grandmother, with " mob cap " to cover back of head —grannie's face on one side and wolf the other.
3. Wee Willie Winkie made as for stockinette dolls, wearing a long, plain flannel nightshirt, and night-cap on back of head, crying on one face, laughing the other.

DANCING PARTNERS

A two to four year old will love a dancing partner doll—made almost as large as him or herself. These dolls have strong elastic loops on their feet, into which the child's feet slip—so that the doll is in effect standing ON the child's feet. The two hold hands and walk together.

As it is essential for the doll to have large, firm feet, a clown makes a very good subject—also he is fun to dance with, as he can be a wobbly and altogether rather a silly person !

Almost any pattern can be enlarged for this purpose—for the original the stockinette doll on page 256 was used, with certain alterations. Choose gay, small-patterned cotton material for the tunic, the brighter the better.

GIANT CLOWN

Height approx. 33 in. Patterns for enlarging, pages 256-7. Illustration Plate 9

Materials :

½ yd. unbleached calico 36 in. wide or similar strong material for the body.
Kapok for stuffing (and wood wool if liked).
7 in. of wood—½ in. dowelling or similar for stiffening neck.

$\frac{3}{4}$ yd. bright cotton material 36 in. wide for tunic.

Large scraps of Vynide or felt for shoes and gloves.

1 oz. (half a ball) " Double Quick Knitting " or rug wool for hair.

$\frac{1}{2}$ yd. gay cotton material 36 in. wide for ruffs (or two pieces 27 in. $\times$ 5$\frac{1}{2}$ in., and one piece 36 in. $\times$ 6 in.).

Scraps of red and white felt for features.

Black, red and blue stranded cotton for features.

Scraps of fur fabric for pom-poms.

Braid, ric-rac or bias binding for trimming.

Method :

Body (fig. 67) :

Using the method shown on page 26 and fig. 9, enlarge the body of the stockinette doll on page 257 to twice its size (i.e. draw the body on one-inch squared paper, then copy on to two-inch squared paper—a large sheet will be needed, so you may prefer to Sellotape several smaller pieces together). When you have the enlarged size pattern follow fig. 67 and shape off the feet so that there are just pointed tips to fit into the shoes. Shape the hands similarly (fig. 67). Cut the arms clean off so that they are separate from the body and placing one of them on a separate piece of paper draw round it, then extend the piece at the top as shown by fig. 67 B. This is because they need to be sewn on separately so that they are more flexible.

Draw these patterns on to double unbleached calico and cut out one pair of bodies and two pairs of arms, allowing $\frac{1}{4}$ in. turning all round. Machine twice round on the pencil line, except for an opening at one side of the body and at the top of each arm ; turn right side out. Stuff the body and legs very firmly, stitch across base twice, insert the wood, gather in the neck and close the opening as shown on fig. 43 C and described on page 114. Stuff the arms firmly, stitching across at " elbow " and finish off and attach to body as shown by fig. 51 and described on page 136.

Face (Patterns page 281 and fig. 68 A) :

1st Method : Cut out the mouth, nose and spots, in red felt. Neatly hem the mouth in place. Gather all round outside edge of nose, pull up and stuff to form a small ball. Stitch to face, working all round several times. Embroider brows, eyes and lines on mouth in two strands of black cotton, and the pupils in blue. Finally sew on the spots.

2nd Method (fig. 68 C) : After making the body, cover the face with a piece of flesh pink stockinette (remains from the dolls in Section VIII). Stretch this round the face, very tightly, seaming up centre back and across top of head, where the stitches will eventually be covered by the hair. Stitch firmly all round neck, turning in raw edges. Cut out the eye patches and mouth in white felt and nose and spots in red. Hem the eye patches, mouth and spots neatly to face. Make the nose as given on page 37. Embroider mouth lines in red, eyes and brows in black and pupils in blue.

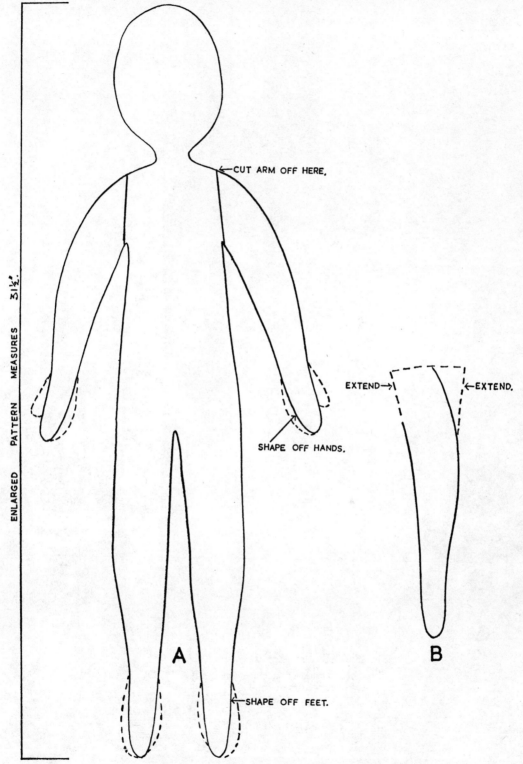

ENLARGED PATTERN MEASURES 31½".

CUT ARM OFF HERE.

SHAPE OFF HANDS.

EXTEND→   ←EXTEND.

A

B

SHAPE OFF FEET.

Fig. 67. *Shaping enlarged pattern for " Dancing Partner " Clowns*

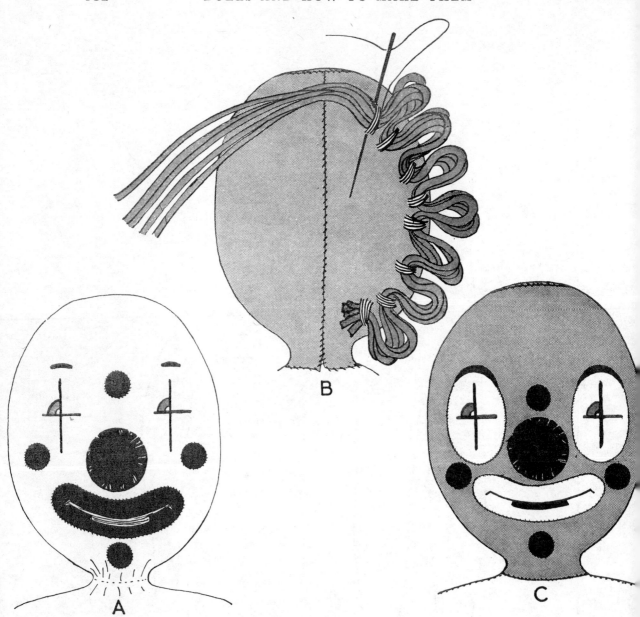

Fig. 68. *Dancing Partner Clowns*
A. Details of face (1st method)
B. Construction of hair
C. Details of face (2nd method)

Hair (fig. 68 B) :

Using a very thick wool in any shade suitable for hair (ginger was used for the original), unroll about one yard, then double this length backwards and forwards on itself until you have five thicknesses of one yard long. Now working in a circle round edge of face and across nape of neck, stitch this wool in a series of loops firmly to head. When you have completed one circle, continue in a smaller circle, working spirally inwards, each row of loops overlapping the previous one and hanging forwards towards the face, except across the back, when they will, of course, be hanging downwards. Keep the loops close together, so as to give a thick " thatch " of hair and so that the head does not show through the wool. Several new lengths of wool will, of course, be needed. Working over a newspaper and using *very* sharp scissors, trim off the ends of the loops, so that the finished " hair " looks rather like a floor mop. Or alternatively, leave the loops intact, to give the effect of curls.

Tunic (fig. 69) :

Lay the body of doll on to the doubled material (fold is along top) and draw all round as shown by broken lines on fig. 69, so as to make a full sleeved and baggy trousered garment rather like Joey's (page 268). Remove doll and double the material again, so as to have a fold right down centre and between legs. Now cut out and you will have both sides alike. Machine up one inside leg seam, across and down the other ; then along under arm and down outside leg seam on both sides. Cut a slit along top fold, for neck, about 2–2½ in. long, and then slit down centre front for 4 in., or until you find you can get the doll into the garment. Do not slit further than is necessary. Ease the doll inside, then ladder stitch the centre front opening and stitch tunic to doll all round neck. Run a gathering thread round base of each trouser leg, pull up to fit and stitch to tip of each foot.

Gloves :

Enlarge the Golliwog's glove pattern on page 272 to twice the size and cut out and make up as given on page 153. Stuff the fingers with kapok instead of using pipe cleaners, then push one glove over the end of each arm, adding any more stuffing that you can get into the palms, and stitch to arm all round wrist. Now gather ends of sleeves turning in raw edges as you work and stitch to gloves, overlapping the joins between gloves and arms.

Shoes :

Enlarge the pattern for Clown's shoe No. 2 on page 47, making it twice the size, and make up according to the directions on page 46. For the original, black Vynide with a brown felt sole was used—stiffened with *very* strong cardboard, such as an old calendar. When stitching the sides together do not work merely from D–C but continue along the top of shoe until only a small opening is left at the heel end, into which the base of leg, complete with trouser, will just fit. Stuff the shoes very firmly, leaving room to insert leg as far as possible. Stitch to leg, working through

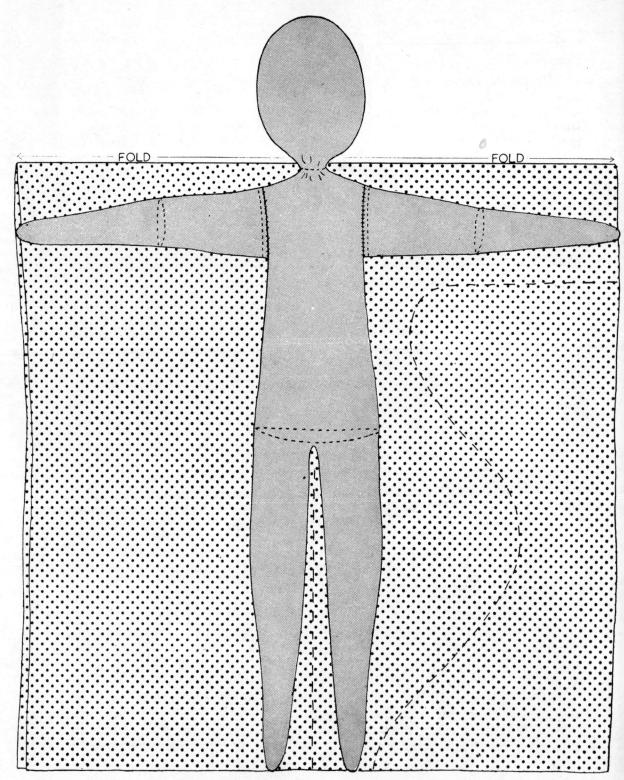

FOLD — — — — — — — — — — — — — FOLD

Fig. 69. *Cutting the tunic for a dancing partner clown*

the trouser, all round top of shoe. Make and attach the other shoe in the same way (The shoes also look well if made up in a gay coloured felt.)

Hat :

Enlarge Clown's hat No. 2 on page 53 to twice the size ; make up according to directions on page 54, but do not press up the edge of brim. Stuff firmly, taking particular care over the point, and stitch to clown's head at a " one-sided " angle.

Ruffs :

Cut a strip of bright cotton material, which blends or contrasts well with the tunic, 36 in. × 6 in. for the neck, and two each 27 in. × 5½ in. for the wrists. Machine a narrow hem along both long edges of each strip, then join short ends neatly to become a circle. Fold in half lengthwise and run a strong gathering thread along the fold. Before pulling up gathers, stitch braid, ric-rac or contrasting bias binding along edges of the strips as a decoration ; or if preferred leave plain. Think carefully before you stitch on any decoration so as to be sure it comes on the " top " of the ruff when it is in position. Pull up the gathers, put on to neck and wrists (the ruff having been folded will be double), and with a very long slim needle, stitch each one firmly in place, working round and round several times.

Pom-Poms :

Make up some pom-poms (fig. 8) in any suitable coloured material you may have available and decorate shoes, hat and front of tunic with them.

Elastic :

Measure the foot of the child for whom the doll is intended, and stitch loops of strong 1 in. wide black elastic to the feet of the clown.

SPINELESS DOLLS

Dolls which are " spineless " and whose heads wobble hopelessly backwards and forwards are fun to make and great favourites with certain age groups. The secret lies in two pieces of wood, one in the neck and one in the body, joined by two staples (fig. 70 A). The arms are merely pieces of string inside the blouse sleeves and the legs softly stuffed " tubes ", so that both flop about. The good lady given here is quite a character with her enormous nose on a caricature of a face, and her great clumsy shoes.

WOBBLY WINNIE

Height 14½ in. Pattern page 284. Illustration Fig. 71

Materials :

Scraps of flesh pink stockinette for the face and hands.
14 in. string for the arms.

Scraps of muslin for moulding face.

    ,,   ,, striped cotton material for stockings.

    ,,   ,, black Vynide for shoes.

Two pieces 13 in. × 4 in. fine black/white striped cotton material for blouse.

One piece 15 in. × 6 in. of grey flannel for skirt.

Oddment of white cotton material or gay print for apron.

8 in. × 8 in. of red woollen material or Folkweave for shawl.

Red felt ⎫

Pipe cleaner ⎬ for hat.

2 in. pill box ⎭

3-ply ginger wool for hair and brows.

Blue, red and white stranded cotton for features.

Some odd pieces of wood and cotton rag for the body.

About three handfuls of kapok.

Method :

Cut out the pieces as given.

Body (fig. 70) :

Cut two odd pieces of wood, one 4 in. × $\frac{3}{4}$ in. and one $1\frac{1}{2}$ in. × $\frac{1}{2}$ in.—both of them about $\frac{1}{2}$ in. thick. Join the two loosely together with two staples so that when the longer piece is held in the hand, the smaller piece (the head) will wobble.

Bind the larger piece from the top downwards with odd strips of rag—securing firmly by stitching *and* sticking the ends.

Arms (fig. 70 B) :

Stitch the string to top of body. Make up the hands by stitching all round A–B–C on the wrong side. Turn right side out and stuff very lightly. Stitch lines to indicate fingers. Push each hand over an end of the string, so that the ends are well down inside, and gathering tops of hands stitch firmly to the strings.

Stockings (fig. 71) :

For the stockings cut two strips of striped cotton material 6 in. × $2\frac{1}{4}$ in.—(stripes running across). Fold them in half lengthwise and on the wrong side join what will be the centre back seam, taking $\frac{1}{4}$ in. turnings so that the completed tube is $1\frac{3}{4}$ in. round. Gather all round one end of each stocking, pull up tightly and fasten off. Turn right side out, stuff and oversew top end.

Shoes (fig. 71) :

Make these exactly as for Clown's shoe No. 4 (page 46), using black Vynide or felt with fawn felt soles. Stuff each one firmly, then push the gathered end of a stocking into each shoe and stitch firmly in place, working round the top of the shoes. Make two tiny bows of black tape and stitch one on top of each shoe as a decoration.

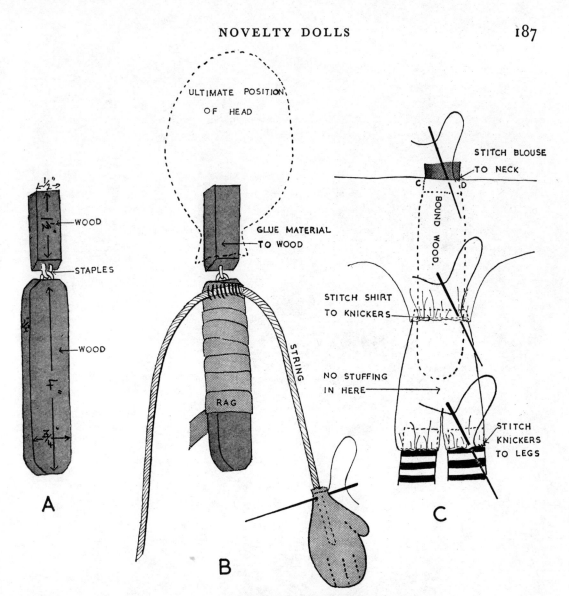

Fig. 70. *Construction of Wobbly Winnie*

A. Two pieces of wood for body and head
B. Position of arms and head
C. Attaching clothes to bound wood

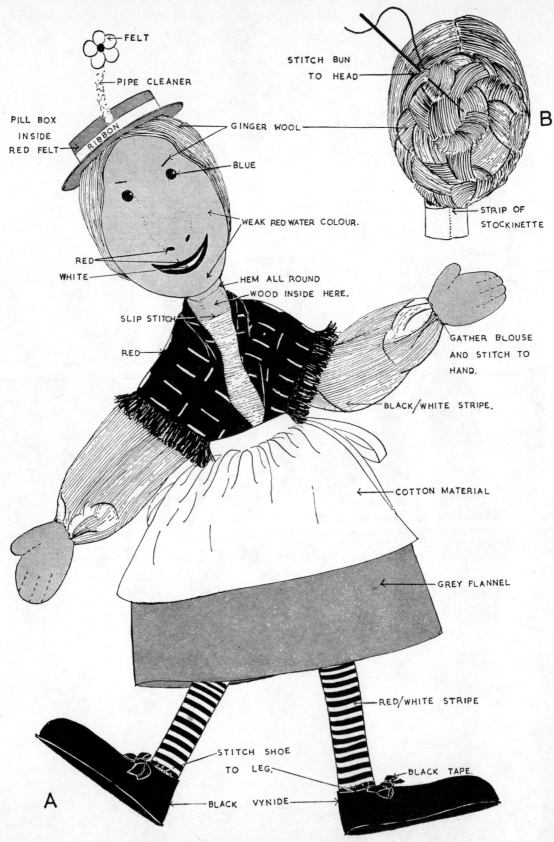

FELT

PIPE CLEANER

PILL BOX
INSIDE
RED FELT

RIBBON

GINGER WOOL

BLUE

WEAK RED WATER COLOUR.

RED

WHITE

HEM ALL ROUND

WOOD INSIDE HERE.

SLIP STITCH

RED

GATHER BLOUSE
AND STITCH TO
HAND.

BLACK/WHITE STRIPE.

COTTON MATERIAL

GREY FLANNEL

STITCH BUN
TO HEAD

STRIP OF
STOCKINETTE

B

RED/WHITE STRIPE

STITCH SHOE
TO LEG.

BLACK TAPE.

A

BLACK VYNIDE

Fig. 71. *Wobbly Winnie*
A. Fully dressed
B. Back of head

Head (fig. 71 A and B) :

Make up a padded head as shown by figs. 10 and 11 and described on page 32, starting with a good double handful of kapok. Ease the small piece of wood up into the neck and glue both muslin and stockinette firmly to this. Now wrap a strip of stockinette right round the neck, turning in the raw edges and hemming top edge to base of head and bottom edge to rag at top of body. Ladder stitch seam at centre back of neck. Test that this is loose enough to still allow the head to wobble. Embroider tiny bead-like eyes in blue with a white highlight, nostrils and lips in red and " gap " indicating teeth in white.

Hair (fig. 71 A and B) :

Stitch on the ginger " hair ", exactly as for Elizabeth (fig. 45 (4)) but with no fringe or Alice band, and have it about 12 in. long. Make into one thick plait at centre back, then wind into an enormous bun covering the whole of the back of the head. Tuck the end underneath and stitch the whole thing firmly in place with matching wool.

Embroider brows.

Blouse (fig. 70 C and 71) :

Fold as shown on pattern and on the wrong side join underarm and side seams A–B. Turn right side out. Slip wooden body piece through the neck slit C–D. Turn in the raw edge of neck slit and slip stitch all round to base of neck of doll. Run a gathering thread round the sleeve edges of blouse, turning in the raw edges as you work, pull up to fit top of hand and stitch so that the sleeves overlap and cover the top raw edges of hands.

Knickers (fig. 70 C) :

Place the two pieces together and on the wrong side join side seams A–B and C–D. Join " hairpin shaped " seam E–F–G. Turn right side out. Run a gathering thread round base of each leg B–E–B and G–D–G, turning in raw edges as you work. Push the top of a stocking into each knicker leg, arranging them so that there is about $\frac{1}{2}$ in. of stocking up inside each knicker leg, and so that the feet turn sharply outwards at a comic angle. Pull up gathers to fit stockings and stitch firmly in place, working all round each knicker leg. Pull the knickers with legs attached on to piece of body wood. Gather round lower edge of blouse, turning in raw edge as you work, pull up to fit wood and so that it covers top raw edge of knickers, stitch securely in place.

Skirt :

Fold the strip in half widthwise and join seam (which will be at centre back). Turn up and herringbone (fig. 6 C) $\frac{1}{2}$ in. hem all round bottom edge. Run a gathering thread round top edge, turning in raw edge as you work. Turn right side out and put on to doll, pulling up gathers to fit and stitching firmly to base of blouse, working all round waist.

Shawl (fig. 71) :

Fringe the outside ½ in. all round the piece of woollen material by drawing threads. Work a row of neat oversewing all round, to secure remaining threads. Fold in half cornerwise and place round doll's shoulders. (The ends will eventually tuck into the top of apron and keep neatly in place.)

Apron (fig. 71) :

Cut a piece of cotton material 8 in. × 4¼ in. Make a narrow hem round the two short and one of the long sides, and gather along the other long side, pulling it up to 3 in. Gather this into a little band ½ in. wide. Sew on two strings each ½ in. × 10 in. and tie on to doll.

Hat (fig. 71) :

Make a " boater " from red felt as shown on pages 54 and 56. Add a yellow ribbon and a felt flower mounted on 1½ in. of pipe cleaner—or a plain flower and leaf. The hat will keep firmly in place by putting the elastic under Winnie's bun. Finally, give her rosy cheeks and chin with a little weak water-colour.

VARIATIONS

You might like to make a husband for Winnie. The meek little man's face shown on page 31 would be suitable for a " Wobbly Willie "—alternatively try making a clown by this method—they are very suitable subjects and look most effective.

JACK-IN-THE-BOX

Box = 3½ in. cube. Pattern pages 279, 281. Illustration Fig. 72 C

Whereas a Jack-in-the-Box is usually a commercially made toy, it *is* possible for the needlewoman to construct one, provided she can obtain a suitable spring. This sometimes presents quite a problem as it must not be too stiff or the little figure will not push right down into the box, and not too weak or it will not stand upright and support the weight of the head. The springs used for the originals were taken from rollers used for setting hair.

Another essential is some *very* strong cardboard from which to make the box. Last year's calendars are good for this, or any cardboard which is too tough to cut with scissors. Cut it with a very sharp knife, run along the edge of a metal straight edge.

Materials :

Six pieces of very strong cardboard 3½ in. square   }for
    ,,   ,,   ,, red felt, very slightly larger than the board squares }the
    ,,   ,,   ,, green ,,   ,,   ,,   ,,   ,,   ,,   ,,   ,, }box.
One round ball-like button.

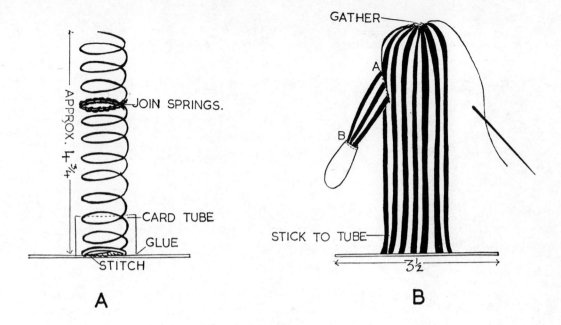

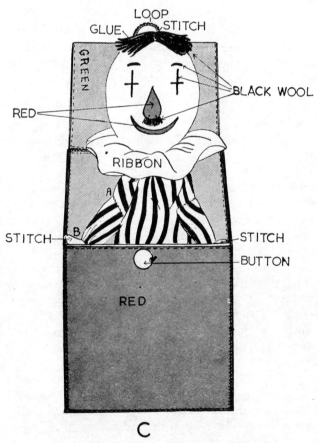

Fig. 72. *Construction of Jack-in-the-Box*

    A. Joining and attaching spring
    B. Construction of " body "
    C. Completed toy

Scrap of white felt ⎫
Tiny piece of red felt ⎪
A few yards of black darning wool ⎬ for the head.
A handful of kapok ⎭

Two springs from hairdresser's rollers ⎫
A scrap of green/white striped cotton material ⎪
12 in. yellow ribbon 1½ in. wide ⎬ for the body.
A cardboard tube (inside of toilet roll) ⎭

Method :

Cut out the pieces on page 281 as given. Also the head pieces for felt dolls on page 279 in white and the nose in red.

The Box :

Cover each square of board with the felt—green one side and red the other, by placing the board between the pieces and stab stitching neatly all round the outside. Stitch four of these pieces together to form the four sides of the box—green inside and red outside, and oversew firmly down each join. Take a fifth piece and oversew this to the top edge of one of the four sides. This is the lid and the oversewing will form a hinge. Sew the button to the centre front and make a strong loop to fit it, by buttonhole or blanket stitching tightly along several strands of thread. Place all this on one side.

The Body :

Remove net covering from roller and, with wire cutters, cut one of the springs in half—discard one half. Take the full-length spring and join half the other one to it, by binding the two together with strong thread or fuse wire. The joined spring will then be about 4¾ in. long (fig. 72 A).

Take the sixth side of the box and stitch the base of the spring firmly to the centre of green side, working round the bottom coil several times (fig. 72 A).

Cut 1¼ in. off the cardboard tube, drop this over the spring and glue it firmly to the base of box (fig. 72 A). This will help to guide the spring straight down into the box when it is shut and prevent it from pushing over to one side. Measure a piece of striped cotton material so that it fits *loosely* over cardboard tube and spring, allowing for turnings top, bottom and down centre back seam. On the wrong side stitch centre back seam. Turn right side out. Turn in raw edges all round lower edge, and glue in place. Pull cotton " tube " over spring and stick securely to cardboard tube, spreading the glue all over the cardboard so that the cotton material sticks to its entire surface. Turn in top raw edges, run a gathering thread all round, pull up and fasten off.

Arms (fig. 72 B) :

Fold each piece in half and on the wrong side join seam A–B. Run a gathering thread round the wrist edge (B). Pull up and fasten off tightly. Turn right side

Plate 11.   Sally, Judy and Pam have stopped playing with their dolls and golliwog to watch
Bert and Algy perform

out, and stuff lightly. Turn in the top raw edges and oversew. Sew a hand to each wrist. Stitch one arm to each side of cotton " body tube ".

Head :

Make the head exactly as given for the felt dolls on page 160, working from * to *. Close the bottom opening with ladder stitch. Make up the red nose and attach to face exactly as given for felt dolls on page 160, consulting fig. 72 C for position. Still consulting fig. 72 C embroider the mouth, using one strand of red cotton, and the eye crosses, brows and moustache in black wool, making all " beginnings and end- ings " on top of head where they will be covered by the hair. Cut a little bundle of black wool 2 in. long and lay it on top of head. Back stitch firmly down centre for a parting, then glue the ends of wool to head as they will easily be disarranged when the lid of the box presses on them.

Assembling the Pieces :

Stitch completed head firmly to top of spring, working through the cotton " body tube ", so that you are stitching to the top coil. Join the short ends of the ribbon. Run a gathering thread round one edge, put over the little man's head, seam at centre back. Pull up gathers to fit neck so as to form a ruff and stitch to neck. Now place this completed piece at the base of the top of box, so that the man is standing in the middle, and oversew base of box firmly to the four sides. Stitch the tip of each hand to a corner (see fig. 72 C). This steadies the " Jack " and gives him the appearance of holding on to the box.

VARIATIONS

Jacks-in-the-Box are usually clown or golliwog figures, so you could adapt many of the dolls in other sections to this purpose, altering the size of the head concerned to fit the box, or the size of the box and spring to fit the head.

INANIMATE OBJECTS AS DOLLS

It is not always necessary for a doll to represent a human character, and the possibilities of " humanizing " an inanimate object are often overlooked. One notable success was the much loved " Mr. Turnip " of children's television fame.

Vegetables, flowers and nursery rhyme " objects " such as the dish and the spoon from " Hey Diddle Diddle ", as well as familiar everyday things like a pillar box, may all be given arms, legs and faces and brought to life.

The example given here is a Belisha Beacon, because it was felt that he might serve a useful purpose by helping in the road safety campaign !

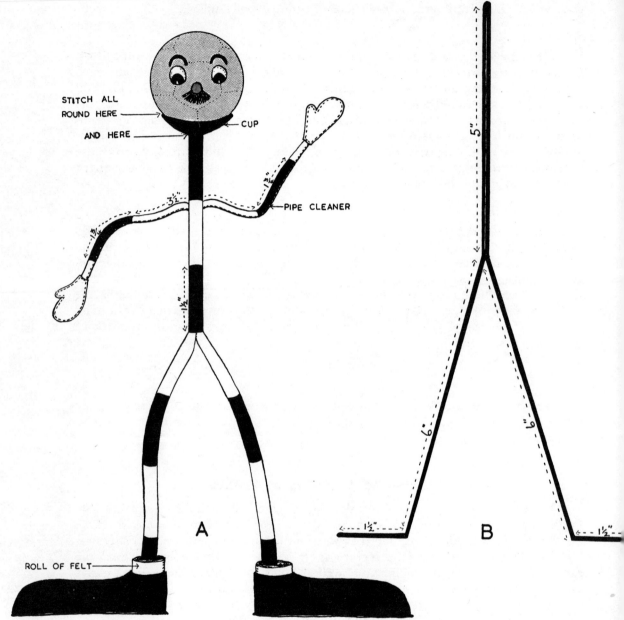

STITCH ALL
ROUND HERE

AND HERE

CUP

3½"

3"

1½"

PIPE CLEANER

A

ROLL OF FELT

5"

6"

6"

1½"

1½"

B

Fig. 73. *Construction of Bertie Beacon*

BERTIE BEACON

Height 12 in. Pattern pages 271, 281. Illustration Fig. 73

Materials :

> 25 in. of wire (gauge 14).
> Odd scraps of orange, black, white and red felt.
> A needleful of black darning wool.
> Two pipe cleaners. A small handful of kapok.

Method :

Head :

Using template E, page 271, cut out twelve patches in orange felt and make them up into a ball as described on page 78 and fig. 26. The patches may be sewn directly together on the wrong side, using a small neat stab stitch and silk or Sylko which exactly matches the material. No paper backings are necessary when making a felt ball. Turn right side out, stuff very firmly indeed and DO NOT close the opening. Place on one side.

Arms :

Cut out the gloves as given on page 281, and placing them together in pairs stab stitch all round except for straight edge A–B. Place on one side.

Take the pipe cleaners and overlap and twist them together so that they are 9 in. long when joined, with the double, twisted part at the centre. Now following fig. 73 join strips of black and white felt together ready for covering the arms. The strips need to be only $\frac{3}{8}$ in. wide—so that they will fit tightly round the pipe cleaners. Have the centre white strip $3\frac{1}{2}$ in. long, then $1\frac{3}{4}$ in. of black at each side, finish with white at each end, which will be partly hidden by the gloves. Roll the prepared strip round the pipe cleaner and stab stitch all the way along, close to the cleaner, using black or white Sylko on the appropriate felt. Push a little stuffing into each glove and push one over each end of arm. Stitch in place, working all round the base of glove. Place on one side.

Body :

Take the wire and bend as shown by fig. 73 B. Cut six strips of black felt $1\frac{1}{4}$ in. wide and $1\frac{1}{2}$ in. long, and five of white, the same size. Join these together on the wrong side, black—white—black for the body and black—white—black—white for each leg.

Bind the wire tightly with adhesive tape as shown in fig. 82 D, working over it several times until the prepared felt strips fit exactly round it. Wrap body strip round and oversew together all down centre back. Cover the legs in the same way, then stitch top of legs to each other and to base of body, working very neatly.

Cut out the " cup " to hold the head (pattern page 281) and piercing a hole in the centre, thread it on to top of wire, pushing it down as far as the top black " stripe ", push the wire up into the head as far as it will go, and stitch the cup to head all round the outside edge of circle. Then ladder stitch top of body to base of cup. Following fig. 73 A stitch arms firmly to back of body and bend and curve them as you wish.

Shoes :

Make up a pair of shoes exactly as given for Wobbly Winnie, page 186, but use felt instead of Vynide. Stuff them very firmly. Roll a strip of white felt round the base of each leg until it exactly fits opening in shoe. Stitch in place with a centre back seam ; this makes the socks. Slip into shoes, working the wire " feet " into the stuffing, and stitch shoes to socks all round top of shoes. Adjust for firm standing.

Face :

Cut out the pieces as given on page 281. Stab stitch each pupil to an eye, and embroider a tiny white highlight on each. Hem neatly to face. Run a gathering thread all round outside edge of nose, pull up and push a tiny piece of stuffing inside to form a little, round " knob ". Sew to face.

With black wool, embroider brows and moustache.

VARIATIONS

1. Bertie could be given a " mat " of black and white striped felt to carry rolled up under his arm. This could be unrolled and laid down in front of him to use as a " crossing ".

2. Try making a pillar box to go with Bertie.

*   *   *

Did you know that the Jack-in-the-Box probably originated at the end of the 13th century from the devil being trapped in a boot ? The late rector of North Marston, Bucks, the Rev. Denis Daly, told an interesting story of John of Shorne (Kent) who was priest in charge of that Parish from 1290 and was famous throughout the country for his miraculous powers in healing skin diseases. Chalybeate wells sprang up in various places in this parish, and one still exists. John's most famous " miracle " was to ask the devil to come to church and then conjure him into his boot. The villagers all made little boots with a toy Jack (Knave ? devil ?) inside, and these are often supposed to be the origin of our modern Jack-in-the-Box. Pilgrims came from far and wide to see and venerate this boot, and replicas were sold to them which they believed would cure them of gout. Among many interesting Inn signs commemorating these events is that of " The Boot " at Winslow, Bucks, on which is depicted a boot with the devil in it and pilgrims climbing the hill beyond, to the North Marston Church of St. Mary—the front of the church on one side of the sign and the back on the other. In those days villagers were so isolated that widely scattered counties all venerated the same Saint and his miracles, and many Inns called the Boot may have been resting places for the pilgrims.

CORSET AND SHOE LACE DOLLS

DOLLS ON A SCALE suitable for use in a doll's house can present something of a problem, either being too large for the size of the rooms and furniture or too stiff and unyielding to look natural. We are all familiar with the enchanting photographs of Victorian dolls' houses, in which a large family of children, forbidding-looking mother and father and a positive bevy of servants and nursemaids, either stood solemnly to attention or leaned in a dead faint against the walls of the various rooms, for their entire lives. Although these fascinating creatures have a charm of their own, they are not so easy to play with as dolls which will sit, stand, bend or lie in any position.

The doll's house family given here is a modern one and consists of a Mother and Father, Grannie (who has come to live with them and give mother a hand !), a little girl called Theresa, the " toddler age " twins Billy and Bunty, and the baby. They are all made on a foundation of corset laces threaded with pipe cleaners, so that they may be bent to any position. The ends of the laces, stuck together and cut, make the most realistic and graceful hands ! As it is essential that this type of doll should stand very firmly, the feet are made from " Blakey's Segs ", sold by the shoemaker to protect the tips of the sole of your shoes, and the weight and " flatness " of these makes an excellent and firm base for the dolls.

At the end of the section ideas are given for turning " the twins " into dolls for the stockinette dolls in Section VIII and golliwogs for the felt golliwogs in Section X. And at the very end instructions are given for making even smaller dolls and golliwogs as playthings for these miniatures.

Needless to say, with metal Segs as feet, this type of doll is not intended for the very young child, as however carefully the doll is made an accident *might* happen and a Seg could easily be swallowed. They are specially designed for the older child of " doll's house age ".

A FAMILY FOR THE DOLL'S HOUSE

Patterns page 268. Illustration Plate 8

Materials for making the whole family :

One corset lace.
Twenty pipe cleaners.
Eight Blakey's Segs, " Tom Thumb " size for the larger dolls.
Four   ,,   ,, " Fairy "   ,,   ,,   ,, twins.
Small quantities of brown and yellow darning wool for hair and features.

Black, white, brown, blue and red stranded cotton for hair and features.
Scraps of material for dressing.
A small handful of kapok for stuffing heads.
Approx. 24 in. of fine wire (fine fuse wire or similar).
Colourless nail varnish.

BASIC ADULT FIGURE (Fig. 74)
Height 5 in.

Arms :

Cut the " tag " off one end of the corset lace, and folding a pipe cleaner in half (fig. 74 A) and pinching it well together with pliers, ease it inside the lace. The easiest method of doing this is to pinch the " creases " each side of the lace, so that it opens out into a tube, and work the lace over the pipe cleaner in the same way as one eases a glove over a finger. (This is much quicker than merely pushing the pipe cleaner into the lace.) Push well in, so that there is about ½ in. of lace left unfilled by the cleaner, and cut off the other end, leaving a similar ½ in. (fig. 74 B). Dip each end for about ¾ in. into a bottle of colourless nail varnish and place on one side to dry. (This takes a *very* long time.) While you are making the other parts of the dolls keep pressing the lace flat, between your fingers, so that it sticks together. When quite dry, cut the end to form a hand (fig. 74 I) and curve the fingers and palm of hand into a natural attitude (fig. 74 J). If necessary paint over with a further coat of nail varnish and allow to harden.

N.B. It is a good plan to make *all* the arms for the dolls you intend to make at this stage, so that by the time you are ready for them, they are really dry and hard.

Legs :

For each leg, fold a pipe cleaner in half and push into the corset lace exactly as you did for the arms, so that you have two pieces looking like fig. 74 B.

Feet :

Take two Segs (" Tom Thumb " size) and with a pair of cutting nippers cut two of the spikes from each one, leaving one spike at the *end* of each (fig. 74 C). (Make sure to cut the spikes off so as to make a *pair* of feet, see fig. 74 L, and not so that they both curl in one direction !)

Take about 4 in. of wire and thread through the two holes in the Seg with the ends emerging on the same side as the spike (fig. 74 D). Bring the front end towards the spike and twist the two ends together at right angles to the spike ; bend the top ends of wire over and press tightly together with pliers (fig. 74 E).

Take the prepared piece of corset lace and bend one unfilled end (the foot) at right angles to the filled part (the leg). With pointed scissors, make a tiny hole under the folded end of pipe cleaner and push the wire up into this (fig. 74 F). Continue pushing until both wire and spike are right inside the lace, then take a few stitches through the hole in the Seg which is nearest the leg, and right through the

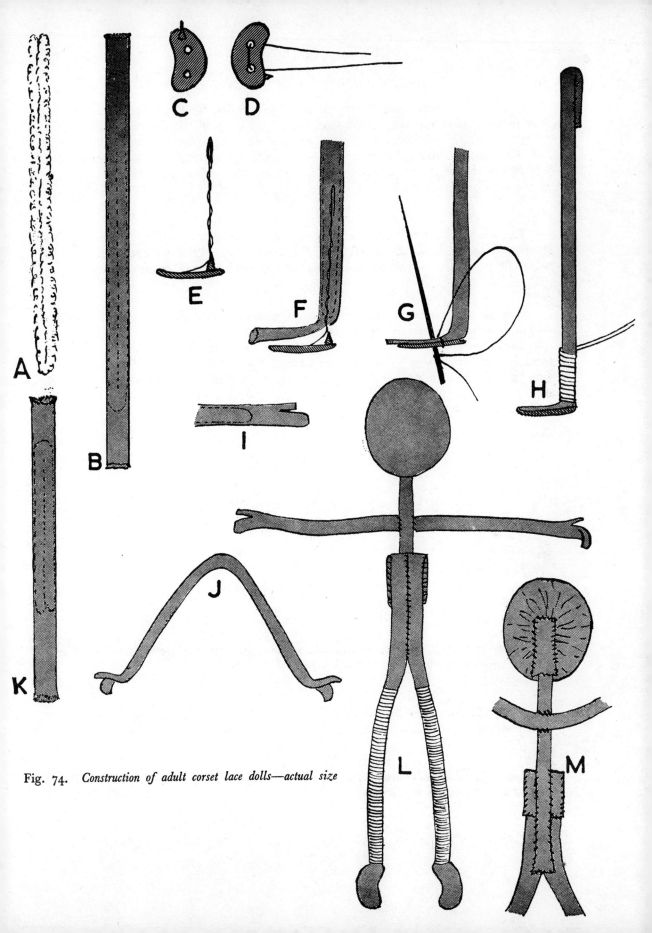

Fig. 74.   *Construction of adult corset lace dolls—actual size*

corset lace which now rests on top of the " foot " (fig. 74 G). For extra security and neatness, stick the lace to the top of Seg and trim off surplus with scissors (fig. 74 H). The legs will later be bound, to represent socks or stockings, which gives added strength. Make the other leg in the same way, then fold back the unfilled $\frac{1}{2}$ in. of corset lace at top of each leg and stitch in place. Stitch the two legs together at the top for about 1 in.

Body :

Cut a pipe cleaner in half and fold one of these pieces in half again, push inside the corset lace and cut off so that there is about $\frac{1}{2}$ in. unfilled one end and 1 in. the other (fig. 74 K). Fold the $\frac{1}{2}$ in. end down and stitch (this is the head end).

Head :

Cut out the piece (pattern page 268) in pink stockinette, or if not available, any soft pink material. (Even the smooth side of pink lint would do.) Run a gathering thread all round outside edge of circle and pull up gathers, stuffing firmly to form a hard little knob. Fasten off gathers at back and stitch top of body in place (fig. 74 M). Now stitch body to legs, leaving about 1 in. exposed between head and top of legs (fig. 74 L). Stitch remaining part of lace, both filled and unfilled, to back of joined legs. Sew arms to back of body $\frac{1}{2}$ in. down from head.

Shoes :

Paint the tops of the feet with any sort of black household paint or enamel and leave overnight to dry.

BASIC " TODDLER " FIGURE (Fig. 75 A)
Height 3 in.

Legs :

Cut a piece of pipe cleaner $5\frac{1}{4}$ in. long and push singly into the corset lace, leaving $\frac{1}{2}$ in. unfilled each end. The piece will look like fig. 74 B, but the cleaner inside will not be doubled.

Feet :

Make up exactly as given for the adult's on page 198, but use " Fairy " size Segs, placing one on each end of the leg piece.

Body :

Fold this completed feet and leg piece in half like a hairpin and stitch together at the top for 1 in. (fig. 75 A).

Head :

Cut out the piece (pattern page 268) and make up exactly as for the adult's on page 200. Stitch to top of body.

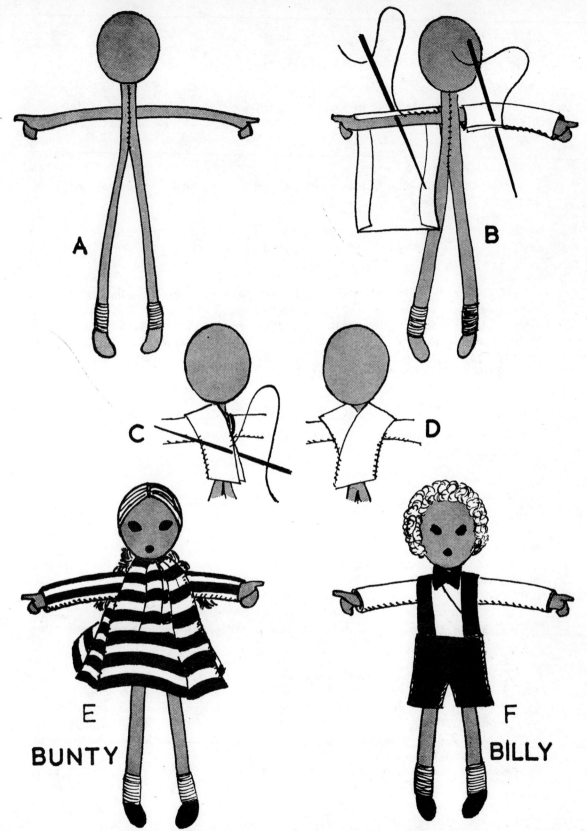

Fig. 75. *Construction of toddler corset lace dolls—actual size*

Arms :

Prepare and make these up exactly as given for the adult's on page 198, but only use 2¾ in. of pipe cleaner—and single instead of folded. Stitch to body about ¼ in. below head.

Shoes :

Paint the tops of the feet with red nail varnish or household enamel, for shoes, and leave overnight.

BASIC "LITTLE GIRL" FIGURE
Height 3¾ in.

Make exactly as given for the toddler on page 200, but use a full-length pipe cleaner single for the legs and Tom Thumb size Segs for the feet. Use 3 in. of pipe cleaner single for the arms and a slightly larger size circle for the head (pattern page 268). If available a red, blue, black or green shoe lace may be used for the legs to give the appearance of coloured stockings and avoid binding later, but these *are* just a little bit " skinny " in appearance.

MOTHER (Fig. 76 A)

Make a basic adult figure (page 198) and bind the lower 2 in. of legs tightly with fawn stranded cotton for stockings.

Features :

Embroider eyes and brows in brown and mouth in red, using one strand of cotton.

Hair :

Cover the head with long stitches in brown stranded cotton or Coton à Broder, making some of them a little longer than the others round the edge of face, to give a feathery effect. Make a 4 in. plait, using six threads. Bind each end and stitch one end to top of head. Curl the rest of plait round and round into a small tight " bun " and stitch securely in place, tucking in the end when you come to it.

Dress :

Take a piece of material with a *small* pattern and cut two little strips 1½ in. wide. Press back ¼ in. turning on each side and stick in place with Gripfix or similar paste, so that the strips are now 1 in. wide and with no raw edges. Place on arm as shown for " toddler " (fig. 75 B)—but Mother's sleeves will be short. Stitch in place along top of arm. Roll strip two or three times round arm, then, tucking in raw edge as you work, oversew neatly along underarm.

Make two similar strips, sticking back raw edges, so that they are finally a little

A
MOTHER

B
FATHER

C
GRANNIE

Fig. 76. *Finished adult corset lace dolls—actual size*

more than ½ in. wide.   Place one across shoulders, and overlapping sleeve, as shown for " toddler " (fig. 75 C) and stitch in place under arm and down opposite side of body.   Place the other piece across the other way (fig. 75 D) and stitch similarly in place.

Cut a piece of material to fit round the doll's waist so as to make a slim skirt, allowing a little piece extra for folding under at back.   Turn back and stick the top and bottom edges so that the skirt is 2 in. long.   Place on to doll, turning the raw edge under and sticking all down centre back.   Take a few invisible stitches all round waist.

FATHER (Fig. 76 B)

Make a basic adult figure (page 198).

Features :

Embroider eyes, brows and moustache in black and mouth in red, using one strand of cotton.

Hair :

Cover the head with long stitches in black stranded cotton, coming to a point on forehead and at nape of neck.   If liked add an odd grey stitch or two at temples and on moustache.

Trousers :

Cut a narrow strip of grey felt to fit round each leg and oversew in place, up inside of leg.

Sleeves :

Make these by rolling navy blue felt several times round arms, as given under Mother's dress, page 202.   Being felt, the edges may be left raw.

Shirt and Tie :

Stitch a tiny piece of white felt across under chin, from top of one sleeve to top of the other, and sew a " tie shaped " piece of bright blue felt in place at centre front.

Rest of Jacket or Blazer :

Cut two rectangles of navy felt the right size to reach from shoulders to hips and loosely across body.   Cut one of these in half lengthwise for the front.   Place the large piece at the back and the two smaller pieces at the front of doll, oversew across shoulders and down each side.   Fold back the tops of fronts for revers and catch to shoulders.   Overlap left front very slightly and stitch down centre front.

GRANNIE (Fig. 76 C)

Make a basic adult figure (page 198) and bind the lower 1 in. of legs with grey stranded cotton for stockings.

Features :

Embroider spectacles and eyes in black and mouth in red, using one strand of cotton.

Hair :

Make up a small " wig " exactly as given for Jane on page 123 but without a fringe, and use white or grey Coton à Broder or stranded cotton. Stitch to head and make two plaits, then bring one up each side, tucking the ends together at top, and stitch securely all round.

Blouse :

Use a fine stripe such as a piece of an old shirt, and make up exactly as given for the top of Mother's dress (page 202) but have long sleeves.

Skirt :

Gather a piece of black cotton or silk material so that it is very *slightly* full (about 4 in. round hem), turn up and stick hem, making the finished skirt 2¼ in. long. Place on doll, stitching round waist, with raw edge turned in and seam stuck at centre back, also with raw edge turned in.

Apron :

Take a piece of plain or very small patterned material and make a rectangle, sticking back a hem all round so that the finished apron is 1¼ in. × 1 in. Stick or stitch to waist. Cut two narrow strips of the same material, stick back a little hem all along edges. Stitch one to each side of waist and tie in bow at centre back.

THE TWINS (Fig. 75)

BUNTY (Fig. 75 E)

Make a basic " toddler " figure as given on page 200 and bind the lower ¼ in. of legs with white stranded cotton for socks.

Features :

Embroider eyes in blue and mouth in red, using one strand of cotton.

Hair :

Using pale yellow darning wool, make a little wig as given for Jane on page 123 but without a fringe. Stitch firmly to head with the two little plaits hanging down back.

Dress :

Striped material looks well for this. Make the sleeves exactly as described for Mother on page 202 and fig. 75 B. Then cut two little pieces of material to reach from the neck to just above knee length, allowing a little extra for turnings, and having each one about $2\frac{1}{2}$ in. wide. Stick up a narrow hem along bottom of each and run a gathering thread along top of each, turning in the raw edge as you work. Pull up gathers tightly and place one piece in the front and one at the back of the doll ; stitch all round neck. Oversew the two pieces together from under arms to hem, turning in raw edges as you work.

BILLY (Fig. 75 F)

Make a basic " toddler " figure as given on page 200 and bind the lower $\frac{1}{4}$ in. of legs with white stranded cotton for socks.

Features :

Work just as for Bunty, page 205.

Hair :

Cover the head with small looped stitches of pale yellow darning wool.

Shirt :

Make just as given for the top of Mother's dress on page 202, but use white felt. No turnings will be necessary. Make long sleeves.

Trousers :

Cut two pieces in red felt (pattern page 268). Oversew the leg seams B–B–C. Place on doll and oversew outside seams. Cut two narrow strips of red felt and sew in place for braces crossing at centre back. Cut a tiny bow tie to match and stitch at centre front of shirt.

THERESA (Fig. 77)

Make a basic " little girl " figure (page 202) using a black shoe lace for legs, or bind these with black stranded cotton (or any bright colour).

Features :

Embroider eyes in black and mouth in red, using one strand of cotton.

Hair :

Make a " pony tail " exactly as given for Pam on page 124, but use brown darning wool and only sew two strands of hair in place at a time.

Jersey :

Make the sleeves as shown on fig. 75 B, using yellow felt. Cut two little squares

Fig. 77. " *Theresa* "
—*little girl corset lace doll—
actual size*

of felt to fit front and back of body, oversew in place along shoulders and under arms. Roll a piece of felt round neck for a polo collar, stitch at centre back and round base. Cut out the skirt (pattern page 268) in jade green felt. Join seam A–B, ease on to doll and stitch round waist.

THE BABY (Fig. 78)

Body and Legs :

Push 4 in. of pipe cleaner unfolded into the corset lace, leaving $\frac{1}{2}$ in. unfilled each end (as fig. 74 B but with single thickness of pipe cleaner). Fold the unfilled pieces at each end back, and tucking in raw ends, stitch (fig. 78 A). Fold the piece in half like a hairpin, and stitch top $\frac{3}{4}$ in. together. Fold the piece into an L shape when viewed sideways, then turn up the ends for feet (fig. 78 B). The baby is in a sitting position.

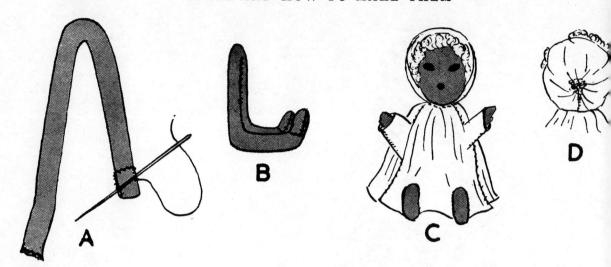

Fig. 78. *Construction of corset lace baby*

Arms :

Make these exactly as for the adult's, page 198, but use only 1½ in. of pipe cleaner and cut the " hands " to a smaller, baby shape.

Head :

Make as for adult's, page 200, but use smaller circle (pattern page 268). Sew to top of body.

Features :

Work just as for Bunty (page 205).

Hair :

Work just as for Billy (page 206).

Clothes (fig. 78 C and D) :

Using fine, white lawn such as a piece of old handkerchief, make a tiny long-sleeved dress as given for Bunty on page 206. If liked, make a little bonnet to match, by gathering a straight strip all along one edge and pulling up gathers at back. Turn back a tiny hem along front edge and stitch to head.

MORE CORSET AND SHOE LACE DOLLS

IDEAS FOR MAKING DOLLS FOR THE DOLLS

All little girls love their dolls to have their own small-scale dolls. The corset and shoe lace " toddler dolls " are particularly suitable for this. The twins, Billy and Bunty, make excellent dolls for the little girl stockinette dolls in Section VIII. Here are some other ideas.

PEGGY (Fig. 79)

Make exactly as given for Bunty on page 205, but copy the hair style given for Elizabeth on page 119. Cut the hair short and do not use an Alice band. Make the frock in a very small patterned cotton material. A whole selection of these dolls may be made, copying hair styles and features from the dolls in Section and varying the material used for the dresses. Be sure to use *very* small patterns or plain materials for the clothes.

PICCANINNY (Fig. 79)

Make exactly as given for Bunty on page 205, but use brown shoe laces instead of pink corset laces for arms and legs, and a tiny scrap of brown material for the head. Copy the features from fig. 79, giving her black and white eyes and scarlet mouth and nose. Make the hair in black darning wool, taking small, looped stitches all over the head until it is completely covered. Use spotted material for the dress (red and white is very effective) and stitch a tiny bow of $\frac{1}{4}$ in. wide ribbon to the top of the head.

THE TEN LITTLE NIGGER BOYS (Fig. 79)

Ten little boys to conform to the well loved nursery rhyme would make a wonderful present if attractively packed in a box. Even a teenager would welcome them for the mantelshelf! They do not take long to make if a system is worked out ; e.g. 1. Make all the arms ; 2. Make all the legs and feet ; 3. Make all the heads ; 4. Assemble the pieces ; 5. Embroider the features and hair ; 6. Dress the figures ; 7. Add final details to each one.

Make the dolls just as given for the Piccaninny, above, but dress them in a shirt made as for Billy, page 206. Striped material is effective for these. Give them little red felt trousers (pattern page 268) and a white felt collar made from a narrow, straight piece stitched tightly round the neck. Vary the expressions on each one after studying the rhyme and make them hold or do appropriate things. Here are some ideas to help you :

> Ten little nigger boys went out to dine ;
> One choked his little self, and then there were nine.

(As shown by fig. 79.)

> Nine little nigger boys sat up very late ;
> One overslept himself, and then there were eight.

(Eyes shut, as on Angel (fig. 42 C) and head leaning sideways on folded hands.)

PEGGY.
(A DOLL FOR A DOLL)

PICCANINNY.

**THE FIRST LITTLE
NIGGER BOY.**

**MINIATURE
FAIRY DOLL.**

Fig. 79.   *More corset and shoe lace dolls—actual size*

Eight little nigger boys travelling in Devon ;
One said he'd stay there, and then there were seven.

(Holding a small suitcase, made from a felt-covered " half-size " match box and labelled DEVON.)

Seven little nigger boys chopping up sticks ;
One chopped himself in half, and then there were six.

(Holding a small chopper made from felt covered cocktail stick and cardboard. Bend arm so that the blade is touching his waist.)

Six little nigger boys playing with a hive ;
A bumble-bee stung one, and then there were five.

(Wearing a bee-keeper's hat with net.)

Five little nigger boys going in for law ;
One got in Chancery, and then there were four.

(Wearing a small judge's wig made from cotton wool or white crêpe hair, and if possible a little black " gown ". A tiny scroll of paper in his hand.)

Four little nigger boys going out to sea ;
A red herring swallowed one, and then there were three.

(Wearing a sailor hat and holding a large fish.)

Three little nigger boys walking in the Zoo ;
A big bear hugged one, and then there were two.

(Holding a miniature teddy bear.)

Two little nigger boys sitting in the sun ;
One got frizzled up, and then there was one.

(Wearing a raffia sun hat and holding a little bottle labelled " Sun Tan Lotion ".)

One little nigger boy living all alone ;
He got married, and then there were none.

(Wearing a miniature top hat and with a white felt flower stitched to his shirt.)

MINIATURE FAIRY DOLL (Fig. 79)

Make exactly as given for Bunty on page 205, using very fine white material for the dress. Make the hair in yellow darning wool, by taking a series of small looped stitches all over head, having the loops slightly longer on top of head to give it a raised " oval " shape, instead of square like the Piccaninny.

Embroider the eyes in blue and mouth and nose in red. Bind a piece of fine wire with white stranded cotton for a wand and stitch a star-shaped, silver sequin to the end, also one to front of head. Decorate the hem with tiny crystal beads.

Fig. 80. *Toy golliwogs for the Golliwog family (and THEIR toy golliwogs!)—actual size*

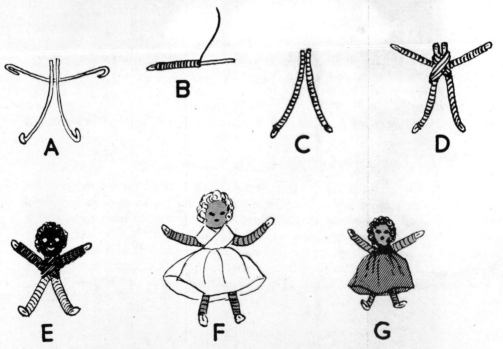

Fig. 81. *Dolls for the dolls' dolls!—actual size*

The Golliwoglet and Girliwoglet on fig. 58 and plate 10 would surely like to own miniatures of themselves with which to play ! These are easily made from black shoe laces.

MINIATURE GIRLIWOG (Fig. 80 A and plate 10)

Make exactly as for Billy on page 206, but use black shoe laces instead of a pink corset lace. Make the " shirt " in red felt and instead of trousers gather a narrow strip of blue felt round waist for a skirt, with the joining seam at centre back. Make a collar from a narrow strip of white felt, stitched tightly round neck. Bind the legs with red stranded cotton or wool, for stockings. Cut a tiny circle of black fur (over from the full-size Golliwogs) and stitch to head for hair. This will probably be too long in proportion to the size of doll, so clip it neatly all over, using very sharp scissors, until it is reduced to about $\frac{1}{4}$ in. in length. Work carefully to get it a good shape. Embroider eyes in black and white, nose and mouth in red, using one strand of cotton.

MINIATURE GOLLIWOG (Fig. 80 B and plate 10)

Make exactly as given for miniature Girliwog, but give him a blue " jacket " and make long red trousers, extending the pattern for Billy's trousers given on page 286 to reach to the ankles.

N.B. A pattern for a miniature Golliwog made entirely in *felt* appears on page 75 of *Modern Soft Toy Making*.

DOLLS FOR THE DOLLS' DOLLS

There seems no reason why these small people should not have their own, even smaller dolls. Bunty and Theresa are holding theirs on plate 8, and the miniature Golliwog in fig. 80 and plate 11 has his own even smaller Girliwog.

Although these minute dolls do not need corset or shoe laces, they are included here, as seeming the most appropriate place. For their basic foundation a small quantity of millinery wire is needed. This is a fine wire, bound with white, and costs only a few pence for a small coil, from most stores. They may be made just as small as you wish, depending really on how nimble your fingers are. One inch is a good length for each leg.

GOLLIWOG (Fig. 81 E)

Cut three pieces of wire. Bend a tiny piece back at one end of two of the pieces for legs, and at each end of the third piece for arms (fig. 81 A). Press these pieces tightly back, with snipe-nosed pliers. Bind each leg tightly with red stranded cotton, starting by carrying the " end " along under the binding and finishing by threading the end into a needle and stitching along under the last few " twists " and back again several times. Bind the arm piece similarly, but use blue stranded cotton.

Place the pieces together as shown by fig. 81 D and bind with several " criss-crosses " of blue stranded cotton.   Stretch a tiny piece of black material over ends of leg wires for a head, drawing together and stitching at back.   (If available, jersey cloth or old black stocking is ideal for this, or a flat shoe lace may be split and used.)

Embroider tiny white eyes and a red nose and mouth and cover top of head with loose stitches in black, stranded cotton for the hair.

GIRLIWOG (Held by miniature Golliwog in fig. 80 B)

Make in the same way as the Golliwog above, but bind legs with blue and arms and top of body with red.   Gather a narrow piece of red ribbon tightly round waist, with seam at centre back, for a skirt.

THE DOLLS (Fig. 81 F and G)

Make these in just the same way as the little Girliwog, but bind arms and legs with pink stranded cotton and use a tiny piece of pink stockinette for the head (you may have some over from the dolls in Section VIII) or split a corset lace and use this.   Give them golden or brown " curls " and blue eyes and red mouths.   If they are very small make a tiny skirt from a piece of ribbon stitched under arms (fig. 81 G), or if the doll is large enough, make a bodice by crossing two pieces of folded ribbon across shoulders before stitching on the skirt (fig. 81 F).

*   *   *

Did you know that in the " bad old days ", when orphanages were institutions giving shelter but no love or security to the children in them, these youngsters were often desperately unhappy and for comfort made little " secret " dolls to carry around in their pockets?

Fashioned from anything which would not be missed, such as scraps of wool, string, paper, feathers, etc., these tiny dolls gave security to a be-wildered and lonely child, who were the only people to know of their existence. When life got too intolerable a small hand would steal into a pocket and feel the only friend (and often the only possession) it had in the world.

" I had a little moppet,
I kept it in my pocket,
And fed it on corn and hay ;
Then came a proud beggar
And said he would wed her,
And stole my little moppet away."
(Old nursery rhyme.)

WIRED FIGURES

THE CHRISTMAS CRIB (Illustration on Frontispiece)

THESE WIRED FIGURES are not truly " dolls "—the word " figures " describes them more accurately. They are not designed to be played with but to be used to illustrate, describe and to form tableaux and groups. The obvious choice seemed to be a Nativity Group which will, it is hoped, fulfil the demand which has existed for a very long time for patterns and designs for making these figures.

It has been said that St. Francis of Assisi first introduced the idea of making a Christmas Crib (or Crêche) but investigations show that they were in existence many years before his time and that figures were used to illustrate the Nativity as far back as A.D. 354, the year which saw the establishing by Pope Liberius of the Festival of Christmas.

A family could accumulate a group of these figures over the years—which *could* become a family heirloom ! For a start just Mary, Joseph and the Baby would be sufficient, the other figures being added year by year.

A group of needlewomen could make a set as a gift for their church—thus keeping the doll makers in step with all the wonderful church work being turned out today by embroideresses and rug makers.

The figures are fascinating to make—each one being built up slowly on a strong wire frame. The work *is* rather specialized, but if the instructions are followed implicitly, and each figure carefully and slowly built, there should be no difficulty.

Take great care when choosing materials to see that they are in keeping. Shiny silks, satins, brocades and lamé are essential for the kings, to make them stand out in a rich contrast to the more humble shepherds. Sequins, beads and " jewels " can be used liberally (see fig. 7 for attaching sequins).

Material for the shepherds' clothes needs choosing just as carefully ; drab, dull, loosely woven material being ideal for their tunics, while their outer garments need to be of gay striped material, with the stripes in the correct proportion for the size of the doll. You will find this in the most unlikely places—striped flannel and similar material sold for men's pyjamas, parts of a folkweave design or a tablecloth, are often very suitable. Above all, don't make the mistake of dressing Mary in silks or chiffons—keep her clothes plain and simple, made only of fine cotton material.

MAKING THE WIRE FRAMES

Height approx. 10½ in. Use for all the male figures in the Christmas Crib.
Pattern page 286. Follow Figs. 82 and 83.

Materials (for each figure) :

> 38½ in. gauge 14 copper or galvanized wire for the frame.
> ¼ in. wide adhesive tape for binding.
> Strips of cotton rag for binding (one side of an old pillow case, torn lengthways into 1½ in. strips, is ideal).
> One 9 in. square of flesh pink felt for body parts.
> Six pipe cleaners for stiffening fingers.
> Two or three handfuls of kapok.

Method :

Cut out the felt pieces as given, using the colour given under each separate figure, and place on one side.

Wire Frame :

Cut the wire into three pieces, 15 in. for the legs, 12 in. for the arms and 11½ in. for the body. You will now need some pliers for bending.

Take the leg piece and bend in half like a hairpin. Now following fig. 82 A bend 2 in. *forwards* at each end (these are shown bent sideways for clarity, but should, in fact, be forwards for the feet). Now bend the end ½ in. back again, so that the " foot " is 1½ in. long.

Take the body piece and bend 3 in. back at each end, so that the reduced length is 5½ in. (fig. 82 C).

Take the arm piece and bend 1 in. back at each end, so that the reduced length is 10 in. (fig. 82 B).

Pinch all the end " loops " tightly together as shown on the exposed wire of arm on fig. 82 D. Now following fig. 82 D hook the body wire on to the legs, and bind the arm wire tightly to the body wire, 2 in. down from the top, with adhesive tape criss-crossed many times at the join. Bind the whole frame with adhesive tape, keeping the hands, feet and head loops very neat and *slim* and criss-crossing where body and legs join, in the same way as you did at neck, until the entire frame is completely firm.

Now take the strips of cotton material and following fig. 82 E bind the frame neatly, turning in one raw edge as you work. Keep the feet very slim, as they have to slip into a narrow felt foot, and only bind the arms as far as the " elbows ". Pad the " chest " and " seat " with a handful of kapok under the binding so that when completed the chest measures approximately 4 in. and the seat 5½ in. *round* (NOT ACROSS !). It is important that this binding should be strong and neat especially at crutch of legs which will eventually be bent and adjusted to make the figure stand, and which has no further covering. Secure the ends with a few stitches.

Hands (fig. 83 A, B and C) :

Place the pieces together in pairs and on the right side, and using a *small* needle and Sylko or pure silk which exactly matches your felt stab stitch very neatly and

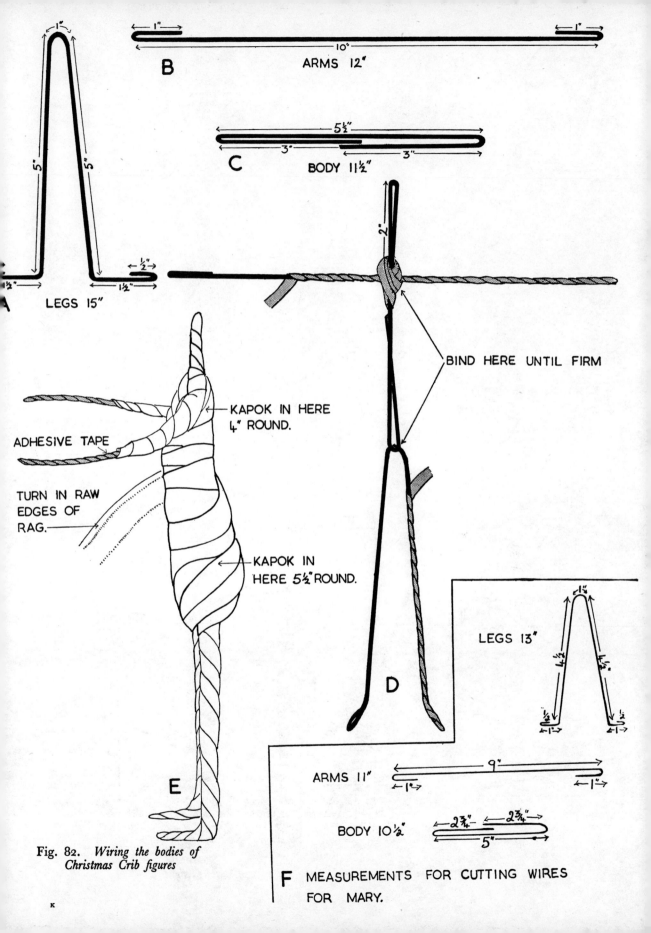

B

1″

10°

1″

ARMS 12″

1″

5″   5″

C

5½″

3″   3″

BODY 11½″

2″

BIND HERE UNTIL FIRM

½″

½″   ½″

LEGS 15″

D

KAPOK IN HERE
4″ ROUND.

ADHESIVE TAPE

TURN IN RAW
EDGES OF
RAG.

KAPOK IN
HERE 5½″ROUND.

LEGS 13″

1″

4½″   4½″

½″   ½″

1″   1″

ARMS 11″

9″

1″

1″

BODY 10½″

2¾″   2¾″

5″

E

Fig. 82. *Wiring the bodies of
Christmas Crib figures*

F   MEASUREMENTS FOR CUTTING WIRES
FOR MARY.

K

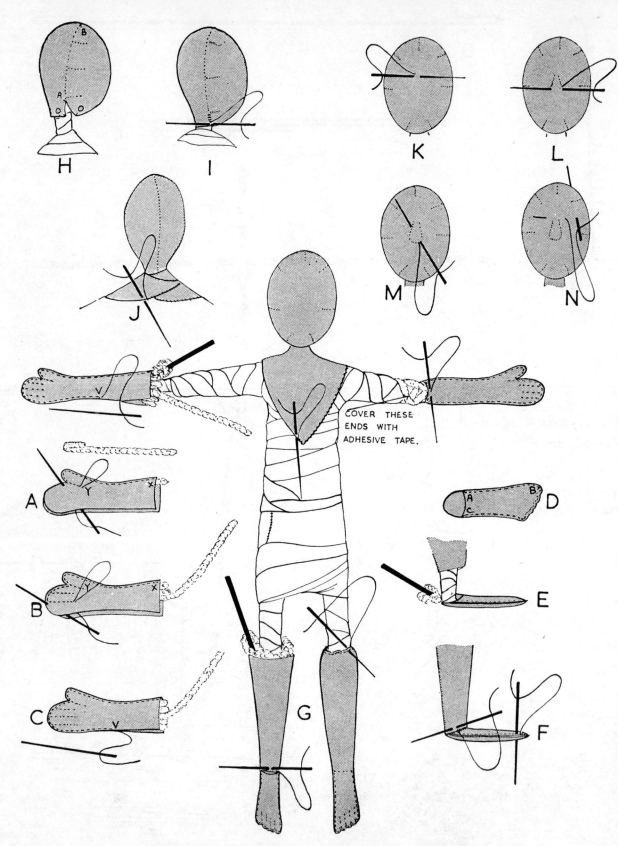

COVER THESE ENDS WITH ADHESIVE TAPE.

Fig. 83. *Construction of head, arms and legs of a wired figure*

with a tiny invisible stitch from X round thumb to Y. Cut two pipe cleaners in half and double back $\frac{1}{4}$ in. at one end of each of these pieces, nipping the "loops" tightly together. Push one of these pieces into the thumb, doubled end first. Now continue stitching, round first finger and down to Z, having slipped your needle between the two pieces of felt to the starting point; push another half pipe cleaner into second finger. Stitch round second finger and this time push a whole pipe cleaner (with the end doubled back) inside it. Continue stitching round third and fourth fingers, pushing half a pipe cleaner into each, until you come to V—do not break off thread. Push hand over one end of arm on prepared frame, easing the bound end of wire carefully in among the pipe cleaners, and with an orange or cock-tail stick insert tiny pieces of kapok so as to make the hand a firm, attractive shape (fig. 83 G). Continue stitching from V to end of arm; insert more kapok, shaping carefully and embedding the pipe cleaners and frame. Twist the long pipe cleaner round the arm so that it ties down the four shorter ends. Stitch end of arm all round to prevent stuffing from escaping, pulling up the stitches tightly. Finally, bind the twisted pipe cleaners with a further piece of adhesive tape to cover the sharp, prickly ends.

Legs :

Fold the pieces in half so that the A's meet and the B's meet and on the wrong side seam A–B. Turn right side out and slip over foot of frame and on to leg with B at centre back at "ankle". Place on one side.

Feet (fig. 83 D, E and F) :

Place each "top of foot" on top of a sole, making sure you have a "pair", and stab stitch all round A–B–C. Push a very little stuffing into the toe end of each, spreading it evenly. Gently insert the bound foot wire (you will now see why it was important to keep it slim), easing the foot into place. With a cocktail stick add a little more stuffing so that the wire is completely embedded. Remember that the figure has to stand eventually, so aim at keeping the base of the foot as flat as possible. Pull the leg piece down to meet the foot and ladder stitch all round, joining them firmly together. Stab stitch to indicate toes as shown by broken lines on pattern. Lastly stuff each leg firmly, avoiding ungainly "knobs" and lumps, and making sure the wire is completely embedded. Gather round top of felt leg, pull up and stitch to rag binding (fig. 83 G).

Head (fig. 83 H, I and J):

On the wrong side join the two back pieces together round the *curved* edge B–C; this will be the centre back seam. Place on one side.

On the front of head piece join the dart X–Y–X and the other six darts simi-larly. Now, still on the wrong side, join the front to the back pieces, matching B's at top and stitching down to A on one side and X on the other. Turn right side out. Stuff firmly, shaping into a neat oval and pushing out the chin firmly as you work. Ease head on to wire frame, pushing well on. Now ladder stitch under chin A–O–X (see fig. 83 H and I). Place the "front of body" piece on frame, well up under the chin so that no gap shows here. Cross the ends at centre back and stitch this piece firmly in place, hemming neatly all round (fig. 83 G and J).

The figure is now complete and ready for the exciting part of adding features and dressing up.

YOUNG SHEPHERD
Pattern pages 222, 286.   Illustration on Frontispiece

Materials :

A completed basic figure made with flesh pink felt face, hands and feet (page 216).

A piece of drab brown woollen material $9\frac{1}{2}$ in. × 15 in. for tunic.

A piece of unbleached calico 9 in. square for head wrap.

A piece of bright, finely striped material 11 in. × $19\frac{1}{2}$ in. for outer garment.

Scraps of brown suède and chamois leather for sandals and belt.

15 in. stout wire for crook.

About $6\frac{1}{2}$ in. fine red cord.

Small quantity "beige" or light brown darning wool ⎫
White, red, black and blue stranded cotton ⎬for features.

Method :

Features (figs. 83 K, L, M and N ; and 84) :

Raise the nose following outline shown on diagram, and sink the eye sockets where shown. Using one strand of embroidery cotton work the whites of the eyes, blue pupil and black iris, with a tiny white highlight. Sew on lids. Embroider mouth and nostrils in red, moustache and eyebrows in beige wool. Embroider the beard in long straight stitches and sew on the ears with tiny hemming stitches.

Sandals :

Make up a pair of rustic sandals (pattern and instructions pages 46, 49) using brown suède for the soles and straps and chamois leather for the linings. Slip these on to the feet and tie round legs. Now adjust the figure for firm standing, bending the knees and bending the head forward so that he is looking down at the Baby.

Tunic (fig. 85) :

Cut a slit 2 in. long in the centre of the brown material, running widthwise ; this is for the neck. Turn in and herringbone, or face, this slit. Fold the material in half widthwise so that A's match and B's match. Join side seams A–C and B–D. Turn a narrow hem all round armholes and base of tunic. Put on to shepherd and tie a narrow strip of brown suède round waist to draw it in.

Outer Garment (fig. 86) :

Cut this piece with the stripes running lengthwise. Cut a slit up centre front

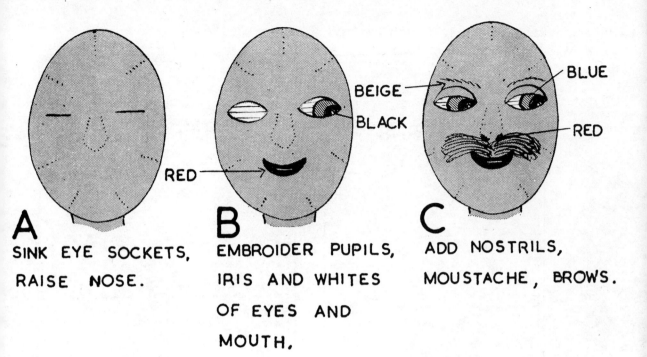

A SINK EYE SOCKETS, RAISE NOSE.

B EMBROIDER PUPILS, IRIS AND WHITES OF EYES AND MOUTH.

BEIGE

BLACK

RED

C ADD NOSTRILS, MOUSTACHE, BROWS.

BLUE

RED

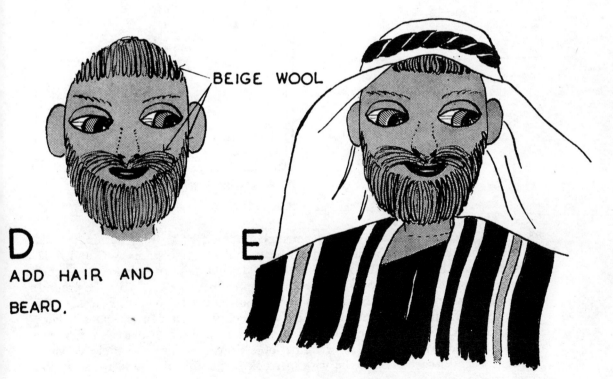

D ADD HAIR AND BEARD.

BEIGE WOOL

E

Fig. 84. *Construction of young shepherd's features—shown actual size*

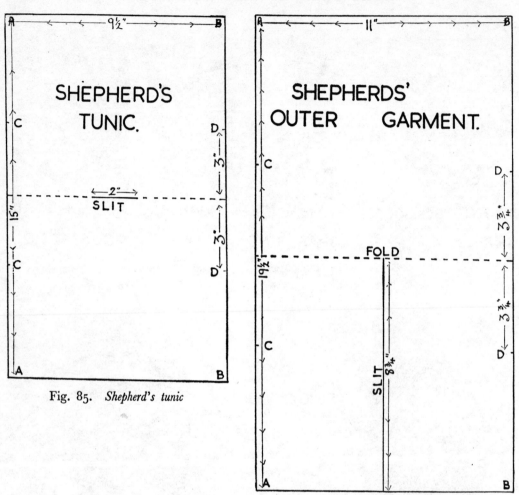

Fig. 85. *Shepherd's tunic*

Fig. 86. *Shepherd's outer garment*

$8\frac{3}{4}$ in. long, i.e. halfway, and face or herringbone this for the front opening. Fold the piece in half so that A's meet and B's meet, and join side seams A–C and B–D. Turn a narrow hem back all round armholes. Try garment on shepherd and turn up hem all round base so that the garment is approximately $1\frac{1}{2}$ in. from the ground. Place on figure and adjust the arms to a natural angle, the left one ready to hold the crook. Make both outer garment and tunic (which is much shorter) hang in loose natural folds, tacking here and there where necessary to keep in place. Make sure the bare bound arm does not show inside loose sleeves, tacking the tunic sleeve to the arm where needed. Bend the wire to crook shape, fold the hand round it and stitch in place.

Head Wrap :

Neatly hem the 9 in. square of unbleached calico. Fold it in half cornerwise and place over head, as shown in fig. 84 E, stitch in place. Tie a narrow red cord round head and stitch this in place.

Now " play " with your shepherd, making final adjustments to his attitude, and making quite sure he stands very firmly.

OLD SHEPHERD
Pattern pages 222, 286. Illustration on Frontispiece

Materials :

A completed basic figure made with light beige or flesh pink face, hands and feet (page 216).

A piece of grey woollen material 9½ in. × 15 in. for tunic.

A piece of tan cotton material 9 in. square for head wrap.

A piece of finely striped material (11 in. × 19½ in.) in a different colour from the young shepherd, for the outer garment.

Scraps of brown suède and chamois leather for sandals and belt.

15 in. stout wire for crook.

About 6½ in. fine yellow cord.

Brown, white and red stranded cotton.

A few inches of white crêpe hair.

Method :

Features (figs. 83 K, L, M and N ; and 87) :

Raise the nose, following outline shown on diagram, and sink the eye sockets where shown. Using one strand of embroidery cotton, work whites of eyes, then brown eyes and white highlights. Embroider mouth and nostrils in red. Sew on lids. Cut a short length of crêpe hair, fluff out and sew to top and sides of head where it will protrude from head wrap. Take another length and sew to chin and face for beard. Sew a very fine piece along upper lip for moustache and smooth this down to mingle with beard. Sew two tiny wisps above eyes for brows, making your stitches as invisible as possible. No ears are necessary.

Make up sandals, tunic, outer garment and head wrap exactly as for young shepherd (pages 220-2). Put the crook in the right hand this time and have the old shepherd standing at quite a different angle. The left hand can be outstretched sideways, as though he is telling the younger man to look at the Baby.

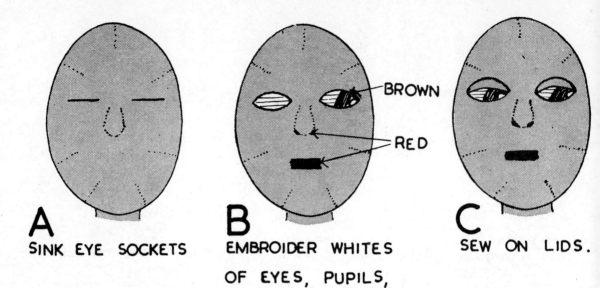

A SINK EYE SOCKETS

B EMBROIDER WHITES OF EYES, PUPILS, NOSTRILS AND MOUTH.

BROWN

RED

C SEW ON LIDS.

WHITE CREPE HAIR

D ADD BEARD, BROWS AND HAIR.

E

Fig. 87. *Construction of old shepherd's features—shown actual size*

FIRST KING
Pattern pages 227, 286.   Illustration on Frontispiece

The first king has an oriental appearance, with a yellow skin.   He is dressed in vivid purple and emerald green, decorated with matching sequins.

Materials :

A completed basic figure made with creamy yellow felt face, hands and feet (page 216).

A piece of purple satin 13 in. × 22 in. for the robe.

Two pieces of emerald green satin 13 in. × 7 in. for the train.

½ yd. 1¼ in. wide braid in matching colours for cuffs, collar and trimming.

Mauve, blue and green sequins⎫
Tiny crystal and green beads ⎬for trimming.
Pearls ⎭

Scrap of silver lamé for crown and gift.

Black, white and red stranded cotton for features.

2-ply black wool for hair, moustache and brows.

Method :

Features (figs. 83 K, L, M and N ; and 88) :

Raise nose, following outline shown on diagram, and sink the eye sockets where shown.   Using one strand of white embroidery cotton embroider whites of eyes, and using red, nostrils and mouth.   Work pupils in black.   Sew on lids—one above and one below each eye—taking care to place these carefully and sew very neatly.   Embroider brows and moustache in fine black wool.   Using about twenty-four strands of wool, plait to make a pigtail 6 in. long and bind each end with matching wool to secure.   Sew to back of head.   Cover this end of pigtail with long, straight stitches in black wool, continuing up as far as the crown will eventually reach.   Sew on ears, just in front of hair.

Mules (Pattern and instructions pages 46, 48) :

Make these using a strong emerald green cotton material.   (Sailcloth was used for the original.)   Decorate with purple sequins and green beads.   Put on to king, adjust for firm standing and stitch heels and toes invisibly to soles.

Robe (fig. 89) :

Fold the piece of purple satin in half widthwise, and measuring 3 in. down from the fold cut 3 in. inwards, then straight down to the bottom corner on each side, curving round under the arms.   Stitch these side seams A–B and C–D.   Turn back a narrow hem all round sleeve edges.   Cut a very small slit at centre of top fold, just large enough to go over head.   Try robe on doll and pin up a hem all round bottom edge.   This can either be straight or can be longer at back to give the effect of a small train.   In any case, the front hem should just clear the feet so that the mules

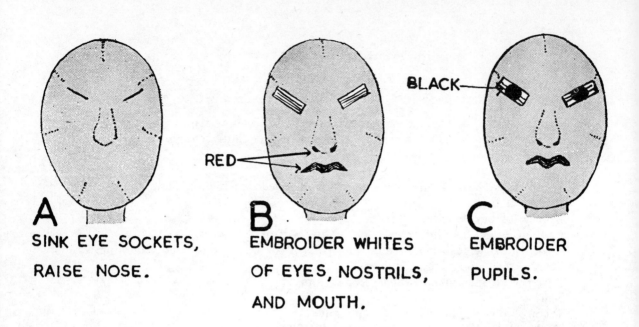

A SINK EYE SOCKETS, RAISE NOSE.

B EMBROIDER WHITES OF EYES, NOSTRILS, AND MOUTH.

RED

C EMBROIDER PUPILS.

BLACK

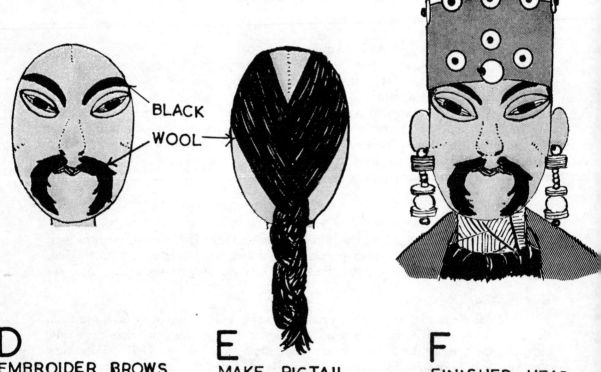

BLACK

WOOL

D EMBROIDER BROWS AND MOUSTACHE, SEW ON LIDS.

E MAKE PIGTAIL, EMBROIDER HAIR.

F FINISHED HEAD.

Fig. 88. *Construction of first King's features—shown actual size*

will eventually show. Remove robe, stitch hem and decorate all round with sequins and beads, making it very rich. Edge the cuffs with $1\frac{1}{4}$ in. wide braid; reserve sufficient braid to go tightly round neck, and if you have any remaining stitch to base of centre of robe running upwards from the hem. Edge this with beads and sequins to match the border. Place the robe on doll; run a gathering thread round neck, turning in a tiny hem as you work; pull up gathers and stitch snugly to neck. Fold the piece of braid reserved for the purpose in half, stretch tightly round neck, stitching at centre back. Fold arms forwards, so that the hands almost meet at centre front ready to hold the gift of frankincense.

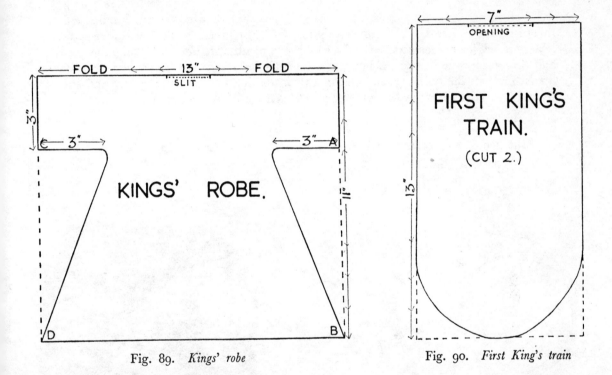

Fig. 89. *Kings' robe*   Fig. 90. *First King's train*

Train (fig. 90) :

Place the two pieces together and round off the corners at one end to make a shaped train at back. Stitch together all round except for a short section at the top end. Turn right side out and slip stitch opening. Press very carefully. Place on king, stitching front corners to front of robe, low down, just in crook of elbows. Stitch a $3\frac{1}{4}$ in. " string " of blue sequins across front, from corner to corner of cloak, to give the appearance of a chain. Sew a large pearl over these stitches, on each corner, to simulate a jewelled clasp.

Crown (fig. 88 F) :

Cut two strips of postcard 4¾ in. × 1 in. Tack a piece of silver lamé over each of these, folding edges at back as shown for the pentagon patches (fig. 24 E). Place the two pieces of covered card together, wrong sides inside, and oversew together all round outside edges. Remove tacking threads. Curl the crown round into a ring, joining short ends. Sew green sequins with a small pearl in the centre of each all round top edge, and decorate the front with one large pearl and three or five purple sequins with a small pearl in the centre. Place crown squarely on head and stitch firmly in place.

Earrings :

Following fig. 88 F, work as follows. With a fine needle and double Sylko, thread up a tiny pearl, eight purple sequins, four tiny green beads, four blue sequins, a large pearl, four green sequins and a tiny green bead in that order. Take the needle and thread *over* the last green bead and insert it back into the first blue sequin and up through all the holes again, coming out at the first pearl. Pull tightly and stitch securely to lobe of ear. Make the second earring in the same way.

Ring :

Stitch a purple sequin with a medium sized pearl to the thumb of right hand to make a ring (fig. 91 C).

His Gift (fig. 91 A, B and C) :

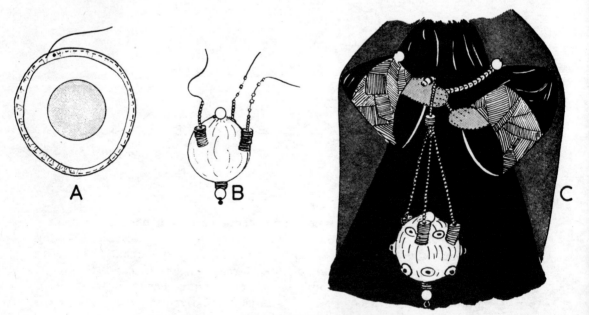

Fig. 91. *Construction of first King's gift*

Make a small hard ball about 1¼ in. diameter by rolling cotton wool in the palm of your hand, or better still, because the weight makes the gift hang better, buy a small wooden ball or large marble. Cover this with silver lamé by cutting a larger circle and gathering this up round outside edge. Sew a large pearl where gathers meet and have this at top. Thread three sequins of a colour to tone with the king's clothes to base of ball, followed by a large pearl and small bead. Thread three needles with double Sylko or strong cotton and attach these threads evenly at three points round side of ball. On to each thread twenty-four sequins, then 1½ in. of small beads ; now thread the three strings together through ten sequins and 1½ in. of beads. Fasten off the ends. Decorate the ball here and there with sequins with a small bead in the centre to give a " spiked " effect. Drape the end of " handle " over the right hand and across to the palm of the left hand. Stitch firmly in place.

Adjust the king for firm standing. He should stand straight and simply, feet a little apart and head erect.

SECOND KING
Pattern pages 227, 233, 286. Illustration on Frontispiece

The second king has a brown skin, with the thick nose and lips typical of a dark-skinned race. He is dressed in gold satin, with a black velvet cloak.

Materials :

A completed basic figure made with brown felt face, hands and feet (page 216).
A piece of gold satin 13 in. × 22 in. for the robe.
A piece of black velvet and black silk each 15½ in. × 7 in. for the train.
1 yd. ½ in. wide black and gold braid for trimming.
Red and silver sequins.
Red " jewels " (with holes at back).
One large pearl.
Bronze bugle beads.
Bronze oval sequins.
Tiny crystal beads.
Nine ½ in. brass rings for bangles and earrings.
One pipe cleaner for " fur " on crown.
2-ply black wool for hair.
Red, white and black stranded cotton for features.
Two tiny black beads for eyes.
One ½ in. pill box for gift.
Scrap of red satin   ,,   ,,
Scraps of orange felt for sandals.

Method :
Features (figs. 83 K, L, M and N ; and 92) :

Raise nose, noting how broad it is, compared with the other figures, and sink

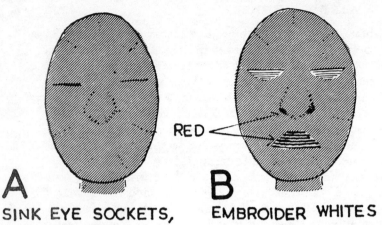

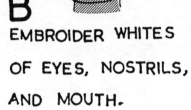

RED

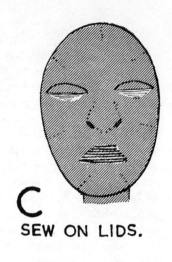

A
SINK EYE SOCKETS,
RAISE NOSE.

B
EMBROIDER WHITES
OF EYES, NOSTRILS,
AND MOUTH.

C
SEW ON LIDS.

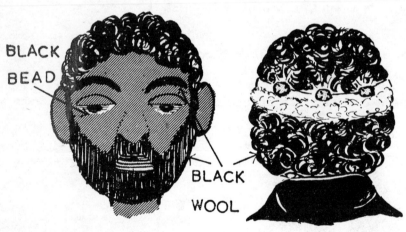

BLACK
BEAD

BLACK
WOOL

D
SEW ON PUPILS.
ADD BROWS, BEARD
AND HAIR.

E
BACK OF HEAD.

F
FINISHED HEAD.

Fig. 92. *Construction of second King's features—shown actual size*

eye sockets. Embroider whites of eyes using one strand of white cotton, and the mouth and nostrils with red. Try to make the mouth thick and slightly protruding. Sew on lids. Sew a tiny black bead just under each lid for an eye—push them, so that they are half underneath. Embroider eyebrows and beard using 2-ply black wool and long straight stitches. Sew on top half of ears, whilst making beard, but leave the bottom half until robe is on, so that the earrings can be inserted. Make the hair by sewing a series of loops of black wool all over the head. Use the wool double and merely keep taking small stitches this way and that, and leaving them loose, until the head is completely covered.

Sandals :

Make up a pair of strip sandals (pattern and instructions on pages 45, 46) using orange felt throughout.

N.B. It is important that the felt used for the straps should be very strong, so use, if possible, a piece of the thick part at selvedge, or use two thicknesses and stab stitch together. Decorate with red sequins and tiny crystal beads. Put on king and stitch to soles of feet. Adjust figure for firm standing.

Robe :

Make this exactly as for the first king, but edge the robe with $\frac{1}{2}$ in. wide black and gold braid. Put on to king and stitch 1 in. of the braid across top of centre front (fig. 92 F) where it will show between front edges of cloak. Gather round edges of sleeves, pull up to fit arm at " $\frac{3}{4}$ length " (fig. 93 D) and stitch to arm. Stitch a piece of braid tightly round these edges for a cuff, with the joins underneath arm where they will not show. Stitch a " string " of red sequins round the remaining piece of braid and stitch round waist to draw in the robe and make a jewelled belt. Bend arms forwards ready to hold the gift at about waist level.

Jewellery (figs. 92 F and 93 D) :

Ease three brass rings on to one arm and four on to the other for bangles, and sew a red " jewel " to the third finger of the right hand for a ring. Finish sewing on ears with a brass ring tucked into each about halfway up.

Crown (fig. 92 E and F) :

Stitch a narrow piece of white tape or ribbon round the king's head—rather low down on the brow, then stitch a series of red " jewels " round this, making a little " pile " of them at the front with one crystal " jewel " at top of pile if available. Add one or two tiny crystal beads round crown if " jewels " are scarce ! Stitch a piece of pipe cleaner all round base of tape for a fur edging.

Train (fig. 94) :

Take the piece of black velvet and the silk and shape them as shown by fig. 94. Make just as for first king's cloak, but, when putting on to figure, place the ends only *just* over the shoulders, at a point about $\frac{3}{4}$ in. below the piece of braid. Stitch in place.   Attach a 2 in. long string of red sequins, one end to each corner, for a " chain fastening ".

His Gift (fig. 93) :

Take the pill box and place it on a circle of red satin cut large enough to cover it.   Run a gathering thread round outer edge, turning in a narrow hem as you work. Pull up gathers and fasten off at centre top of box.   Stitch a large **pearl,** with a sequin and tiny crystal bead on top of it, to the centre for a " knob ".   Decorate the box with oval bronze sequins, round silver sequins with a tiny bead in the centre of each and bugle beads if available.   Stitch to king's hands.

Finally adjust position of king.   This one should stand with knees slightly bent and body bending forward from the waist as if he is about to kneel and offer his gift.

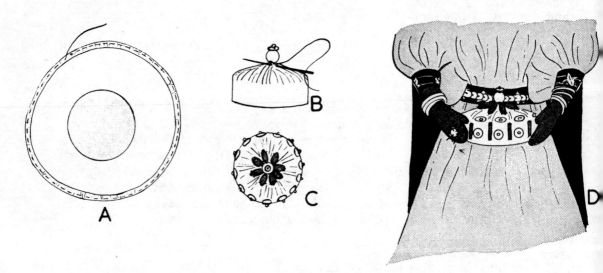

Fig. 93.   *Construction of second King's gift*

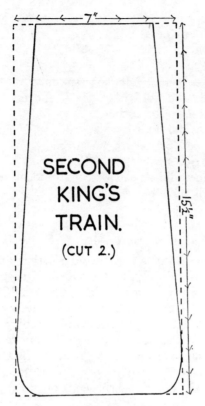

Fig. 94. *Second King's train*

THIRD KING

Pattern pages 227, 286. Illustration on Frontispiece

This king has a " white " skin, with beard and hair made of tow. This may be bought from an ironmonger, or a plumber will often supply the small handful which is needed. He is dressed in old rose taffeta, with a ruby velvet cloak lined with magenta silk.

Materials :

A completed basic figure made with flesh pink face, hands and feet (page 216).
A piece of old rose taffeta 13 in. × 22 in. for the robe.
  ,, ,, ,, fancy rose/white striped silk 11 in. × 3½ in. for front panel of robe (this is optional).
A piece of ruby velvet, 16½ in. × 7 in., for the train.
  ,, ,, ,, magenta silk ,,   ,,   ,, ,, ,,
Pink, gold and green sequins.

Tiny crystal beads.

One oval wooden bead painted gold.

Two large white beads.

Some crystal "jewels".

$\frac{1}{2}$ yd. white/gold braid, $\frac{1}{4}$ in. wide, for trimming.

Scraps of magenta silk and gold lamé for headdress, sandals and casket.

One small-sized match-box for casket.

A small handful of tow for hair and beard.

Red and brown stranded cotton for features.

Two tiny black beads for features.

Short length of gold metallic thread or cord (chocolates are sometimes tied up with a thread which may be used).

Method :

Features (figs. 83 K, L, M and N ; and 95) :

Raise nose and sink eye sockets. Embroider lashes and brows in light brown stranded cotton using one strand only, and mouth and nostrils in red. Sew on lids. Sew tiny black beads in place for eyes, tucking them half under the lids to give a mystic " eastern " expression. Sew on ears. Make the beard by taking small wisps of tow, doubling them in half like a hairpin and stitching the looped ends to face very neatly with matching Sylko. Continue in this way round back of head for the hair, sewing the tow sufficiently high on the head so that the headdress will cover stitching. Sew one wisp across top of upper lip for moustache and smooth ends downwards to mingle with the beard. Trim ends of tow to a good shape with sharp scissors.

Sandals :

Make up a pair of oriental sandals (pattern and instructions on pages 49, 50) using magenta silk for the upper sole, with matching stranded cotton for the straps and fawn felt for the lower sole. Stitch heel of foot to sole. Now bend the figure so that it is kneeling on the left knee.

Robe :

Make this exactly as for the first king, but to add variety stitch the piece of striped silk all down centre front to make a " panel ". Cover these stitches by sewing a " string " of pink sequins down each side where striped silk and taffeta join. Decorate the bottom two inches of this panel by sewing on four or five rows of pink sequins, with a crystal bead in the centre of each. Edge taffeta part of tunic with narrow white/gold braid. Put on to figure and pull up gathers round neck ; stitch in place. (These stitches will be covered by beard and hair and no trimming will be needed to disguise them.) Pull up gathers to fit wrists and stitch a string of sequins round each arm to cover stitches and form a jewelled cuff. Arrange the front of robe so that the king's right foot is partly showing and stitch hem to foot in this position. Bend arms forward ready to hold casket.

A SINK EYE SOCKETS RAISE NOSE

B EMBROIDER BROWS, LASHES, NOSTRILS AND MOUTH.

LIGHT BROWN

RED

C ADD BEARD, LIDS EYES AND EARS.

BLACK BEAD

TOW

D ADD MOUSTACHE.

E BACK OF HEAD.

F FINISHED HEAD.

Fig. 95. *Construction of third King's features—shown actual size*

Train (fig. 90) :

This time the two pieces are used straight with no shaping at the end. Make up just as for the first king (but realize the measurement is different). Place round king's shoulders and stitch in place to front of robe. Sew a piece of gold cord across front, from corner to corner, for a fastening, making a small loop in each end and covering the stitches with a gold sequin and tiny crystal bead. Arrange "train" so that it sweeps round to one side and the end shows from the front. Stitch here and there to hem of robe at one side, to keep in this position.

Jewellery :

Following fig. 95, make up each earring by threading on to double Sylko a fancy gold bead (or part of the clasp of a broken necklace), a large white bead, six green sequins, six tiny crystal beads, two green sequins and one tiny crystal bead. Take the needle and thread *over* the last bead and back up through all the others again, emerging at the first gold bead ; stitch to ear lobes. Stitch a "jewel" to third finger of left hand for a ring.

Headdress (fig. 95 F) :

Cut a circle of magenta silk the size of a teacup. Run a gathering thread all round outer edge, pull up gathers to fit head, and, stuffing with a little piece of cotton wool to keep it in shape, stitch firmly to head. Stitch a piece of narrow white/gold braid tightly round head to cover edge of silk, with the join at centre back and stitch a narrow gold cord round top edge of this braid. Decorate the headdress with crystal "jewels".

His Gift (fig. 96) :

Fig. 96. *Construction of third King's gift*

Using a " half-size " match-box or rectangular block of wood, make a casket. Stand the box on a suitable-sized piece of gold lamé, and fold " envelope " corners underneath so as to cover it. Stitch the flaps in place. Sew an oval wooden bead, painted gold, to top of casket for a handle and decorate with gold sequins with a tiny crystal bead in the centre of each. Place casket between the hands, bending these to a natural-looking attitude, and stitch in place.

JOSEPH
Pattern pages 239, 286. Illustration on Frontispiece

Joseph is made just like the other figures, but is very simply dressed in a plain " drab " coloured garment.

Materials :

A completed basic figure made with flesh pink face, hands and feet (page 216).
A piece of natural coloured crash or scrim 11½ in. × 21 in. for the main part of garment.
A piece of natural coloured crash or scrim 13 in. × 4½ in. for the cowl.
Scraps of brilliant yellow material (or gold lamé) for the halo.
A few inches of brown crêpe hair for beard and hair.
Brown stranded cotton for lashes.
Scraps of brown suède and chamois leather for sandals.
A straight twig 10 in. long for his staff.
16 in. rough string for his girdle.

Method :
Features (figs. 83 K, L, M and N ; and 97) :

Raise nose and sink eye sockets. Embroider lashes with one strand of brown cotton. Sew on lids. Unravel and fluff out the crêpe hair and sew short lengths round face for beard. Sew a length across top lip for moustache and mingle these ends with the beard. Sew more to head for hair, working as with the wool for the doll's hair on page 76. Leave the forehead bare to give the impression of a receding hair line. Sew on two tiny pieces for brows. Bend the head forward in a meek, submissive attitude.

Sandals :

Make up a pair of rustic sandals (pattern and diagram page 49) using brown suède for the soles and straps and chamois leather for the " linings ". Tie on to figure and adjust for firm standing.

His Garment (fig. 98) :

Fold the larger piece of linen crash in half widthwise and measuring 3 in. down from the fold on each side cut 2¼ in. inwards and 7½ in. downwards on each side to

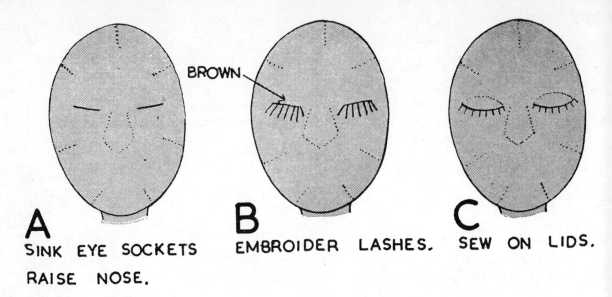

A SINK EYE SOCKETS RAISE NOSE.

B EMBROIDER LASHES.

BROWN

C SEW ON LIDS.

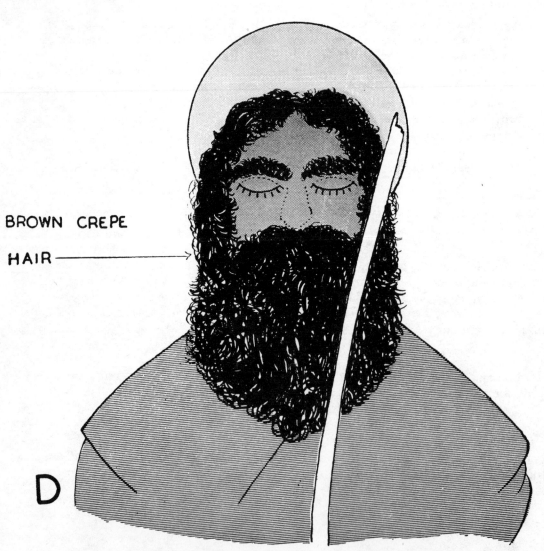

BROWN CREPE HAIR

D

Fig. 97. *Construction of Joseph's features—shown actual size*

make the sleeves, curving round under the arms. Stitch sleeve and side seams A–B–C and turn back a narrow hem round edges of sleeves. Turn right side out and cut a short slit at front of garment only just large enough for the head to go through. Try on and pin up hem so that it shows the feet as far as the ankles. Remove garment and stitch hem. Place garment permanently on to the figure and stitch all round neck, tucking in the raw edge as you work. Close front opening, where it will be hidden by the beard. Tie the string loosely round waist with the ends hanging down one side for a girdle. Make a knot about 1 in. from each end and fray this inch out to look like a tassel.

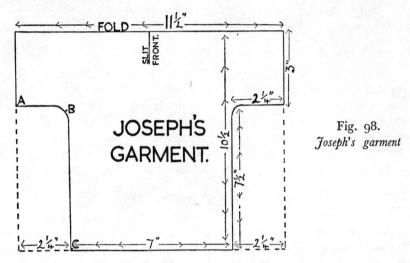

Fig. 98.
Joseph's garment

His Cowl :

Fold the smaller piece of crash in half lengthways and stitch across one end and down the long side. Turn right side out and close the other short end. Place round Joseph's shoulders, crossing at centre front and hanging down the back to form a cowl. Stitch in place at front and attach lower part of cowl to waist at centre back, just above girdle.

Halo :

With a compass draw and cut out two circles of cardboard of 2 in. diameter. Cover these with bright yellow cotton material as shown by fig. 19 A, B and C. Place these together right sides outside and oversew very neatly all round outer edge. Ladder stitch this to Joseph's head, taking care to find the best position for your own particular figure.

Final Adjustment :

Bend the arms forward so that the hands touch and stitch the staff between them. Adjust where necessary to achieve a look of bowed reverence, bending the figure from the waist.

MARY
Pattern pages 242, 286–7.   Illustration on Frontispiece

Materials :

The same as for the basic wired figure on page 216, except that only 34½ in.
of wire and two pipe cleaners are needed.
A piece of soft blue cotton material such as poplin, 21 in. × 15 in., for the robe.
A piece of soft white lawn (a handkerchief is ideal) 8 in. square for her veil.
One skein of brown Coton à Broder for the hair.
Brown and red stranded cotton for features.
Two scraps of brilliant yellow material for her halo.

Method (Use the measurements given for wires in fig. 82 F) :

Make up a wired figure exactly as given on page 216, but slightly smaller.   Make
up and add the head and " front of body ".   Make up the hands using the smaller
size (pattern on page 287) and only inserting a pipe cleaner into the thumbs—not
the fingers as these are too slender.   DO NOT MAKE UP FEET AND LEGS
as these would be completely hidden beneath the robes, but bind these parts *very*
thoroughly with the rag as they will have no further covering.   Now bend the figure
at the " knees " and adjust to a natural kneeling position.

Features (figs. 83 K, L, M and N ; and 99) :

Take great care over the face and hair.   Sink the eye sockets and raise nose.
Using one strand of brown embroidery cotton, work the tiny lashes and finely " etched "
brows.   Sew on lids.   Work nostrils and mouth, using one strand of red cotton.   If
necessary, to improve expression, sink the top of bridge of nose a little with one or
two tiny stitches and give the impression of a tiny chin by raising it a little in the
same way as the nose.   Take the skein of Coton à Broder, and removing the paper
band, cut through *one* end.   Open out flat and lay across front part of head.   Back
stitch in place down a " centre parting " with flesh pink Sylko.   Comb hair smoothly
downwards and slightly forwards and catch invisibly at lower part of face each side,
using matching brown Sylko.   Bring each end forwards over the shoulders and with
sharp scissors taper to a point at each end, so that the hair varies in length.

Her Robe (fig. 100) :

Take the blue material and fold in half widthwise, cut to shape shown on fig. 100
to make the sleeves.   Join underarm seams A–B–C and make a narrow hem all round
edge of sleeves and bottom of robe.   Cut a little slit at *back* of top of body only and
slip over the figure's head.   Stitch neatly round neck and down back slit, turning
in the raw edges as you work.   The back slit will be covered by veil.   Bend hands
forwards to a praying attitude at about waist level, and stitch flat together.   Adjust
robe so that Mary is kneeling on it and so that it falls in soft folds from the shoulders.
Tack in place here and there where necessary, particularly at points at base of wide
sleeve edges.

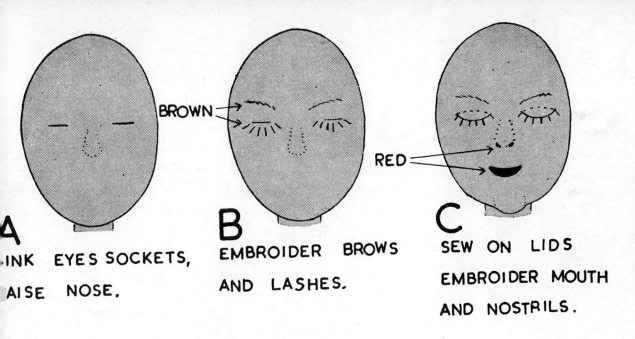

A — INK EYES SOCKETS, RAISE NOSE.

B — EMBROIDER BROWS AND LASHES.

BROWN

C — SEW ON LIDS EMBROIDER MOUTH AND NOSTRILS.

RED

BROWN COTON À BRODER

E

Fig. 99.   *Construction of Mary's features—shown actual size*

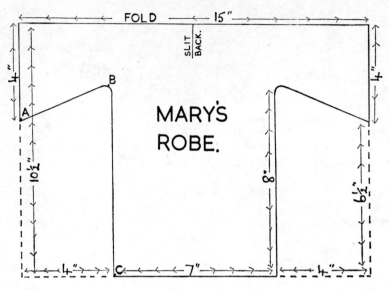

Fig. 100.   *Mary's robe*

Her Veil (fig. 99) :

Take the square of white lawn and make a tiny hem all round the outside edge. Fold in half cornerwise and place on Mary's head, rather far back so that ¾ in. of the centre parting shows.   Arrange this in graceful folds at back, taking time and trouble to get these exactly right for your own particular Mary.   Tack invisibly here and there to keep in place.

Halo :

Cut and make up exactly as given for Joseph (page 239) and stitch to back of Mary's head.

THE MANGER
Illustration on Frontispiece

Materials :

A packet of small lolly sticks (actual size shown, page 243) will be needed. Glue.

Method (fig. 101) :

The manger shown in the photograph was made with " Kenroy " lolly sticks, but if not available a larger size may be used.   Cut odd sizes as shown on fig. 101 with a penknife.   Make two sides like A and two ends like B (criss-crossing thread on B as well as gluing), then add three further pieces to A, so that it looks like C.

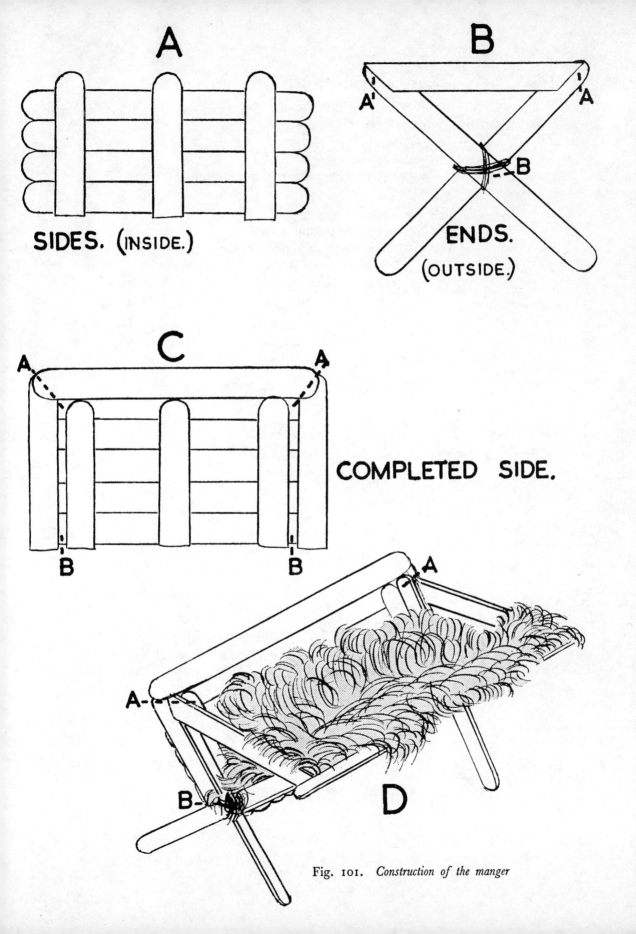

A

SIDES. (INSIDE.)

B

ENDS.
(OUTSIDE.)

C

COMPLETED SIDE.

D

Fig. 101. *Construction of the manger*

Glue ends to completed sides all down A–B—the "edge" of the stick on the ends, fitting into the "groove" on the sides—(A–B).

THE BABY
Pattern page 286.   Illustration on Frontispiece

Materials :

    Scraps of flesh felt for head and body.
      ,,   ,, bright yellow material for the halo.
      ,,   ,, white lawn for the swaddling clothes.
    Red and brown Sylko for features.

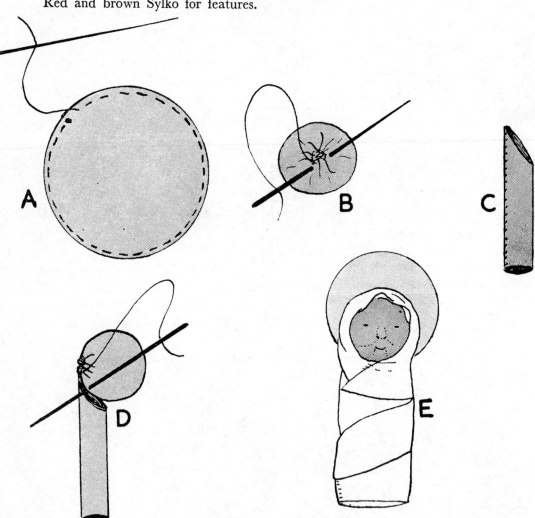

Fig. 102.   *Construction of Baby for the Crib*

Method (fig. 102) :

Cut out the head and body as given.

Run a gathering thread all round outside edge of head ; pull up gathers stuffing the little " knob " firmly. Roll up the body piece, using it lengthwise, so that you have a tight little roll 1½ in. long. Sew down " seam ". Take this roll and cut one end off at an angle (fig. 102 C) so that it will fit on to head. Stitch to back of head.

Features :

With matching flesh-coloured Sylko model a tiny face, sinking eyes and raising a minute nose as shown on page 218. Model tiny cheeks and a chin, raising them in the same way as you have the noses on the large figures. With brown Sylko, make two tiny stitches for eyes, two even smaller ones for nostrils and one for the mouth.

Swaddling Clothes :

Using fine white lawn such as a handkerchief, tear strips about 1 in. wide and completely " bandage " the little figure, only leaving the face exposed, and turning in the raw edges as you work. Bind the body several times to make it look plump and finally fasten end with a few stitches at the back.

Halo :

Make a halo exactly like Joseph's and Mary's but have the circle only one inch in diameter. Stitch to back of the Baby's head.

Place a little " tow " or fine hay in the manger, lay the Baby in it and cover with more " hay ".

A LAMB
Pattern page 287. Illustration on Frontispiece

Materials :

One 9 in. square of white felt for body.
One skein of black stranded cotton for hoofs, eyes and nose.
A handful of kapok for stuffing.

Method :

Cut out the pieces as given and work in stab stitch on the right side throughout, using a small needle and white Sylko in order to achieve a tiny, neat stitch.

Join the two body gussets together C–D on the **wrong side.** Now work through-out on the **right side.** Join 2nd body gusset to 2nd side D–T–S–N–O–P–Q–R–C. Then join 1st body gusset to 1st side C–M–H–I–J–K–L–D. Insert head gusset A–B, joining it to both sides of head, but when you come to F–E slip an ear between gusset and side of head matching the letters, and stitch right through the three thicknesses. Insert under chin gusset, A–G, stitching it to each side of head, then join the two sides together, G–C. Stuff the lamb firmly, pushing tiny pieces of kapok into the legs with an orange stick. Make up the tail by joining the two pieces together all round except for short straight end, and stuffing firmly. Continue stab stitching along back of lamb B–D, inserting tail at D and stitching right through the four thicknesses. Embroider eyes and nose with one strand of cotton following pattern on page 287 for shape ; then, using three thicknesses of black cotton, completely cover the base of each leg with satin stitch, to represent the hoofs.

Consulting frontispiece, turn the lamb's head sideways and ladder stitch it in this position. Bend the shepherd's arm and tuck the lamb underneath it, trying to give it the appearance of being " wriggly " and rather heavy !

These figures are only a beginning, and having grasped the principle you will be able to invent other characters for yourself.

*   *   *

Have you ever been to Nuremberg at Christmas time and seen the golden angels for sale in the Christ Child Market ?

These little wooden dolls were first made three centuries ago by a poor doll maker as a gift for his wife. When their little daughter died just before Christmas, the doll maker's wife was completely grief stricken and she became so ill that no one could cure or comfort her, whilst he himself could not settle to his work for worrying about her.

One day he was whittling absent-mindedly at a piece of wood, when he suddenly found it was turning into the little figure of an angel with the features of his dead daughter. He painted the doll gold and put it beside his wife's bed, so that it would be the first thing she saw on waking. From that moment the poor mother improved and was comforted, while her husband found joy in making other similar dolls for sale, replicas of which still appear on the stalls of the Christkindlsmarkt.

How has YOUR doll turned out? If he or she does not look exactly like the pictures in the book, stop and think for a moment of all the millions of people in the world—no two looking exactly alike, unless they are identical twins. This comes about by the most minute differences in measurements. How easily, then, will your doll vary from the one you are trying to copy, and if this has happened, why worry? It is much more commendable that your doll should have his or her own individual personality than that it should be one of a crowd. So use the diagrams as a basis from which to branch out and create your own characters.

The satisfaction of knowing that YOUR doll is the only one in the whole wide world who looks " just like that " is indeed great, and in this day and age of mass production cannot but give pleasure to those of us who love working with our hands.

*   *   *

Have you ever given serious thought to the quite extraordinary names children sometimes give to their dolls and wondered just how they think of them? One sad and " wobbly " little knitted doll of the author's acquaintance was christened " Meridian Bend " on sight! When her five-year-old " father " was asked why he had made this choice he replied immediately: " Because ' Meridian ' is a straight line through the centre of the earth and she came a long way, but because her neck is wobbly and she can't hold her head up straight, her second name is ' Bend ' " !

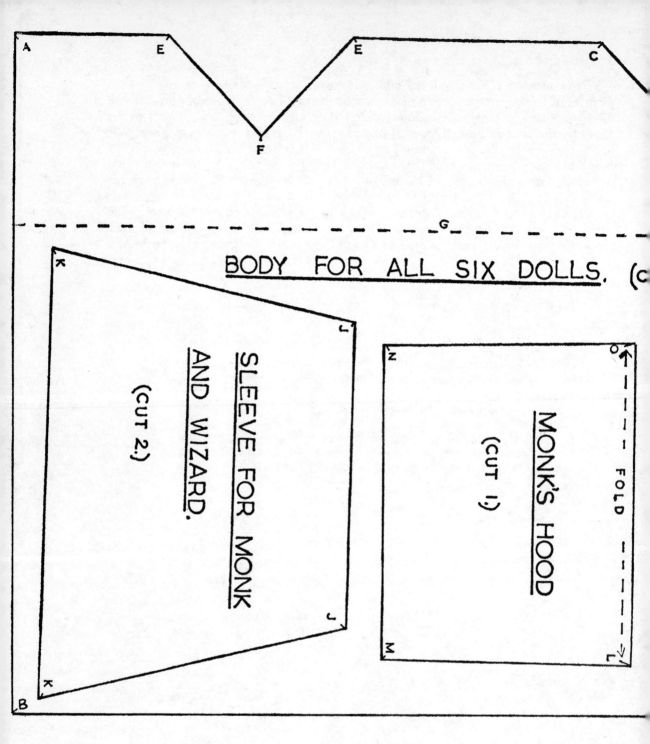

BODY FOR ALL SIX DOLLS. (c

SLEEVE FOR MONK AND WIZARD.

(CUT 2.)

MONK'S HOOD

(CUT 1.)

FOLD

FLAT BASED

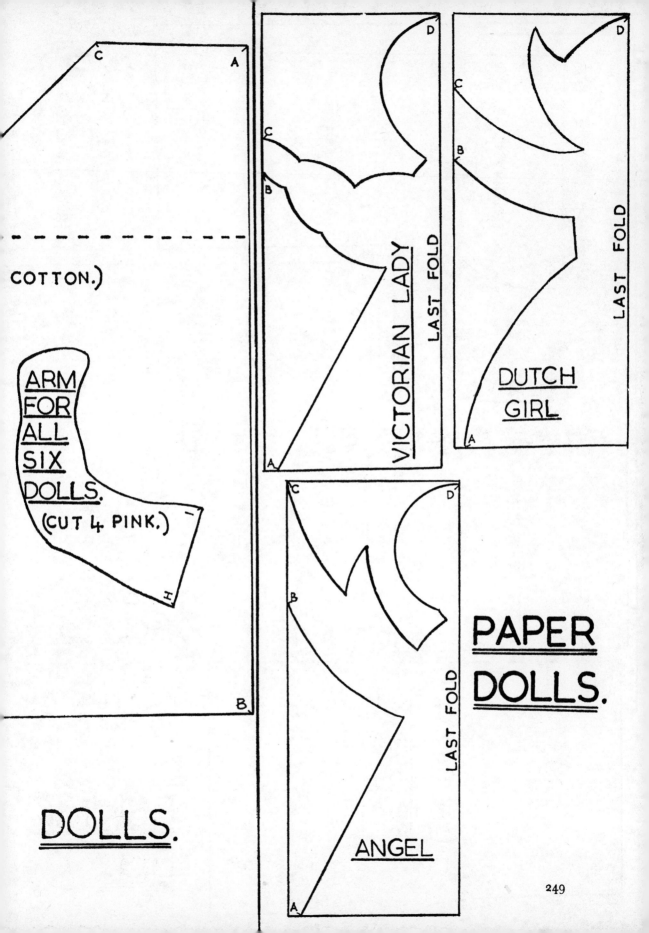

COTTON.)

ARM
FOR
ALL
SIX
DOLLS.
(CUT 4 PINK.)

DOLLS.

VICTORIAN LADY
LAST FOLD

DUTCH
GIRL
LAST FOLD

ANGEL
LAST FOLD

PAPER
DOLLS.

249

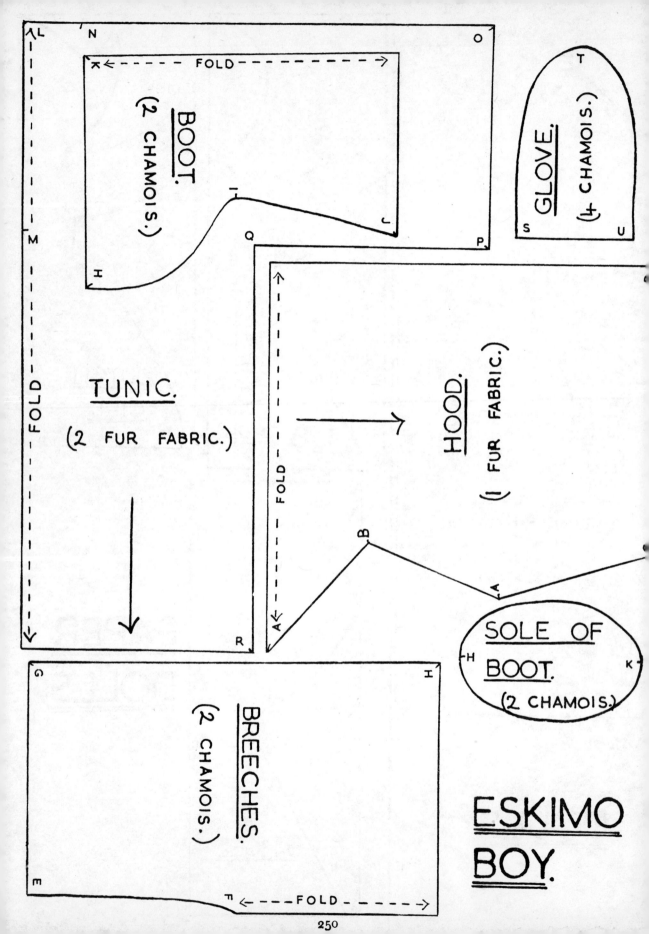

BOOT.
(2 CHAMOIS.)

GLOVE.
(4 CHAMOIS.)

TUNIC.
(2 FUR FABRIC.)

FOLD

HOOD.
(1 FUR FABRIC.)

FOLD

SOLE OF
BOOT.
(2 CHAMOIS.)

BREECHES.
(2 CHAMOIS.)

FOLD

ESKIMO
BOY.

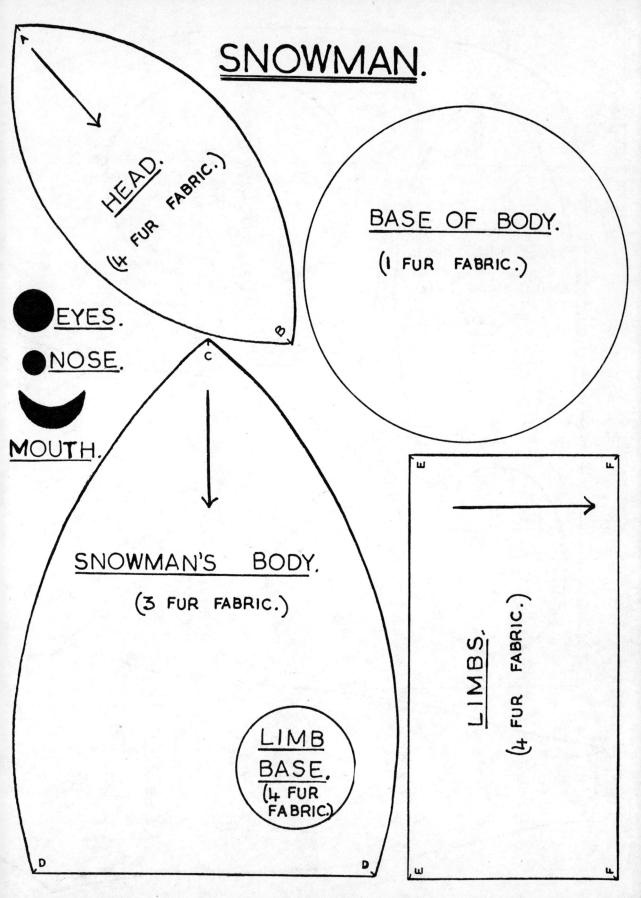

SNOWMAN.

HEAD.
(4 FUR FABRIC.)

BASE OF BODY.
(1 FUR FABRIC.)

EYES.

NOSE.

MOUTH.

SNOWMAN'S BODY.
(3 FUR FABRIC.)

LIMB BASE.
(4 FUR FABRIC.)

LIMBS.
(4 FUR FABRIC.)

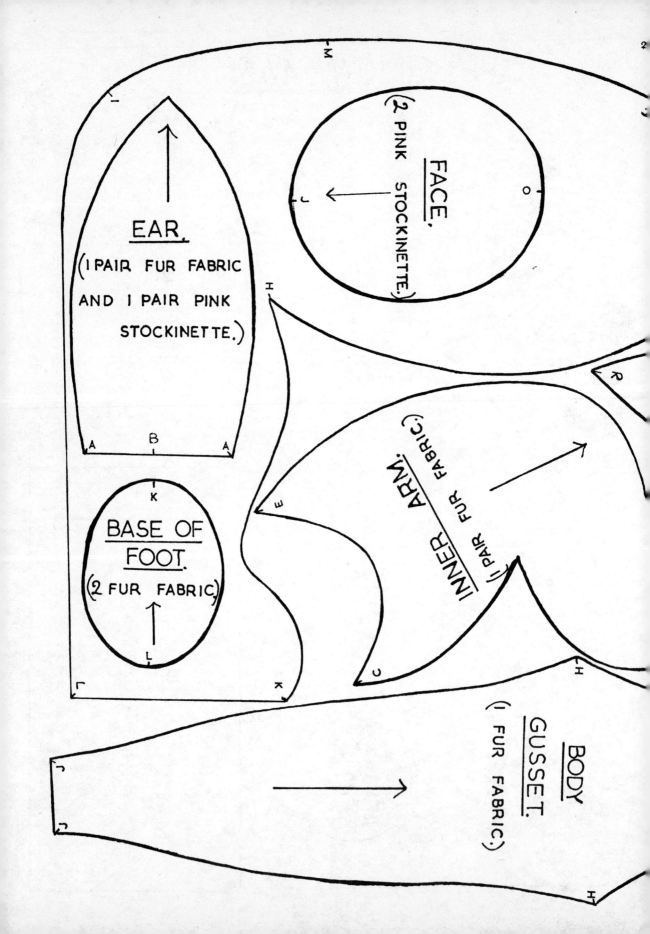

EAR.

(1 PAIR FUR FABRIC AND 1 PAIR PINK STOCKINETTE.)

FACE.

(2 PINK STOCKINETTE.)

BASE OF FOOT.

(2 FUR FABRIC)

INNER ARM.

(1 PAIR FUR FABRIC.)

BODY GUSSET.

(1 FUR FABRIC.)

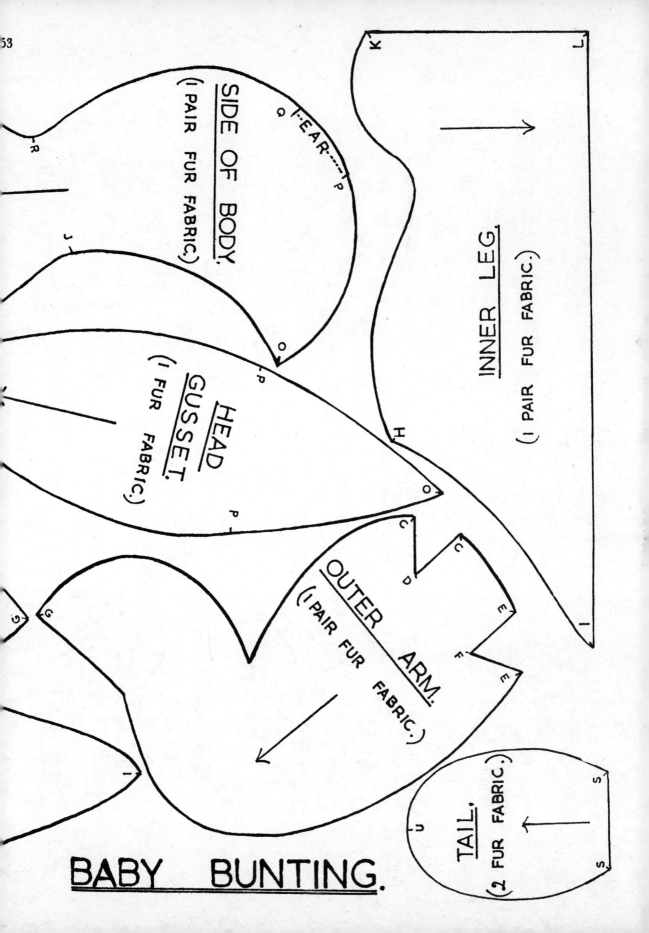

53

SIDE OF BODY.
(1 PAIR FUR FABRIC.)

EAR

INNER LEG.
(1 PAIR FUR FABRIC.)

HEAD GUSSET.
(1 FUR FABRIC.)

OUTER ARM.
(1 PAIR FUR FABRIC.)

TAIL.
(2 FUR FABRIC.)

BABY BUNTING.

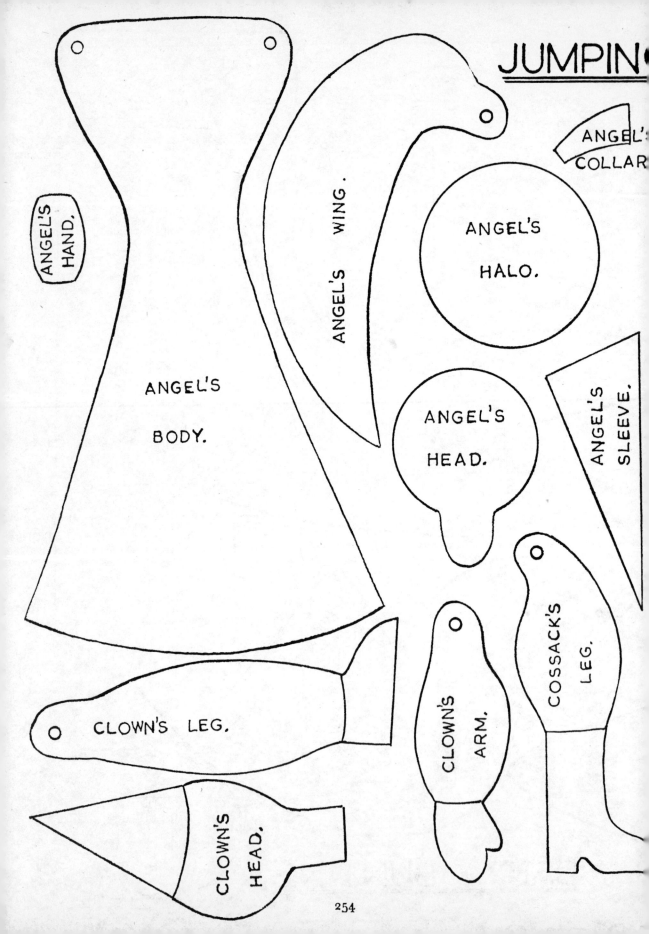

ANGEL'S HAND.

ANGEL'S WING.

ANGEL'S HALO.

JUMPIN

ANGEL'S COLLAR

ANGEL'S BODY.

ANGEL'S HEAD.

ANGEL'S SLEEVE.

CLOWN'S LEG.

CLOWN'S ARM.

COSSACK'S LEG.

CLOWN'S HEAD.

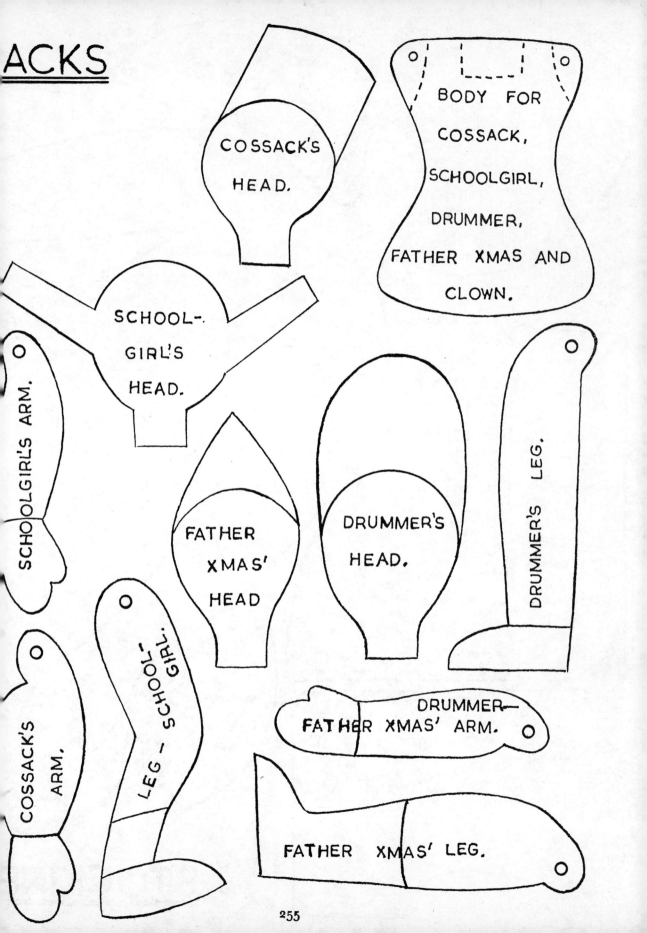

ACKS

COSSACK'S HEAD.

BODY FOR COSSACK, SCHOOLGIRL, DRUMMER, FATHER XMAS AND CLOWN.

SCHOOL-GIRL'S HEAD.

SCHOOLGIRL'S ARM.

FATHER XMAS' HEAD

DRUMMER'S HEAD.

DRUMMER'S LEG.

COSSACK'S ARM.

LEG — SCHOOL-GIRL.

DRUMMER—FATHER XMAS' ARM.

FATHER XMAS' LEG.

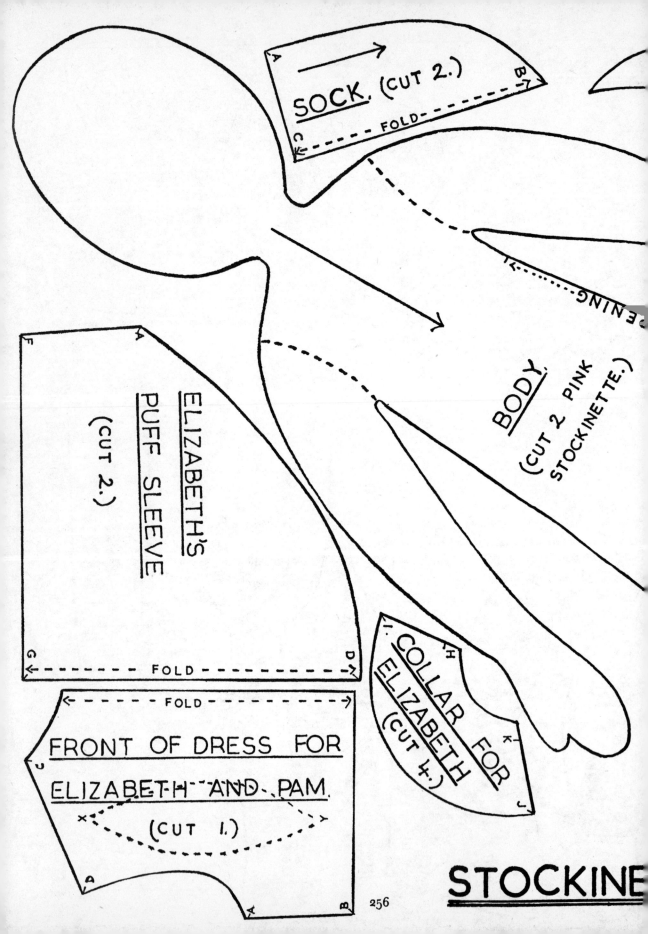

SOCK. (CUT 2.)

FOLD

BODY.
(CUT 2 PINK STOCKINETTE.)

OPENING

ELIZABETH'S
PUFF SLEEVE
(CUT 2.)

FOLD

COLLAR FOR
ELIZABETH
(CUT 4.)

FOLD

FRONT OF DRESS FOR
ELIZABETH AND PAM.
(CUT 1.)

256

STOCKINE

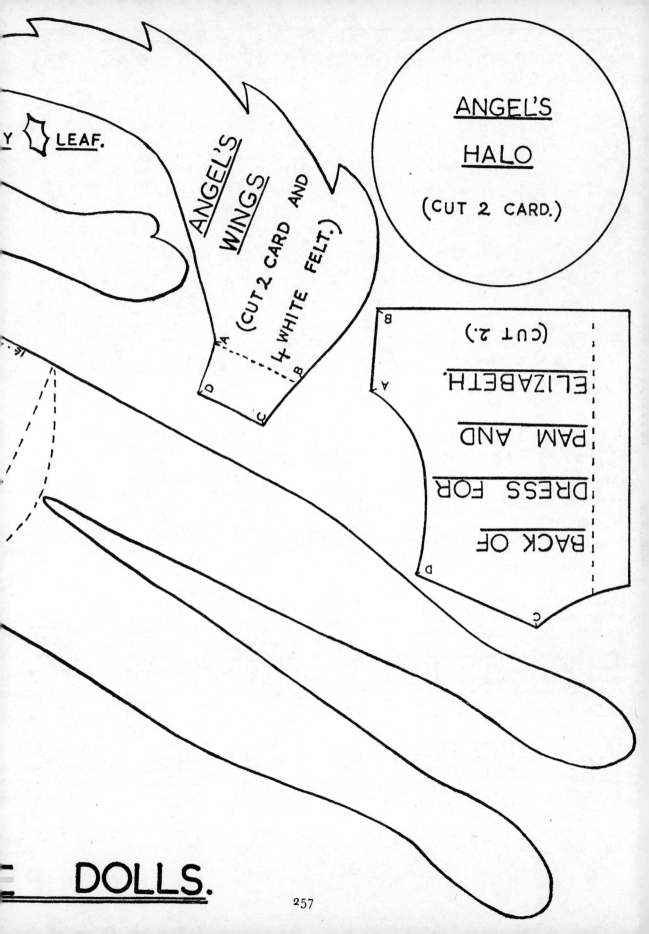

Y <u>LEAF.</u>

<u>ANGEL'S WINGS</u>
(CUT 2 CARD AND 4 WHITE FELT.)

<u>ANGEL'S</u>
<u>HALO</u>
(CUT 2 CARD.)

<u>BACK OF</u>
<u>DRESS FOR</u>
<u>PAM AND</u>
<u>ELIZABETH.</u>
(CUT 2.)

<u>DOLLS.</u>

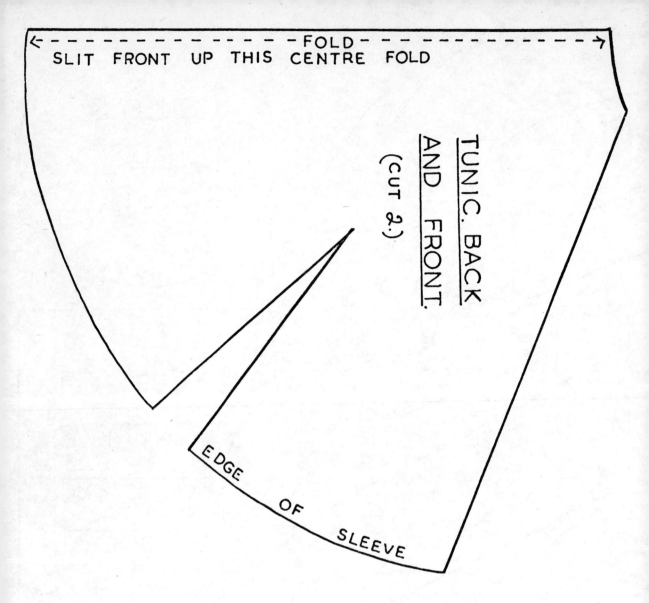

FOLD

SLIT FRONT UP THIS CENTRE FOLD

TUNIC. BACK
AND FRONT.
(CUT 2.)

EDGE OF SLEEVE

SUGGESTED CLOTHES FOR

AN ORIENTAL CHILD.

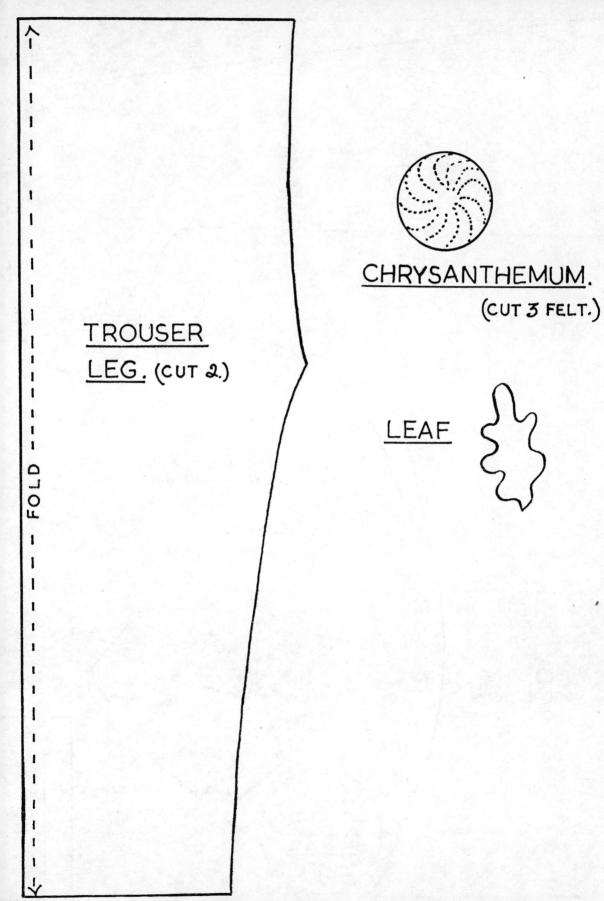

TROUSER
LEG. (CUT 2.)

FOLD

CHRYSANTHEMUM.
(CUT 3 FELT.)

LEAF

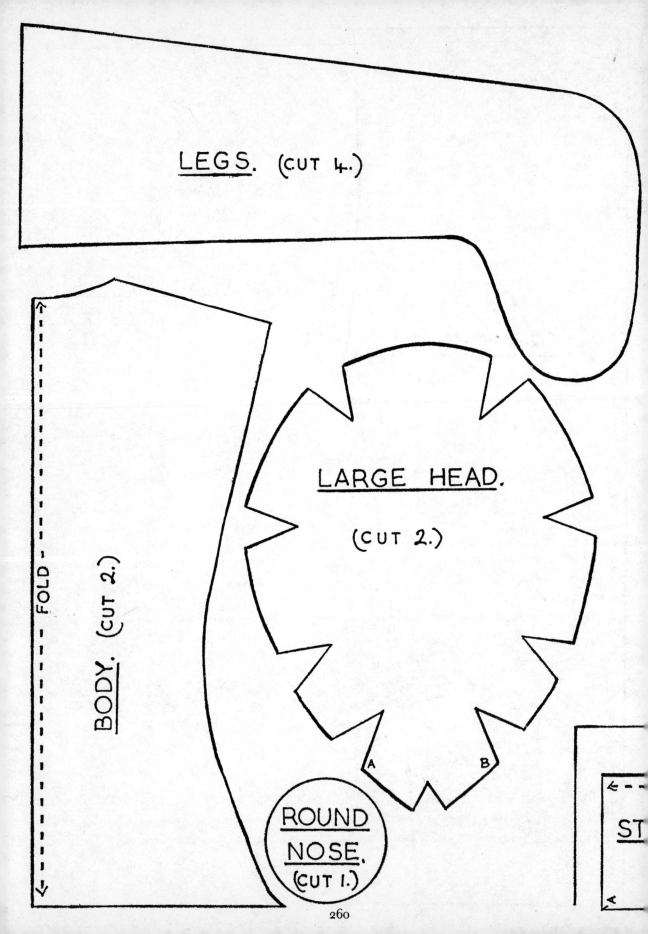

LEGS. (CUT 4.)

FOLD

BODY. (CUT 2.)

LARGE HEAD.

(CUT 2.)

A   B

ROUND
NOSE.
(CUT I.)

ST

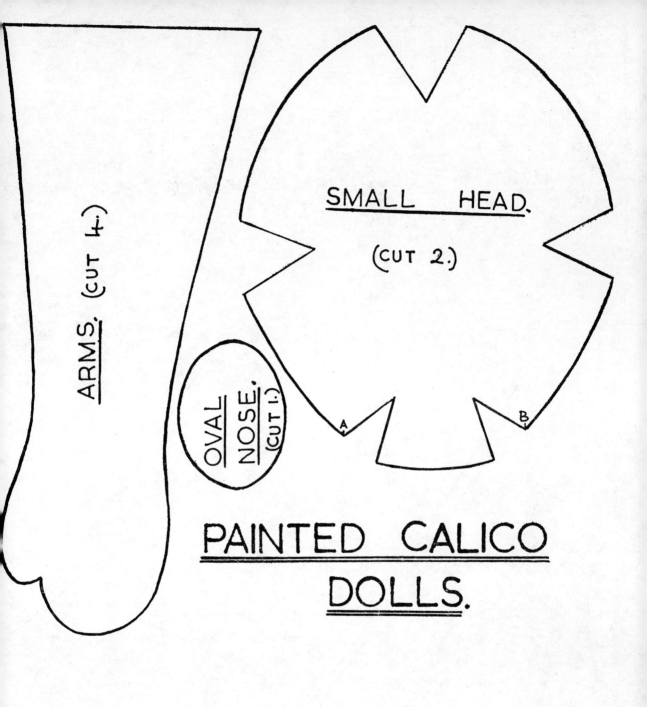

ARMS. (CUT 4.)

SMALL HEAD.

(CUT 2.)

OVAL NOSE. (CUT 1.)

A

B

PAINTED CALICO
DOLLS.

- - - - - - FOLD - - - - - - - - - - - - - - - - - → B

ING FOR TONI AND BERT. (CUT 2.)

BACK OF COAT. (CUT 2 BLACK/WHITE CHECK AND 2

FRONT OF "DICKY" SHIRT. (CUT 2 WHITE FELT.)

FRONT OF WAISTCOAT. (CUT 2 ORANGE FELT.)

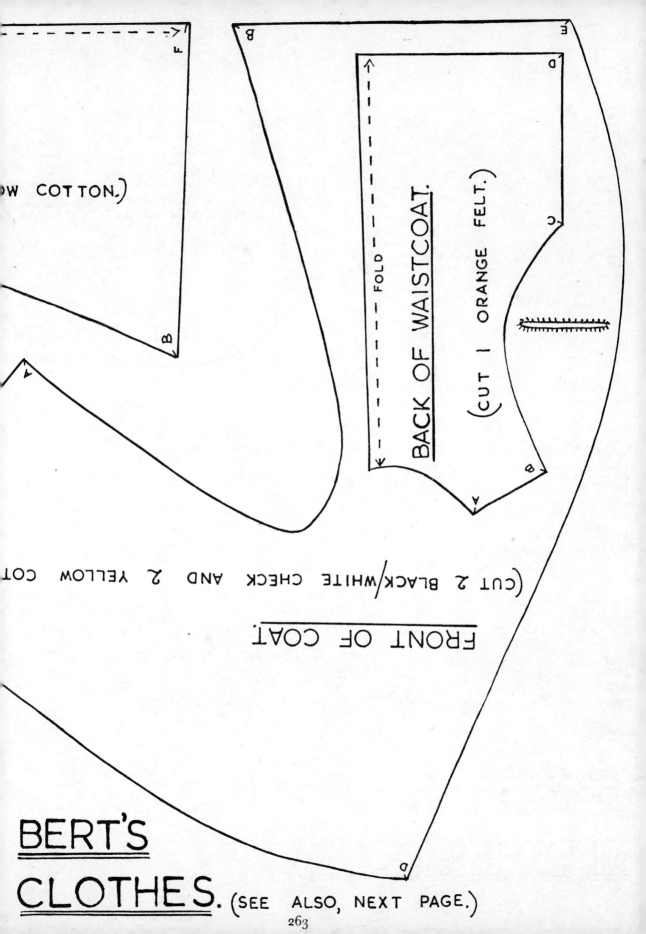

BACK OF WAISTCOAT.

(CUT 1 ORANGE FELT.)

FOLD

ow COTTON.)

(CUT 2 BLACK/WHITE CHECK AND 2 YELLOW COT

FRONT OF COAT

BERT'S
CLOTHES. (SEE ALSO, NEXT PAGE.)

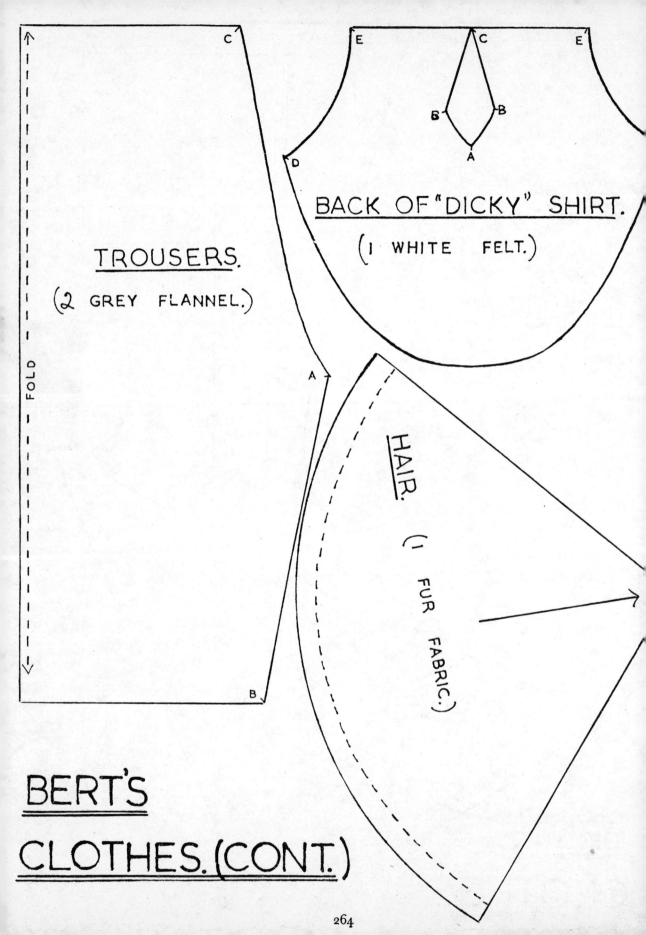

TROUSERS.

(2 GREY FLANNEL.)

FOLD

BACK OF "DICKY" SHIRT.

(I WHITE FELT.)

HAIR. (I FUR FABRIC.)

BERT'S

CLOTHES. (CONT.)

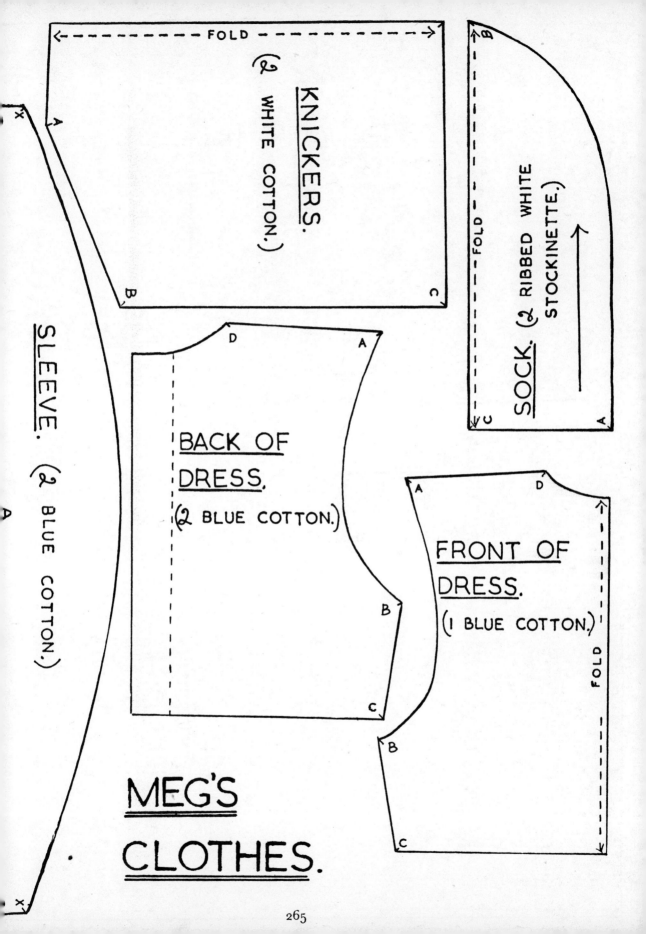

FOLD

KNICKERS.
(2 WHITE COTTON.)

A

B

X

C

SLEEVE. (2 BLUE COTTON.)

X

A

SOCK. (2 RIBBED WHITE STOCKINETTE.)

FOLD

B

C

A

D A

BACK OF DRESS.
(2 BLUE COTTON.)

B

C

A D

FRONT OF DRESS.
(1 BLUE COTTON.)

FOLD

B

C

MEG'S CLOTHES.

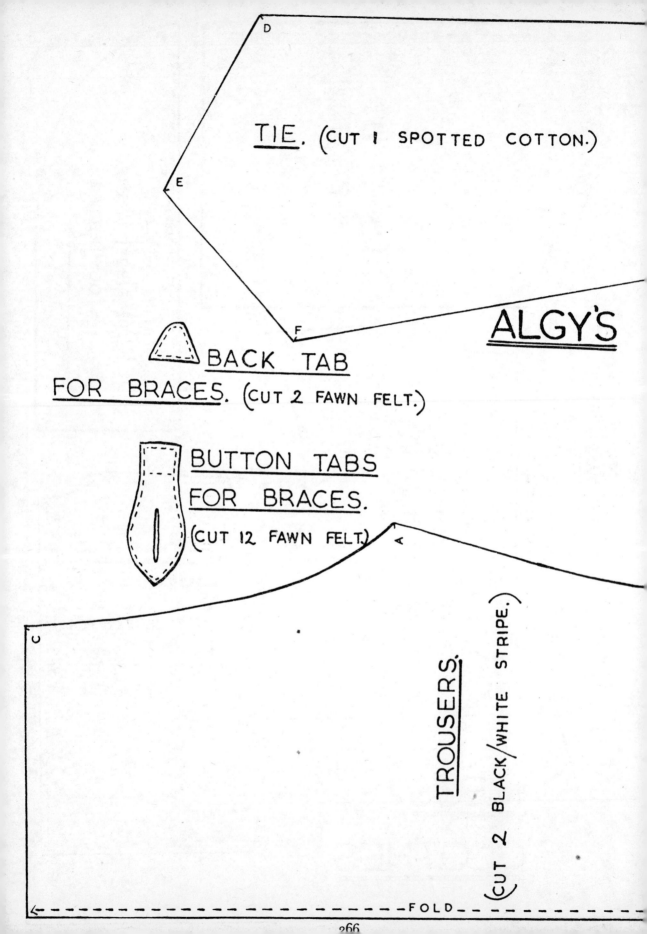

TIE. (CUT 1 SPOTTED COTTON.)

ALGY'S

BACK TAB
FOR BRACES. (CUT 2 FAWN FELT.)

BUTTON TABS
FOR BRACES.
(CUT 12 FAWN FELT.)

TROUSERS.

(CUT 2 BLACK/WHITE STRIPE.)

- - - - - FOLD - - - -

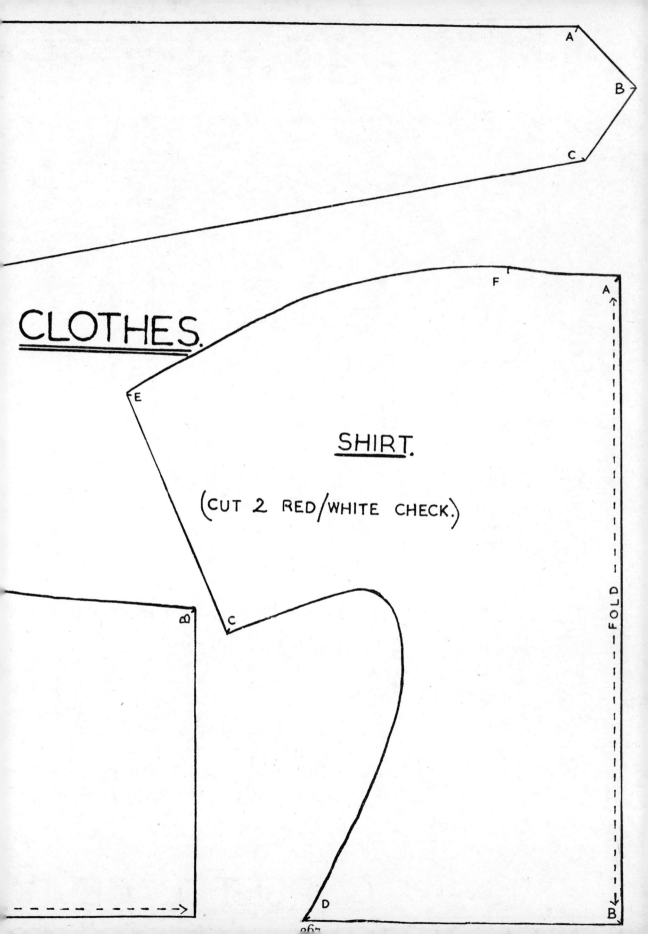

CLOTHES.

SHIRT.

(CUT 2 RED/WHITE CHECK.)

FOLD

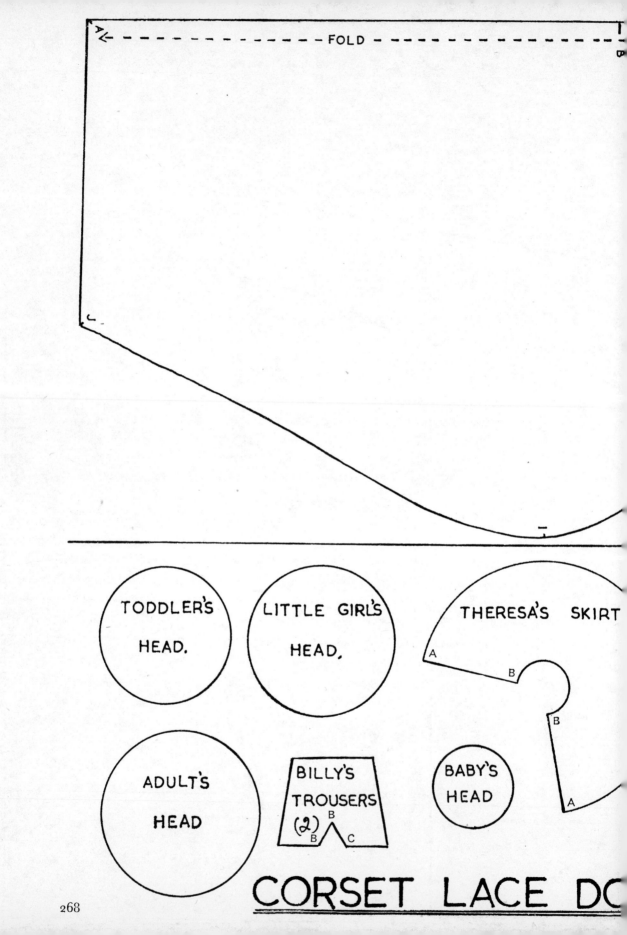

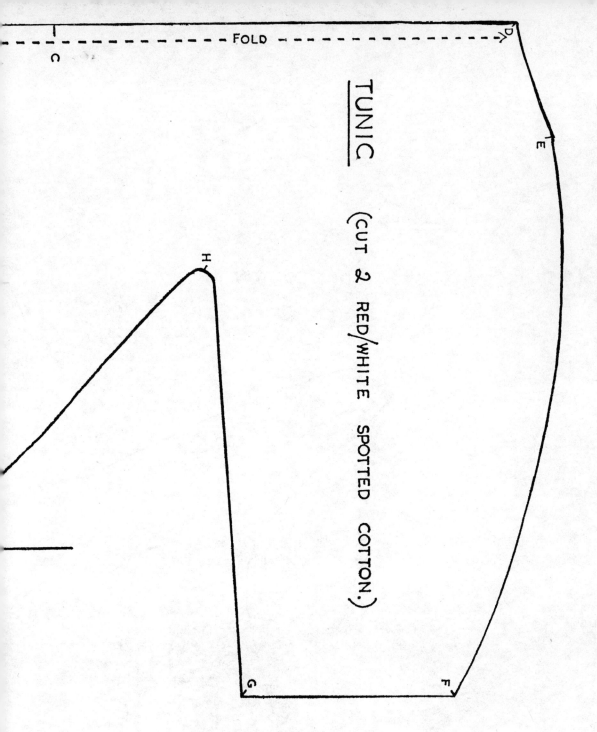

TUNIC

(CUT 2 RED/WHITE SPOTTED COTTON.)

FOLD

JOEY'S TUNIC

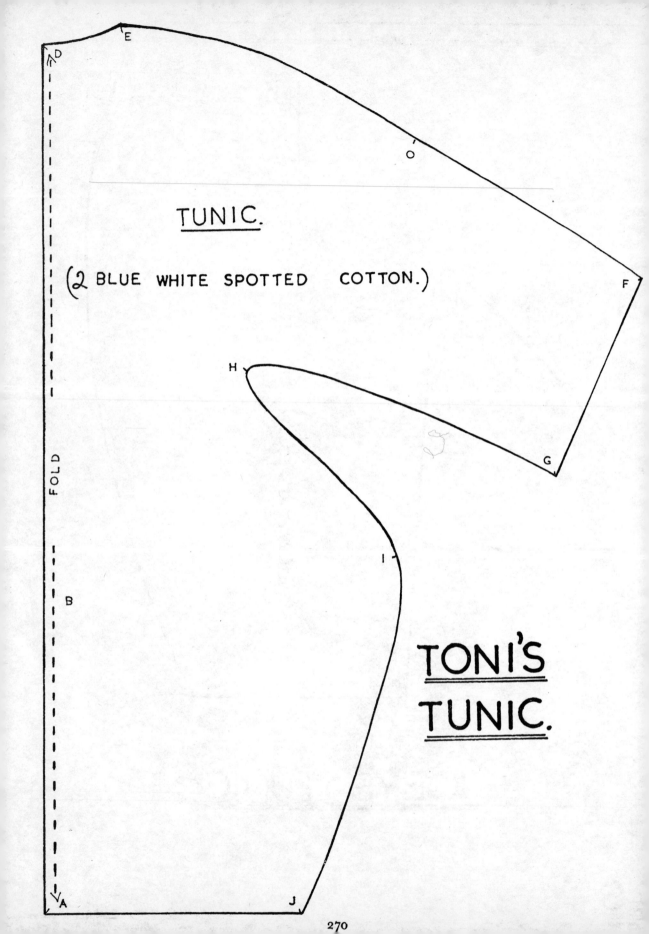

TUNIC.

(2 BLUE WHITE SPOTTED COTTON.)

TONI'S
TUNIC.

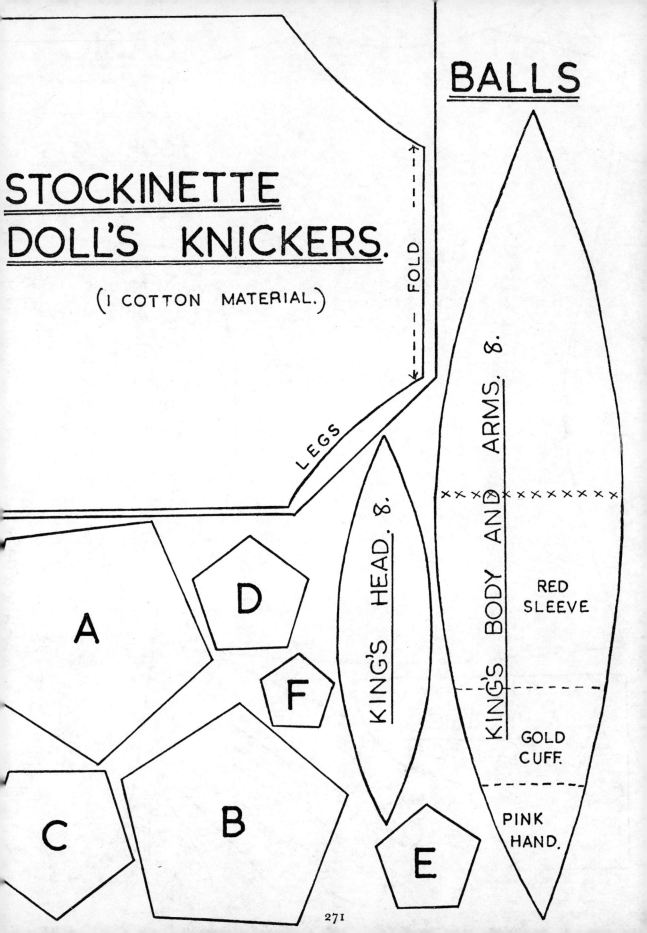

STOCKINETTE DOLL'S KNICKERS.

(1 COTTON MATERIAL.)

FOLD

LEGS

BALLS

KING'S BODY AND ARMS. 8.

RED SLEEVE

GOLD CUFF.

PINK HAND.

KING'S HEAD. 8.

A

D

F

C

B

E

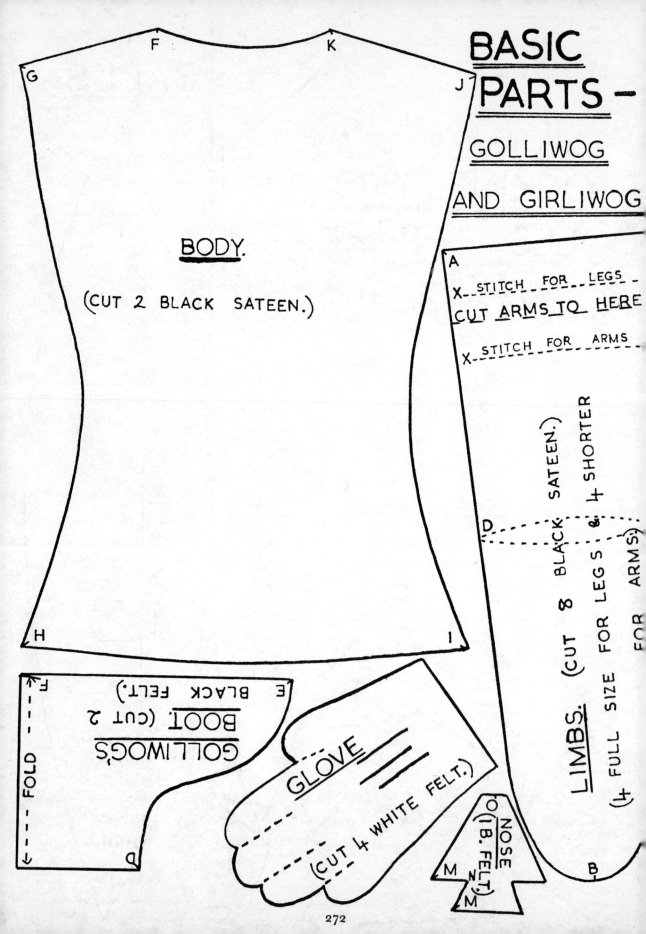

BASIC PARTS –

GOLLIWOG

AND GIRLIWOG

BODY.

(CUT 2 BLACK SATEEN.)

F K
G J

A

X STITCH FOR LEGS

CUT ARMS TO HERE

X STITCH FOR ARMS

D

H I

LIMBS. (CUT 8 BLACK SATEEN.)

(4 FULL SIZE FOR LEGS & 4 SHORTER FOR ARMS.)

GOLLIWOG'S BOOT (CUT 2 BLACK FELT.)

F E

FOLD

D

GLOVE

(CUT 4 WHITE FELT.)

NOSE (1 B. FELT.)

O

M N M

M

B

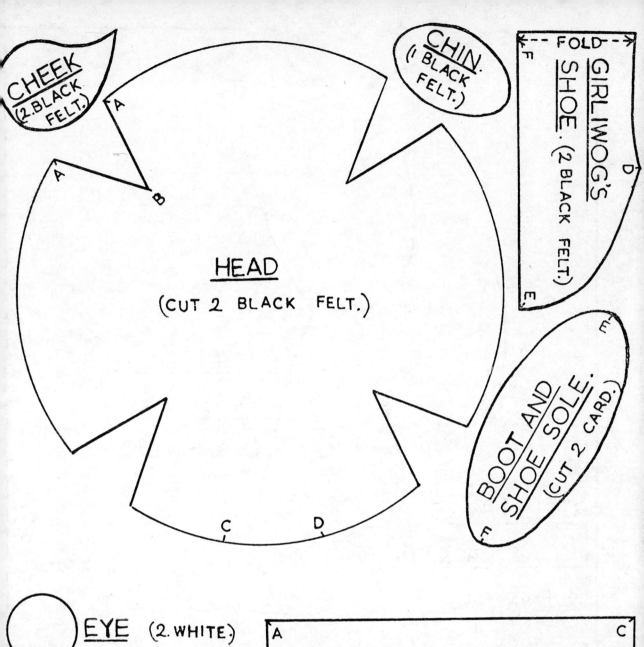

CHEEK
(2. BLACK FELT.)

CHIN.
(1 BLACK FELT.)

GIRLIWOG'S SHOE. (2 BLACK FELT.)

FOLD

HEAD
(CUT 2 BLACK FELT.)

BOOT AND SHOE SOLE. (CUT 2 CARD.)

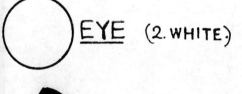

EYE (2. WHITE)

PUPIL (2 BLACK.)

MOUTH.
(1 RED.)

GIRLIWOG'S KNICKERS.

(2 BLUE FELT.)

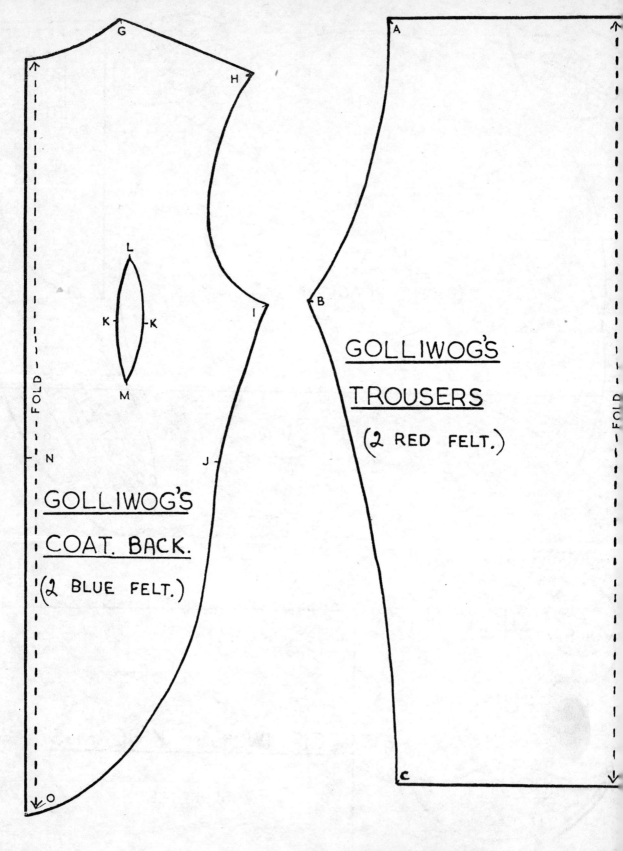

GOLLIWOG'S
TROUSERS

(2 RED FELT.)

GOLLIWOG'S

COAT. BACK.

(2 BLUE FELT.)

CLOTHES FOR

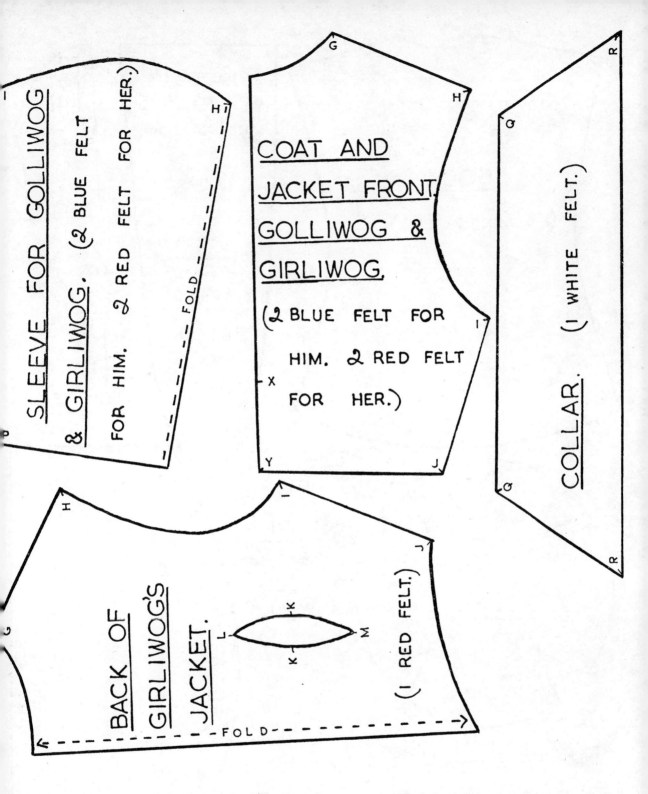

SLEEVE FOR GOLLIWOG & GIRLIWOG. (2 BLUE FELT FOR HIM. 2 RED FELT FOR HER.)

FOLD

COAT AND JACKET FRONT GOLLIWOG & GIRLIWOG.

(2 BLUE FELT FOR HIM. 2 RED FELT FOR HER.)

COLLAR. (1 WHITE FELT.)

BACK OF GIRLIWOG'S JACKET.

(1 RED FELT.)

FOLD

GOLLIWOGS AND GIRLIWOGS.

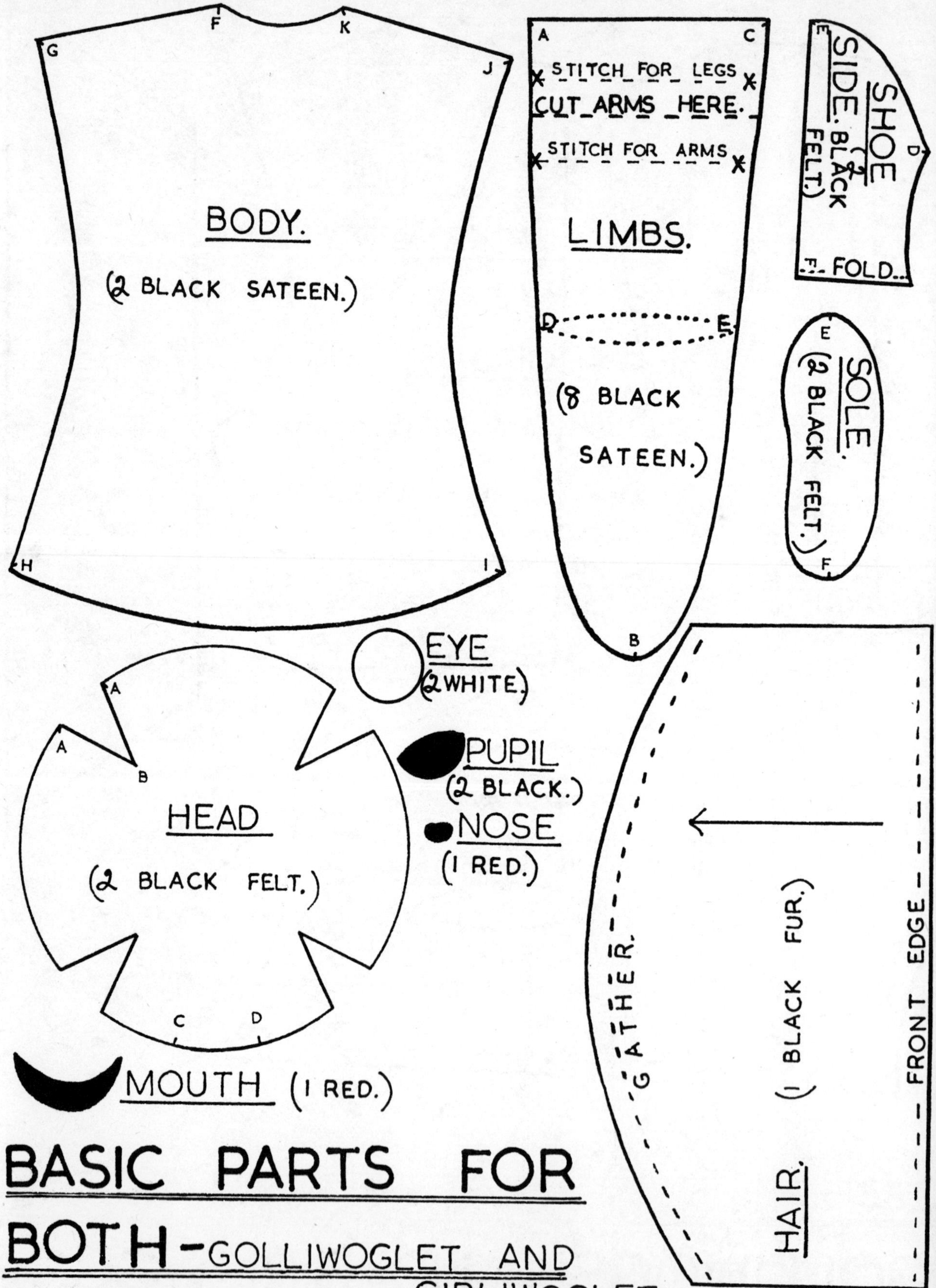

BODY.

(2 BLACK SATEEN.)

G F K J

H I

LIMBS.

A C

STITCH FOR LEGS

CUT ARMS HERE.

STITCH FOR ARMS

(8 BLACK SATEEN.)

D E

B

SHOE (BLACK FELT.)

SIDE.

E D

F FOLD.

SOLE.

(2 BLACK FELT.)

E

F

EYE (2 WHITE.)

PUPIL (2 BLACK.)

NOSE (1 RED.)

HEAD

(2 BLACK FELT.)

A A B

C D

MOUTH (1 RED.)

HAIR. (1 BLACK FUR.)

GATHER.

FRONT EDGE.

BASIC PARTS FOR
BOTH - GOLLIWOGLET AND
GIRLIWOGLET.

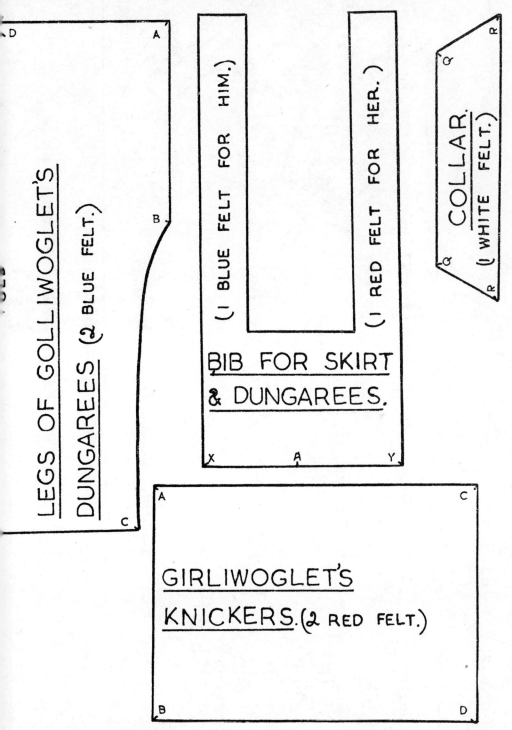

LEGS OF GOLLIWOGLET'S DUNGAREES (2 BLUE FELT.)

(1 BLUE FELT FOR HIM.)

(1 RED FELT FOR HER.)

BIB FOR SKIRT & DUNGAREES.

COLLAR. (1 WHITE FELT.)

GIRLIWOGLET'S KNICKERS. (2 RED FELT.)

CLOTHES FOR GOLLIWOGLET.

AND GIRLIWOGLET.

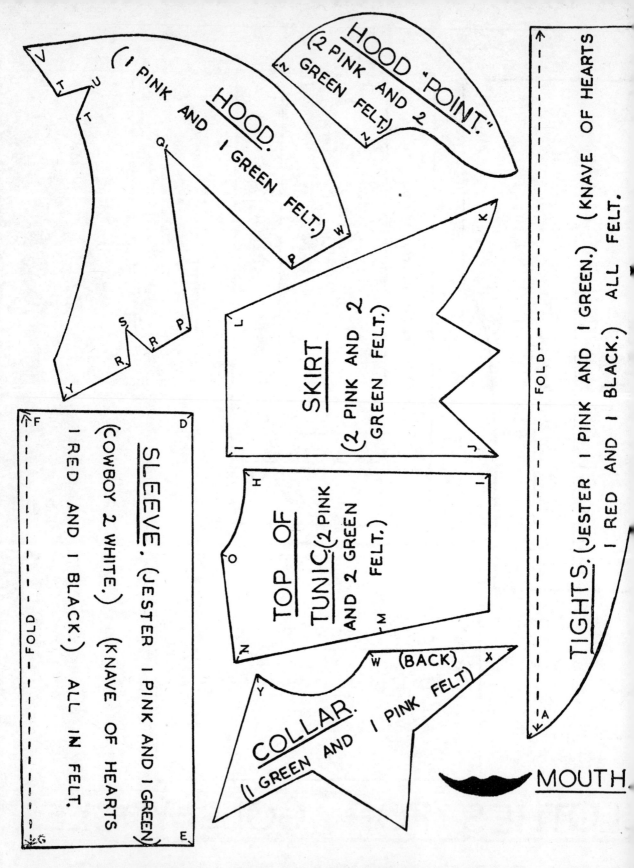

HOOD. (1 PINK AND 1 GREEN FELT.)

HOOD "POINT." (2 PINK AND 2 GREEN FELT.)

SKIRT (2 PINK AND 2 GREEN FELT.)

TOP OF TUNIC (2 PINK AND 2 GREEN FELT.)

SLEEVE. (JESTER 1 PINK AND 1 GREEN) (COWBOY 2 WHITE.) (KNAVE OF HEARTS 1 RED AND 1 BLACK.) ALL IN FELT.

FOLD

COLLAR. (1 GREEN AND 1 PINK FELT)

TIGHTS. (JESTER 1 PINK AND 1 GREEN.) (KNAVE OF HEARTS 1 RED AND 1 BLACK.) ALL FELT.

FOLD

MOUTH.

JESTER'S CLOTHES.

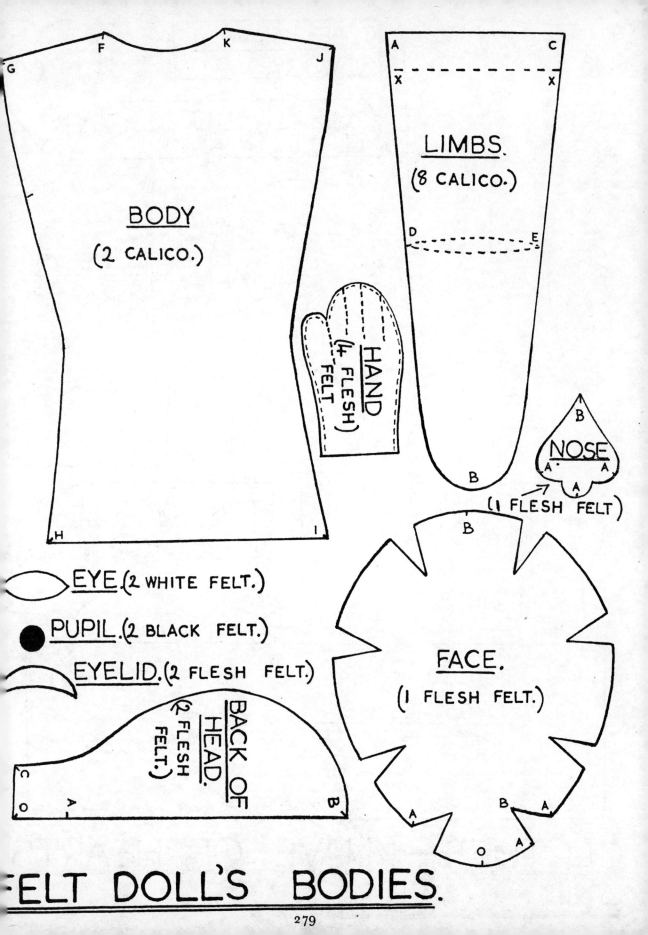

BODY
(2 CALICO.)

LIMBS.
(8 CALICO.)

HAND
(4 FLESH FELT)

NOSE
(1 FLESH FELT)

EYE. (2 WHITE FELT.)

PUPIL. (2 BLACK FELT.)

EYELID. (2 FLESH FELT.)

BACK OF HEAD.
(2 FLESH FELT.)

FACE.
(1 FLESH FELT.)

FELT DOLL'S BODIES.

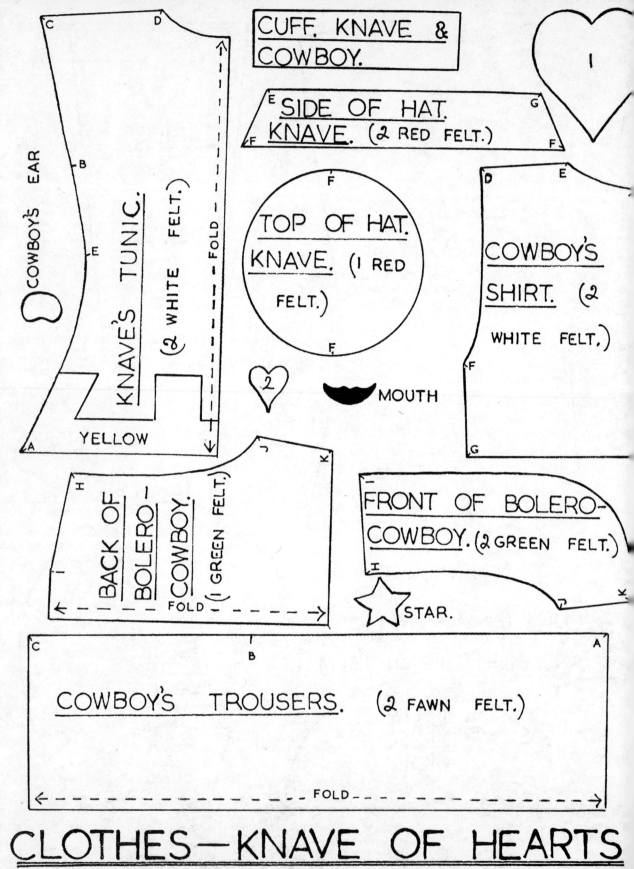

CUFF. KNAVE & COWBOY.

SIDE OF HAT. KNAVE. (2 RED FELT.)

E G

F F

1

COWBOY'S EAR

D

TOP OF HAT. KNAVE. (1 RED FELT.)

F

F

F

COWBOY'S SHIRT. (2 WHITE FELT.)

D E

F

G

C D

B

E

A

KNAVE'S TUNIC.

(2 WHITE FELT.)

FOLD

YELLOW

2

MOUTH

H

BACK OF BOLERO—COWBOY. (1 GREEN FELT.)

FOLD

J K

FRONT OF BOLERO—COWBOY. (2 GREEN FELT.)

I

J K

STAR.

C B A

COWBOY'S TROUSERS. (2 FAWN FELT.)

FOLD

CLOTHES—KNAVE OF HEARTS AND COWBOY.

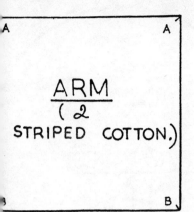

ARM
(2
STRIPED COTTON.)

HAND. (2 WHITE FELT.)

JACK-IN-THE-BOX.

GLOVE.
WHITE
FELT.)

PUPIL.
(2 BLACK
FELT.)

EYE.
(2 WHITE
FELT.)

NOSE.
(1 RED
FELT.)

CUP.
(1 BLACK FELT.)

BERTIE BEACON.

NOSE.
(1 RED FELT.)

EYE.
(2 WHITE
FELT.)

MOUTH. (1 RED OR 1
WHITE FELT.)

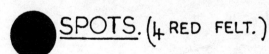

SPOTS. (4 RED FELT.)

DANCING   PARTNER CLOWN.

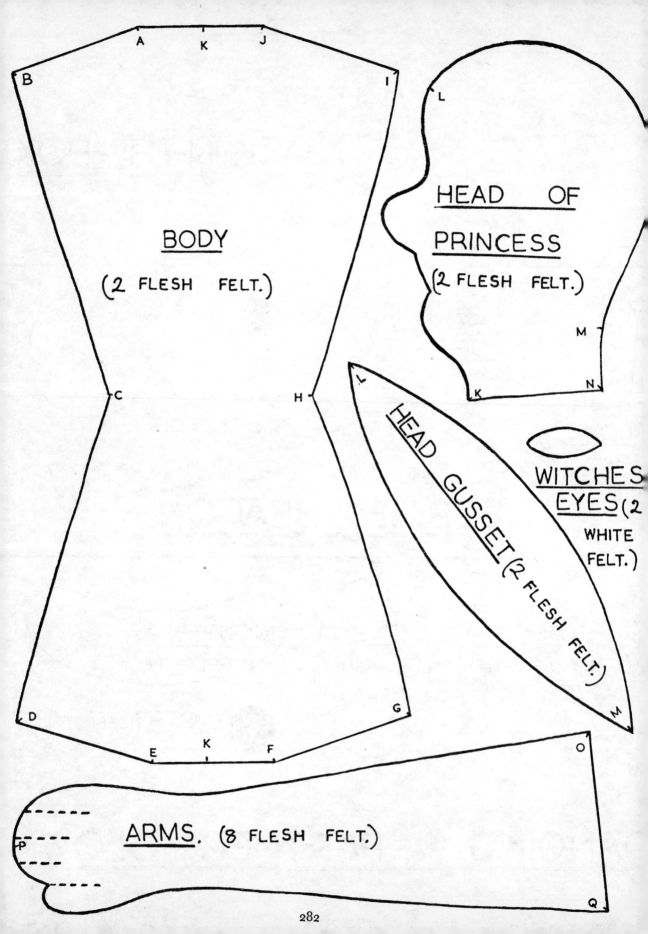

BODY

(2 FLESH FELT.)

HEAD OF PRINCESS

(2 FLESH FELT.)

HEAD GUSSET (2 FLESH FELT.)

WITCHES EYES (2 WHITE FELT.)

ARMS. (8 FLESH FELT.)

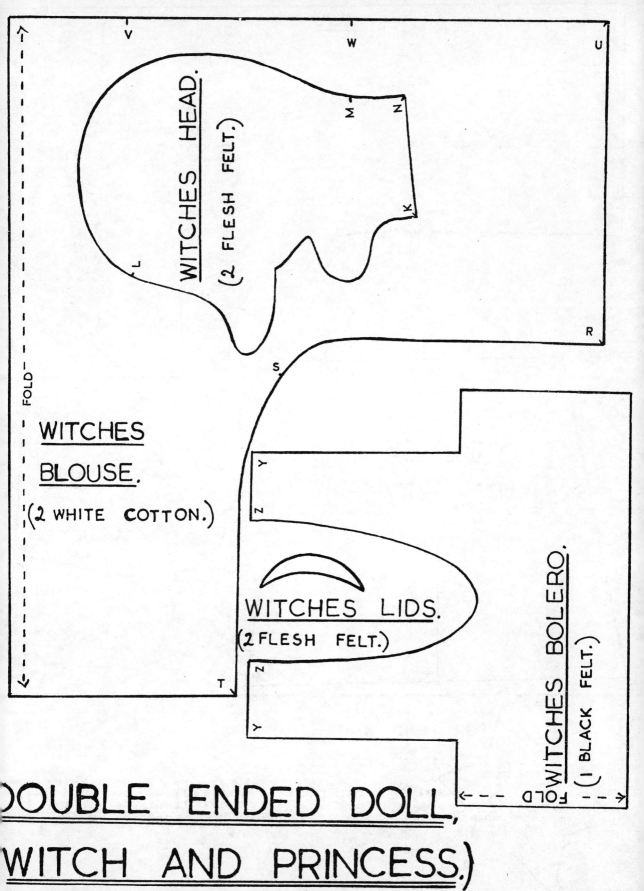

WITCHES HEAD.
(2 FLESH FELT.)

FOLD

WITCHES
BLOUSE.
(2 WHITE COTTON.)

WITCHES LIDS.
(2 FLESH FELT.)

WITCHES BOLERO.
(1 BLACK FELT.)

FOLD

DOUBLE ENDED DOLL,
WITCH AND PRINCESS.)

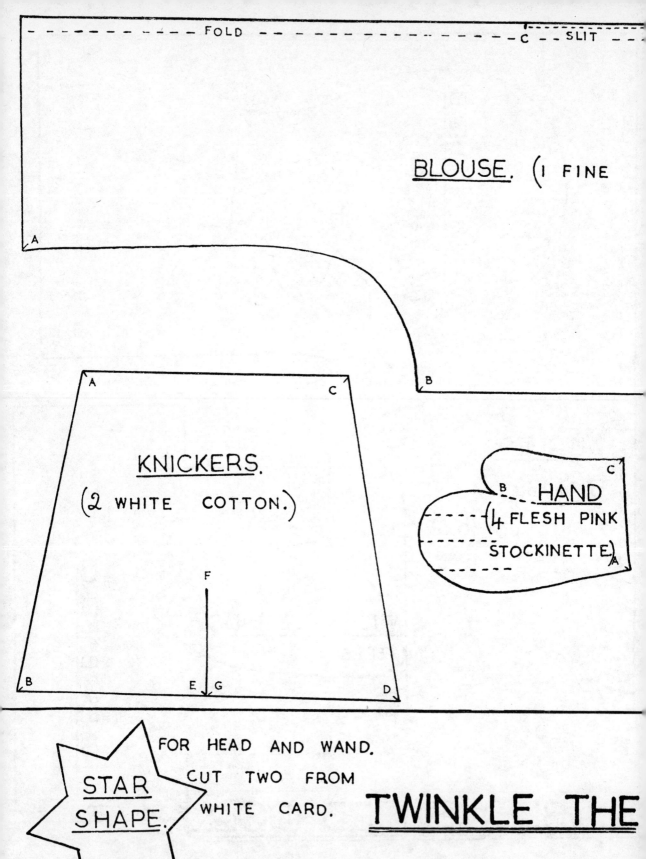

FOLD - - - - - - - - - - - - - C - - SLIT - - -

BLOUSE. (1 FINE

A

B

A   C

KNICKERS.

(2 WHITE COTTON.)

B   C
HAND
(4 FLESH PINK
STOCKINETTE)
A

F

B   E G   D

FOR HEAD AND WAND.

CUT TWO FROM

STAR
SHAPE.   WHITE CARD.   TWINKLE THE

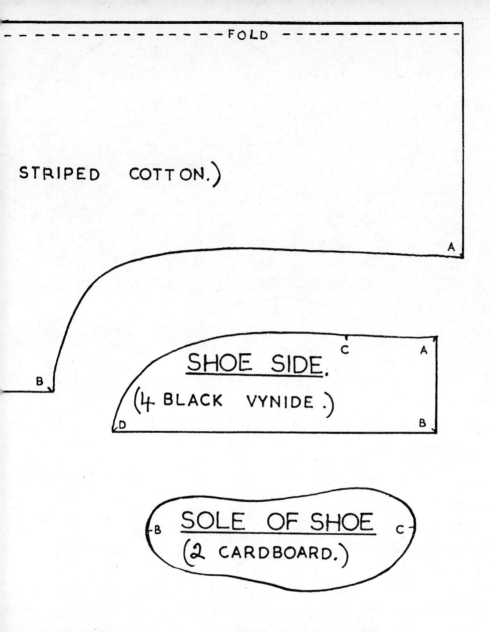

STRIPED COTTON.)

A

SHOE SIDE.

C   A

(4 BLACK VYNIDE.)

D   B

B

SOLE OF SHOE

B   C

(2 CARDBOARD.)

WOBBLEY WINNIE.

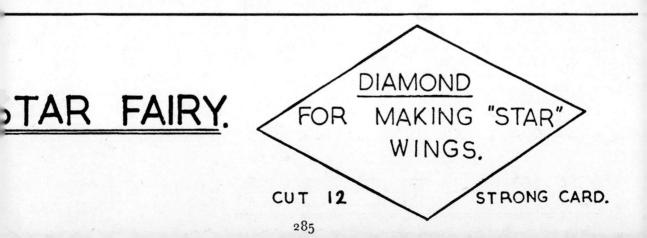

STAR FAIRY.

DIAMOND
FOR MAKING "STAR"
WINGS.

CUT 12   STRONG CARD.

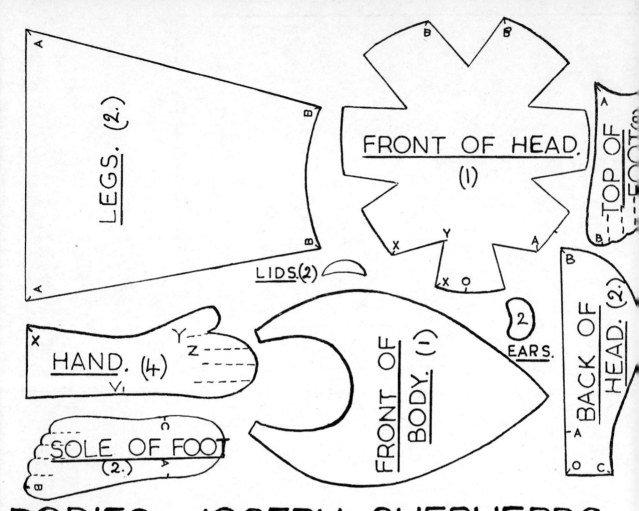

LEGS. (2.)

FRONT OF HEAD. (1)

TOP OF FOOT

LIDS. (2)

X Y A

X O

HAND. (4)

X Y Z V

FRONT OF BODY. (1)

2 EARS.

BACK OF HEAD. (2.)

B A O C

SOLE OF FOOT (2.)

BODIES—JOSEPH, SHEPHERDS AND KINGS. (CUT ALL PIECES IN FLESH FELT.)

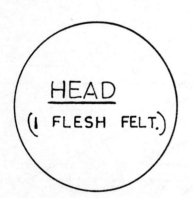

HEAD
(1 FLESH FELT.)

BODY.
(1 FLESH FELT.)

CRIB — THE BABY

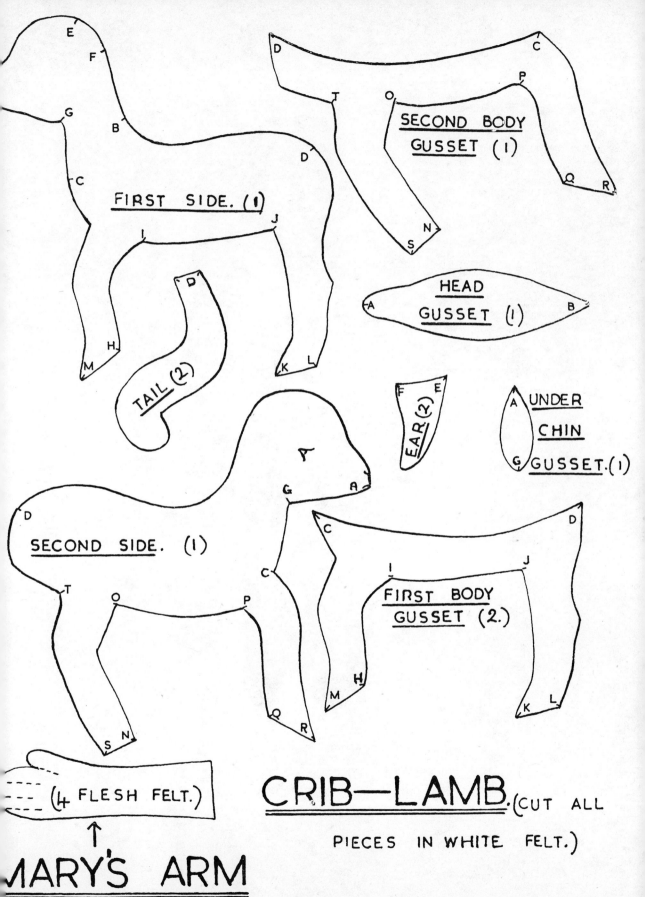

E
F
G
B
C

FIRST SIDE. (1)

I
J

H
M

TAIL (2)

D

K
L

D
C
P
O
T

SECOND BODY
GUSSET (1)

N
S
Q
R

HEAD
GUSSET (1)

A
B

A

SECOND SIDE. (1)

D

G
A

F
E

EAR (2)

A
UNDER
CHIN
GUSSET.(1)
G

T
O
P

C

C
I
J

FIRST BODY
GUSSET (2.)

D

H
M
Q
R
N
S
K
L

(4 FLESH FELT.)

↑

MARY'S ARM

CRIB—LAMB. (CUT ALL

PIECES IN WHITE FELT.)

287

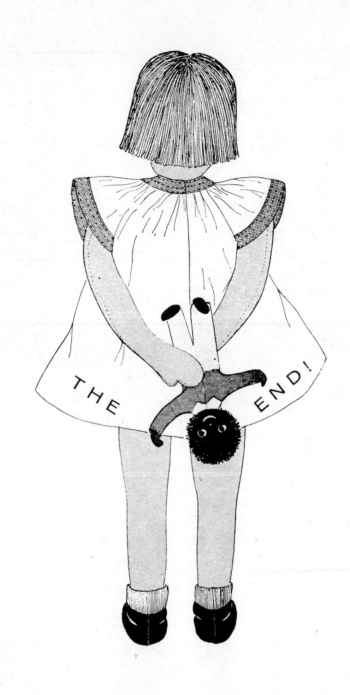